Personal archiving

g:

Preserving Our Digital Heritage

DISCARD

D0792576

Advance Praise for *Personal Archiving*

"*Personal Archiving* addresses all of the significant decisions individuals must make regarding personal (and family) memories and memorabilia. The volume serves as a welcome, much needed how-to for individuals looking to preserve and share their photo albums and shoeboxes of slides with friends and family, near and far, today and future generations."
—Barbie E. Keiser, information resources management (IRM) consultant

"Multiple authors bring a wide range of perspectives that challenge us to consider how our stories are embedded in the increasingly digital but also physical trail that is a byproduct of our lives. Organizing it, understanding it, and sharing it in a way that is meaningful provides ample opportunity for reflection—about ourselves and those whose lives and work will be visible to future generations."
—Judy Luther, president, Informed Strategies LLC

"The new online life has great potential for creating a personal record of digital activities. *Personal Archiving* is a timely collection of excellent chapters from multiple perspectives that cover many aspects of personal digital archiving."
—Greg R. Notess, reference librarian, Montana State University Library

"This thorough examination of the world of digital archiving is an excellent resource for anyone, personally or professionally, who is responsible for preserving their personal and collective stories. It emphasizes the importance of capturing and preserving our stories and the resulting complications, particularly since the digital realm is so impermanent."
—Cherilyn P. Fiory, director, Upper Dublin (PA) Public Library

"Don Hawkins and his contributors provide the knowledge and advice that can ensure that your digital footprints in the sand don't wash away with the next wave of technological change. If you care about your personal written and artistic legacy, learn from this work."
—Stephen Abram, CEO, Federation of Ontario Public Libraries, and president, Lighthouse Consulting Inc.

Personal Archiving: Preserving Our Digital Heritage

Edited by
Donald T. Hawkins

Information Today, Inc.
Medford, New Jersey

First Printing, 2013

Personal Archiving: Preserving Our Digital Heritage

Copyright © 2013 by Donald T. Hawkins

All rights reserved. No part of this book may be reproduced in any form or by any electronic or mechanical means, including information storage and retrieval systems, without permission in writing from the publisher, except by a reviewer, who may quote brief passages in a review. Published by Information Today, Inc., 143 Old Marlton Pike, Medford, New Jersey 08055.

Library of Congress employees do not own a copyright in the works that they create within the scope of their employment because they are U.S. Government personnel. Under the U.S. copyright statute, 17 U.S.C. Section 105, copyright protection is not available in the United States for any work of the U.S. Government. Therefore, Chapter 3, "The Library of Congress and Personal Digital Archiving," is in the public domain.

Publisher's Note: The editor and publisher have taken care in the preparation of this book but make no expressed or implied warranty of any kind and assume no responsibility for errors or omissions. No liability is assumed for incidental or consequential damages in connection with or arising out of the use of the information or programs contained herein.

Many of the designations used by manufacturers and sellers to distinguish their products are claimed as trademarks. Where those designations appear in this book and Information Today, Inc. was aware of a trademark claim, the designations have been printed with initial capital letters.

Library of Congress Cataloging-in-Publication Data

Personal archiving : preserving our digital heritage / edited by Donald T. Hawkins.
    pages cm
 Includes bibliographical references and index.
 ISBN 978-1-57387-480-9
 1. Personal archives. 2. Archival materials--Conservation and restoration. 3. Archival materials--Digitization. 4. Digital preservation. 5. Records--Management. 6. Electronic records--Management. I. Hawkins, Donald T., editor of compilation.
 CD977.P47 2013
 651.5'9--dc23

2013026748

President and CEO: Thomas H. Hogan, Sr.
Editor-in-Chief and Publisher: John B. Bryans
VP Graphics and Production: M. Heide Dengler
Cover Designer: Denise Erickson

infotoday.com

To Pat,
Michael and Lisa,
and Sean, Rebecca, Ethan, and Emma
for their constant love and unfailing support

And to the memory of my father, Donald S. Hawkins,
who taught me how to take slide photographs

Contents

Acknowledgments

This book would not exist if it were not for the work of the contributors, all of whom were very enthusiastic about the project and willingly gave their time to bring us the benefit of their knowledge and their insights into personal archiving. Thank you for your support of the project and for submitting your chapters in a timely manner to keep it on schedule.

Tom Hogan Sr. has created an excellent and supportive working environment at Information Today, Inc. (ITI). The past 15 years of my career, when I have been affiliated with ITI, have been some of the most enjoyable ones. Thank you, Tom, for your friendship and support.

ITI's Book Division—comprised of John B. Bryans, publisher and editor-in-chief; Amy Reeve, managing editor; and Brandi Scardilli, editorial assistant—is a great asset to the company. John brought great enthusiasm to this project from the first day I proposed it to him, and he has been a constant source of advice and information. I have published many articles, but this is my first book, and I thank John for all his support. Amy and Brandi have carefully and efficiently shepherded this work through the production process.

Thank you all.

Foreword

Brewster Kahle
Founder, Internet Archive

Between digitizing the boxes in our basements, filling hard drives with photos, and uploading our videos and email on cloud services, we are creating a bountiful and disorganized mess of our personal histories. Currently, we lack the tools and approaches to save our own histories, much less those of our families and other people we care about. Fortunately, entrepreneurs, archivists, and motivated individuals are developing approaches to saving and presenting these collections.

One obvious solution to the problem of preserving physical documents is to digitize a collection, but decisions about what to digitize are influenced by cost and privacy; often the goal of digitization is one of trying to offer access. Trying to build a comprehensive digital record is much more difficult than curating a set of pictures and documents for an event.

Some experiments on digitizing boxes of archival materials received at the Internet Archive (archive.org) revealed a cost of approximately 25 cents per page, or rather $500 per box, depending on many variables. Preliminary research projects to collect Twitter feeds, blog posts, photo sites, and social media sites are now in the prototype stage and could eventually become commercial or nonprofit services.

But once we have assembled collections of data, how are we supposed to preserve them? Long-term data storage has shifted from CDs and DVDs to external hard drives and internet-based services, each of which has uncertain longevity and expenses. Some prototype preservation services are starting to make estimates and do trials. Commercial services such as GeoCities, Apple MobileMe, Yahoo! Video, Google Video, and many other sites have vanished from the online world, and only snapshots in the Internet Archive's Wayback Machine (archive.org/web/web.php) provide ongoing read-only access. Long-term data storage, especially for personal-scale projects, is evolving with new ideas, but it is safe to say there is no consensus yet on how to protect our personal collections.

The work of organizing and tagging archived files is being aided by some automated tools for reading printed materials and face recognition. Presenting materials in a timeline format, or ideally in relation to other people's archives, is in its infancy. Facebook has started some approaches to this that are quite exciting.

Jeff Ubois of the MacArthur Foundation has led two conferences on personal digital archiving, hosted at the Internet Archive. The participating academics, web developers, and corporate researchers showed how much interest there is in this topic from many different angles. These meetings may come to be seen as foundational in this new field, and we are fortunate to have some of the presenters contribute chapters for *Personal Archiving: Preserving Our Digital Heritage*.

This timely book brings together various approaches to the digitization, collecting, preservation, and presentation of personal archives. Excitement is growing as researchers learn from one other and welcome the type of sharing culture that comes before commercial players enter a field. Pioneering user interfaces are being proposed for existing digital collections, and methods are being developed that would collect our digital legacy from websites and services. As new approaches and products emerge in this young and increasingly critical field, we have much to look forward to. *Personal Archiving* is a great place to begin the journey.

Introduction

Donald T. Hawkins

When I was about 10 years old, my parents gave me a simple box camera, and I began to take snapshots. Then in the mid-1950s, my father bought a 35mm camera for his own use, and he also taught me how to use its features to do more advanced photography. From that simple beginning, a large collection of slides grew, eventually numbering about 30,000. I took on the task of organizing and storing them—the beginnings of a personal archive—and eventually became the family's *de facto* photographer and archivist.

Now, of course, with the proliferation of digital cameras and cell-phone cameras, photography has become much more widespread, and interest in personal archives of all types—not just photographs—has grown. The image that follows is a tag cloud (learn more at en.wikipedia.org/wiki/Tag_cloud) of the approximately 77,000 words comprising the text of this book. (The size of each word indicates its frequency of occurrence.) It provides a convenient visualization of the major subjects encompassed by personal archiving. For example, it rapidly becomes evident that, other than the words in the title of the book, *email, people, information,* and *content* are the next most-often used terms. One name, *Shneiderman,* also appears because of its prominence in Chapter 7.

Personal Archiving **tag cloud created using Wordle software (www.wordle.net)**

As often happens in an emerging field, conferences were organized. The three initial Personal Archiving Conferences drew information professionals from a variety of environments. Many of the chapters in this book are authored by speakers from the 2011 and 2012 conferences.

Personal Archiving: Preserving Our Digital Heritage contains reviews of research, legal issues, activities of libraries and academic institutions, relevant services and software products, and case studies of activities by individuals. The book is intended to appeal to a broad spectrum of readers, including:

- Consumers who want to know how to prepare an archive of family or personal history

- Academic researchers studying digital scholarship in the information science field

- Libraries of all types—research, public, and academic—that serve consumers and researchers

- Historians and authors who are collecting biographical materials on prominent people

- Public officials and local historical societies compiling histories of their towns

In fact, anyone who has a mass of digital information and wants to organize and preserve it should find *Personal Archiving* useful.

Traditionally, libraries and other cultural institutions have played major roles in preservation, but individuals have now become interested in preserving their digital heritage. Three significant technological developments have been instrumental in this shift:

- The widespread use of digital cameras, especially those integrated in cellphones, has resulted in large collections of unorganized digital photographs on users' cameras, phones, and computers.

- Extensive use of email has produced huge files of digital conversations. Many people are beginning to realize that these files can be sources of valuable historical information about people and events.

- Decreases in the cost of data storage and the recent emergence of cloud storage services have removed many of the difficulties formerly associated with storing and managing large information data sets.

In response to these trends, commercial software packages for the preservation of family and individual histories have begun to appear, and the general public's awareness of, and interest in, personal archiving is rapidly increasing. The Library of Congress has begun a major outreach program and is offering services to help people archive their important documents and compile family histories. In the academic area, some libraries are working on preserving the history of noted alumni.

About This Book

Jeff Ubois, organizer and convener of the first three Personal Archiving Conferences, introduces the subject in Chapter 1 by briefly surveying the concept and proposing a new definition of personal archiving. He then discusses five significant issues facing archivists.

In Chapter 2, Danielle Conklin, an independent information professional and owner of Cotton Gloves Research, describes four different individuals and how they have taken different approaches to their personal archiving projects (including me and my own 30,000-slide scanning project). She shares some of the issues they faced and the lessons they learned in areas such as organization, access, and long-term storage. She concludes with an interesting application of personal archiving: tracing the history of one's house.

Mike Ashenfelder, digital preservation project coordinator at the Library of Congress (LC), describes some of LC's outreach activities toward those who want to preserve their digital archives in Chapter 3. He also discusses some of the causes of data loss and how to address them, and he provides practical advice on how to undertake a personal archiving project. He discusses LC's outreach at the National Book Festival and Personal Archiving Day activities, and the lessons that have been learned at these events.

In Chapter 4, I review software and services currently available for personal archiving. The chapter is organized by different types of media collection systems: for photos and documents, for notes, for email archives, and for home movies and videos.

In Chapter 5, Evan Carroll, creator of The Digital Beyond, a website devoted to the legal issues of a digital legacy, delves into exactly those issues. As many authors do, he notes the differences between digital content and tangible assets, and he discusses not only the legal issues involved but also some practical ones. He also reviews the current status of relevant legislation in several states and describes the concept of a digital executor.

Catherine C. Marshall from Microsoft Research in Silicon Valley looks at social media issues that relate to our digital legacy in Chapter 6. She describes three studies that she and her colleagues have done—on curation by benign neglect, causes of personal data loss, and ownership and control—and based on these, she identifies current social norms affecting archiving and makes a case for the role of institutions in personal archiving.

In Chapter 7, Jason Zalinger from the University of South Florida, Nathan G. Freier from the Microsoft Corporation, and Ben

Shneiderman from the University of Maryland describe a fascinating analysis of an archive of nearly 45,000 of Shneiderman's email messages in an effort to create a narrative approach to analyzing a text archive. The chapter presents an account of the issues they considered, how they addressed them, and the lessons they learned in the process. As they conclude, "Narrative elements exist in all email archives: We just need to help others find them."

Chapter 8, by Ellysa Stern Cahoy from The Pennsylvania State University Libraries, looks at how academic institutions are responding to the need to archive the records of faculty and researchers. She outlines programs designed to increase faculty members' awareness of the importance of digital preservation and describes archiving activities at such prominent universities as Harvard, Stanford, MIT, and Emory, as well as a project at her library to develop a model of research workflow that integrates archival practices.

Sarah Kim, a PhD candidate at the University of Texas at Austin, goes into considerable detail on personal archiving activities and research in Chapter 9. She examines the value of personal documents and describes the challenges of managing and preserving them. She reviews much of the research currently underway to address these issues and provides an extensive bibliography on the subject.

Aaron Ximm, an engineer at the Internet Archive, describes the Archive's activities in Chapter 10 and develops the concept of active personal archiving. The Archive is best known for its Wayback Machine, an archive of the internet extending from 1996, but the organization has recently branched out into other areas. Ximm describes the processes and issues that have confronted the Archive, and he discusses possible roles that it could play in personal archiving.

In Chapter 11, Richard Banks from Microsoft Research in Cambridge, U.K., begins by discussing his feelings upon inheriting his father's PC (they may be surprising to some readers) and goes on to identify the differences between physical and digital objects, which are not always obvious. He then takes us behind the scenes of four research projects that are developing new devices to make digital content more available in our physical environments.

Chapter 12 describes two current research projects, which may become significant new products: myKive for automatic aggregation of personal data from several different services, discussed by Christopher Prom from the University of Illinois, and Project MUSE for email archiving, discussed by Peter Chan from Stanford University. In the brief introduction to this chapter, I also look at an interesting project by Cesar Kuriyama, 1 Second Everyday, in which he uses his smartphone to record one second of video from his daily activities and describes the significant impact the project has had on his life.

Clifford Lynch, executive director of the Coalition for Networked Information, concludes the book with Chapter 13, a look at the future of personal archiving, including current challenges and how they are being addressed. He discusses how private materials become public and how future searches for personal data must include not only a person's possessions but also digital sources, such as publications, medical histories, and government records.

My hope is that you will enjoy reading *Personal Archiving* and that it will help you as you build your own personal digital archive.

CHAPTER 1

Personal Digital Archives: What They Are, What They Could Be, and Why They Matter

Jeff Ubois
MacArthur Foundation

Personal Archiving is a timely book highlighting some of the most interesting work that has been done in the domain of personal digital archives. It outlines recent accomplishments in digital preservation, an agenda for future research and development, ideas about the new role of archival institutions, and practical information for those wishing to archive their personal histories. By helping to build a common understanding of personal archives, this book supports collaboration between diverse types of institutions and individuals working in different disciplines.

Science and culture in the 21st century are born digital; today's Einsteins, Rembrandts, and Bachs create and record their works on digital devices. The works of yesterday's eminent individuals are rapidly being digitized, and there is a growing expectation that all of humanity's creative works are or will be instantly accessible in digital form.

The minute-by-minute, day-to-day record of our lives is becoming richer all the time. More than 1 billion camera phones will be sold in 2013, and by one estimate, more than 10 percent of all the photographs ever taken were taken in 2012.[1] Personal digital archiving may focus on genealogical data, but it includes much more: What we have written, what we have read, where we have been, who has met with us, who has communicated with us, what we have purchased, and much else is recorded digitally in increasingly greater detail in personal digital archives, whether they are held by individuals, institutions, or commercial organizations, and whether we are aware of those archives or not.

The ability to create, collect, and preserve personal archives—once a privilege of elites—has now been extended to billions of people around the world, and increasing numbers of them are concerned about the long-term prospects of their data. In the past, individuals who wished to send a message to their descendants or to future generations needed vast sums of money (and perhaps stonemasons and slaves). Not anymore. Personal digital archives democratize access to the future and, for some, fulfill the deeply human urge to leave a legacy.

There is a corollary to all this, which is that the events that will eventually be regarded as historically important are now often first recorded by ordinary individuals. The personal is becoming social and collective. Like Abraham Zapruder, the individual who by chance filmed John F. Kennedy's assassination with his home movie camera, many of us are recording events as they occur and sharing them with the world, sometimes before the mainstream media can, as witnesses present in Cairo's Tahrir Square or at the July 2005 London Underground bombings and other recent global events have done.

The ideal of the *archive* is in the zeitgeist. People casually refer to themselves as archivists; movie plots refer to archives as repositories of truth and hidden knowledge. Newspapers and radio stations routinely refer to their archives, and sometimes the only fees they charge are for access to them. Archives have become a counterweight to the sense that we are awash in the fake; the archive promises some kind of authenticity—none more than the personal archive.

Given a little technical help with production, the memories of individuals with few obvious claims to fame can become compelling stories, an important part of the historical record, or even the basis for popular entertainment. For example, the StoryCorps archive in the American Folklife Center at the Library of Congress (www.loc.gov/folklife/storycorpsfaq.html) contains 45,000 interviews of individuals from diverse walks of life, along with many supplementary materials. With 30,000 hours of audio, it is one of the largest "born digital" collections of oral histories in the world. Radio program segments based on these interviews are heard by 14 million listeners on National Public Radio every week, and the organization is far along in its mission to provide Americans of all backgrounds with the opportunity to record, share, and preserve the stories of their lives.

Clearly, the concept of the personal digital archive is on the minds of many, from authors and artists to historians and genealogists, and from entrepreneurs and engineers to funders and managers of memory institutions. Over the last few years, a common language, shared awareness, and a new field of study centered on personal archives have begun to take shape through the work of a new community of digital archivists. But it has yet to be fully defined or realized.

Not long ago, there was little question that personal archives were the sum of published and unpublished material written and collected by an individual. That definition has become inadequate as the boundaries between what is personal and what is social have blurred. It may now be more accurate to say that personal digital archives are collections of digital material created, collected, and curated by individuals rather than institutions.

It is important that we create a shared understanding of personal archives, appropriately set expectations about them, and most of all, bridge the gap between our imagined ideal and the imperfect tools and services we use to preserve the data we care about. That will require solving some difficult problems that are interrelated in complicated ways.

It will also turn on the resolution of two much-contested issues: copyright and freedom of expression. Each threatens the other, and few of the interests lined up on each side of those debates have personal archives and collections at the center of their concerns. Still, those who love free expression should love the personal archive. And if there is not a lot that archivists can do to affect the outcome of the conflicts over copyrights and over free expression, there are some problems that can be addressed in the more immediate term.

Five issues stand out: 1) funding and costs, 2) the relation between the commercial and noncommercial sectors, 3) the relation between individuals and institutions, 4) technology and design, and 5) culture and expectations.

Funding and Costs

Economics is one of the enduring questions surrounding personal archives. Who pays, how much, for what exactly, and why? Archiving has always been driven by the anticipated future value of information, which in the end is based on a guess. Calculating the costs associated with perpetual storage—or very-long-term access—is also incredibly difficult. And as the cost of information capture and storage continues to decline, the default course of action is to save more and more.

Governments, libraries, archives, and research organizations have collectively spent millions of dollars to develop cost models for digital archives because an ability to predict costs is essential for any organization that wants to promise long-term access. Often, these models are too complex for practical use by smaller organizations. What's needed are "pay once/store forever" services. These are not yet widely available, though a few universities now offer them to faculty. This pricing model seems likely to become more common, in part because agencies that fund scientific research and cultural production are requiring their grantees to provide a plan to preserve project data.

But there is a gap in the way various funding systems work. Science, culture, and scholarship are typically funded on a project basis for a limited term, not in perpetuity. Traditionally, libraries promised long-term access to scientific, cultural, and other scholarly publications, but much of what is being produced now does not fit as well into that system. Closing the gap between project-based funding and preservation in perpetuity is as much a matter of economics or economic understanding as it is a matter of technology.

What many people need are simpler models that make it possible to decide what they can afford to save, which will mean getting to commodity prices and to fixed unit costs, particularly for ingesting (taking in and assimilating the data) and its storage. How much does it cost to digitize an average-sized box of papers? How much does it cost to store a terabyte, forever? We need to know.

Market Solutions

Facebook's Timeline reaches a billion people. It is effectively a personal archive. Few of the more serious attempts at archiving from a traditional perspective will reach that many people as fast or as soon, but it would be foolish to assume that commercial services will continue to improve to the point where all personal archiving needs might be met by the market.

Commercial organizations have a poor record of caring for personal collections; their mission is to turn a profit, which is reflected in their terms of service. When commercial service providers state that they accept no responsibility in the event of data loss, they mean it. Commercial organizations, particularly startups that promise continuity and persistence over time, are suspect, or should be, and entrusting the task of long-term preservation solely to businesses is unwise. However comfortable it may be to imagine that data is safe with today's billion-dollar service provider, when corporate priorities change, personal data may be deleted, as former users of Yahoo!'s GeoCities and many other services can testify.

But we must not say that commercial services have no role in personal digital archives. A factory-like approach to ingest, like ScanCafe (www.scancafe.com), can usually do a better job of scanning photos than most individuals can. Software that automates metadata extraction for purposes such as speech and facial recognition will be valuable, too. Copyright clearance may be another area that is best handled by commercial services. There is also a vibrant trade in manuscripts; although digital archives may lose the aura of authenticity that a handwritten diary has, some personal digital archives are contained in physical devices. The laptop or memory card containing photos and email that once belonged to a famous author may become valuable in the way manuscripts have. The U.S. market for paper scrapbooking is declining, but in 2003, the business still earned $2.5 billion.[2]

In the end, markets are about exchange, and while personal digital archives may be something we use while we are living, much of their value (or promise) is in their ability to allow communication with our descendants. It is hard to envision a market between people who are dead and people who are not yet born, and the nonmarket motivations will be critical to the future of personal archives.

New Relationships Between Institutions and Individuals

The institutions that have traditionally taken on responsibility for digital preservation—libraries, museums, and archives—must face questions over whether they have a new responsibility to collect digital personal materials. One approach has been for leading institutions to provide guidance to individuals who are interested in preserving their own digital materials. For example, the Library of Congress hosts Personal Digital Archiving Day events, which are drawing many people who have already taken on the problem of preserving their own material as best they could.

That kind of learning can go in both directions. Amateurs working outside the system often create the most interesting approaches to personal archiving. There are many fine examples of this, but the Grazian

Archive is my favorite. The general concepts behind it are explored with great wit and understanding in "The Personal Archive: On Retrieving Valuable Cultural Resources" (www.grazian-archive.com/projects/archvpt.html).

Institutions are also developing ways to get help from the public, particularly through crowdsourced cataloging projects. The Church of Jesus Christ of Latter-day Saints has a well-known digital archive focused on individuals that is now more than 10 petabytes in size and is growing by millions of images per month. Those images have been annotated by more than 100,000 volunteers (see www.family search.org).

Crowdfunding is another intriguing possibility. Rather than bank-rupting institutions that care for cultural materials, personal archives and individual donations could become a source of support. With a "pay once/store forever" cost model, individuals might be able endow a terabyte, rather like the more common "buy a brick" programs muse-ums and others have used for years. Universities might also provide a terabyte with tuition and thus tie their alumni into the university in a much deeper way.

Tools, Technology, and Services

The future of personal archives will depend heavily on technologies and services developed for other purposes, particularly for capture and storage. New interfaces that include better timelines, maps, social net-work diagrams, automatic indexing, and data extraction technologies for face, voice, and handwriting recognition are other examples of technologies that will probably be developed for other markets but will also be useful to personal archivists.

Another set of technical needs has to do with integration of multi-ple sources of information and multiple types of media. Not long ago, personal archives consisted mostly of written materials, augmented by a few photographs, sound recordings, or perhaps home movies. Integrating the many kinds of digital data individuals now collect into a meaningful whole is hard, yet it is clear that the future of personal digital archives will depend on integrating the multiple types of data we create, collect, and disseminate through our daily activities.

Institutions also have technical needs, and many of the basic functions of traditional libraries and archives have yet to be implemented in software. For example, libraries and archives have managed patron data and the privacy of it for a very long time. The American Library Association Code of Ethics from 1939 (www.ala.org/advocacy/proethics/history/index5) describes why patron data is so important: "It is the librarian's obligation to treat as confidential any private information obtained through contact with library patrons." That is exactly the opposite sensibility from the way in which many organizations handle data, and tools that embody the ethical sense of librarians and archivists still need to be built. The donor agreements governing what archives may do with an individual's papers may require that materials are kept closed for some period of time, or until some number of years after the death of the author, or even after the deaths of all those mentioned in the collection. No software exists to manage that. There are also new designs required for university scholars who need to preserve their own work and to look back on the lives of eminent persons. The Mellon Foundation is now funding a series of projects in this area, but there is clearly more to be done to address the needs of different types of users.

Culture, Expectations, and the Future

Memory shapes our view of the world, and memories are contested by those in power or those who seek it. Memory institutions, such as libraries and archives, have therefore been at or near the center of debates about freedom of thought, freedom of expression, human rights issues, and privacy. The personal digital archive makes us all stakeholders in the outcome of these debates: If, as part of your practice as a personal archivist, you record your interaction with the police, there may be dire consequences.

Discussions about personal archives often turn on questions relevant to individuals, such as, "What happens to your data when you die?" or "What would you pay for a video of your great-great-grandparents?" But the question of what happens when personal archives are joined together has yet to be explored. It may be that we create a new kind of social memory or historical record, one with the potential to change public discourse and political choice. The personal testimonies of 50,000 Holocaust survivors held by the Shoah Foundation (sfi.usc.edu) are the tip of that iceberg.

The development of personal digital archives will affect the long-term preservation of cultural heritage, the future of cultural and scientific production, and freedom of expression. It will change the balance between commercial and noncommercial efforts to ensure open, long-term access to information, and change the relationship between institutions and individuals concerned with preservation. And on our best days, personal archiving may even help us fulfill the Confucian responsibility of being good ancestors to our descendants.

Endnotes

1. Jonathan Good, "How Many Photos Have Ever Been Taken?" 1000memories, September 15, 2011, accessed May 15, 2013, blog.1000memories.com/94-number-of-photos-ever-taken-digital-and-analog-in-shoebox, and "Global Mobile Statistics 2012 Part A: Mobile Subscribers; Handset Market Share; Mobile Operators," mobiThinking, March 2013, accessed May 15, 2013, mobithinking.com/mobile-marketing-tools/latest-mobile-stats/a#phone-shipments.

2. The market estimates vary, and they are changing, but see Eugene Fram, "The Booming Scrapbooking Market in the USA: Despite Phenomenal Growth, the Future's Unclear," *International Journal of Retail and Distribution Management* 33, no. 3 (2005): 215–225, accessed May 15, 2013, www.emeraldinsight.com/journals.htm?articleid=1464122&show=html.

CHAPTER 2

Personal Archiving for Individuals and Families

Danielle Conklin
Cotton Gloves Research

People want to preserve memories of the past: personal memories, family memories, and even broader historically or culturally significant memories. It's not a new phenomenon. Institutional archives and household attics alike are filled with testaments in the form of preserved letters, journals, photographs, scrapbooks, vital documents, family Bibles, and more.

Thanks to ever-evolving technology, however, preserving the memory of yesteryear has gone beyond the careful storage and handling of paper-based materials. Just this year, the Museum of London discovered a rare collection of sound recordings by a middle-class family dating back to 1902.[1] In an article in *Nature*, Jeremy Leighton John of The British Library writes, "With the emergence of personal computing in the 1970s, more and more people are passing on details of their lives to future generations as digital files."[2]

There have always been preservation concerns that individuals and families—however well-meaning—tend to overlook without education and training on the subject. When I think back to my own family's earliest attempts at saving pieces of personal history for posterity,

I can appreciate the genuine heartfelt attempt, while at the same time wishing that my forebears had the advantages we have now. Just as many personal archivists are doing today, they did the best they could with the information and resources they had at the time.

My maternal grandmother treasured her collection of early family photographs. She kept them in a tin box, not necessarily organized in any fashion, but away from moisture and light. Thanks to the generally long life of black-and-white photos printed on sturdy paper and the simple-but-adequate storage my grandmother provided, they held up remarkably well over several decades.

Her concern was keeping memories alive. Rather than labels and written files, the descriptive information for each image was passed along through oral history. As a family, we looked through what was essentially just a pile of pictures while my grandmother, along with the older relatives of her generation, would identify the people and places shown. This ensured that we, the younger generation, would remember our ancestors and their homes by sight even though we'd never met them in person or set foot in their long-gone homes.

In a sense, my grandmother's collection had some benefits over today's personal archives. Because it was long before the time of digital cameras and mobile phone photography, there were fewer photos to maintain. Her collection was small and manageable. Photos were taken more conservatively: snapshots of special occasions, group photos, and carefully staged memories.

There were, however, many disadvantages to my family's early archive. There were no digital backups, few duplicates, and certainly no informational metadata recorded. That situation puts a collection in a very vulnerable position. An image would be gone forever if the sole print was lost or destroyed. The descriptions of the images would be lost as soon as there was no one left who remembered.

The worst-case scenario happened in our family's case: fire. Like many people in the Northeast region, my grandparents lived in a 200-year-old wood-framed house with wood-stove heating. One winter night, a spark ignited within the chimney and the fire soon spread.

Although my grandparents escaped without harm, the house was reduced to ashes. All the pieces of family history contained therein—the photos, household items passed down through the generations, and the house itself—were gone.

With the advent of widely available digital technologies, individuals and families have a new way to preserve and share their history with others: personal digital archiving. They can upload their images to social networks by pressing a button, save entire photographic collections on a hard drive, and easily print and distribute copies. While they have the challenge of massive digital—as well as print—collections to organize and maintain, they also have the benefit of many applicable resources. With guidance and support, the average person or family can create an impressive personal archive.

The Challenges of Personal Archiving

Personal archiving, albeit rewarding, is not without challenges. As Bill LeFurgy of the Library of Congress so aptly put it, "It's fair to say the vast majority of people need help figuring out how to manage their personal digital collections."[3] Similarly, Sumit Paul-Choudhury noted in an article written for *New Scientist*, "We have learned how to create vast digital legacies but we don't yet know how to tidy them up for our successors."[4] This was evident in the case of Vernon James, as described by Mike Ashenfelder of the Library of Congress. James undertook a monumental scanning project, only to encounter many complications.[5]

James had purchased a scanner and began diligently scanning decades' worth of photos, slides, documents, and letters—an admirable undertaking. His son, however, upon reviewing the project, quickly saw a number of red flags. The massive collection of files was unorganized, the scanner software had marred the images with descriptions literally imprinted over the front of the photographs, and, in terms of scanning quality, the resolution was too low. In Ashenfelder's estimation, "The problem was more a scarcity of consumer-friendly personal archiving information that clearly addressed what Mr. James and millions of others were trying to do—create a digital archive of their personal stuff."

With personal archives, people no longer have to worry solely about the safety of print materials. In the past, the main concern was keeping photos clean, dry, and protected from fire. Now, there is the need to protect both paper-based collections and an unwieldy mass of digital files. Without the education and specialized training possessed by institutional archivists, most individuals are in the unenviable position of simply doing the best they can.

Organization

A common obstacle for new personal archivists is organization. How should they arrange their electronic folders and files? What terms and keywords should they use to describe their materials? What are they to do with the originals?

Professionals in a library setting have the benefit of rules and standards. As a former cataloging librarian, I have experience with national and international cataloging guidelines and formatting structures. The resources used by catalogers indicate where to find the descriptive information on physical materials or within electronic records. They define the order of information and the format, so that records will be uniform. There are thesauri and classification schemas that allow for accurate and predictable keywords. All of this ensures that digital bibliographic records are complete, uniform, and nearly interchangeable across multiple institutions. Books, once cataloged, are then shelved in a reliably consistent manner.

In other words, library patrons and staff members alike are able to find what they are looking for in a collection and locate similar materials using the catalog, and they can even visit other repositories that follow the same standards and continue their search without facing a learning curve. Individuals and families, unfortunately, are not presented with a handbook at the start of their personal archiving projects.

They don't get on-the-job training or a delineated list of do's and don'ts.

Professional archivists, although using a different set of guidelines than cataloging librarians, also have the benefit of rules and training. In preservation and archival work, there are multiple levels to consider when safeguarding and organizing materials, and ultimately making them easily accessible. Processing archival materials at an institution involves the following series of steps:[6]

- The newly accessioned records are arranged and described.

- Conservation and reformatting may be done to protect the original.

- Ultimately, the materials are stored in a way that shields them from damaging external elements and makes them available for reference.

- Digitized and born-digital records are carefully organized and backed up.

The organizational principles that professionals follow have been thoughtfully prepared by committees of experienced practitioners. They have been written, edited, and rewritten for clarity and to keep up with changes in the field. The average person is likely unprepared to create self-imposed standards for the order of operations or descriptive consistency. As a result, a personal archiving project can seem overwhelming and unmanageable.

Long-Term Storage and Access

A preservation management professor once shared an anecdote that spoke to the challenges individuals can face in preserving their digital heritage. She told the story of a determined and well-intentioned man who had spent countless hours digitizing his extensive photograph collection. He had his images saved to floppy disks. Within a matter of years, he no longer had a floppy drive—or any way to access his photos. This story is in no way unique, and therein lies a problem that plagues individuals just as it does institutions: obsolescence. Preserving our digital heritage is not as simple as saving our files to a disk and patting ourselves on the back for a job well done. It is a constant process. "Digital records are more like an oral tradition than traditional documents," Paul-Choudhury contends. "If you don't copy them regularly, they simply disappear."[7]

In "A Fond Farewell to the Floppy Disk," Wendy Grossman echoes that sentiment, while at the same time suggesting the difficulties that obsolescence can pose to personal archivists. She asserts, "If the data matters to you, you must check frequently to make sure you can still read it and transfer it to new media as old ones die off. Libraries have archivists to manage this; families don't."[8] Individuals are responsible for keeping their digital files viable. That's a tall order for nonprofessionals.

Kodak, a company known for making photography accessible to the public since 1888, has weighed in on the new world of digital imaging.[9] In its Digital Learning Center, Kodak states that "As long as the storage media remains intact and there is a device that can replay it, the digital pictures will exist as you saved them."[10] While this is true, those variables are significant and present a major obstacle to the average person undertaking a personal archiving project.

For many, preserving the integrity of the storage device is an uphill battle. Disks can become damaged. As Bill LeFurgy points out, "That's because disks are fragile constructions that were never designed for permanence."[11] Hard drives can crash. USB flash drives can get lost. And even if a person is able to safeguard the storage device itself, there is still that threat of obsolescence. According to Elizabeth Leggett, "Storage devices for digital information become obsolete quickly, lasting not hundreds of years, but as few as ten."[12]

In summer 2012, I attended a large gathering of scrapbookers. The group was a mix of traditional scrapbooking enthusiasts, digital scrappers, and those who do both. The room was abuzz with shared tips, techniques, success stories, and anecdotes collected over years of practice. The ladies (in this case, the group was entirely made up of women) chatted about the preservation of paper-based photographic materials, as well as digital image files.

A common concern for many of the scrapbooking enthusiasts, however, was the pervasiveness of mobile phone-based photos to the exclusion of all other photography types. This is not to say that they were opposed to cellphone photography; they appreciated the convenience of a quick and portable way to capture memories. The concern was what happens to those images once they are captured.

The images end up saved on a tiny SD card or in the phone itself. With many mobile phones, images can be uploaded directly to social media sites. The concern voiced most among that group of scrapbookers was that, especially for younger people, the process stops there. The photos are not printed, downloaded to another device, or backed up in any way.

One participant shared the story of a family friend's teenaged child. The young girl had a massive collection of photos, all taken with her cellphone. She uploaded them to Facebook, essentially creating a photo journal of her life. After posting the images to her social network, she deleted the originals. The scrapbooker, a professional, helped the teenager download all of the pictures from her Facebook profile and ultimately organize those images into a scrapbook. Although this was a good recovery effort for the collection and a valuable lesson for the young girl, the downloaded photos were of relatively poor quality. After being uploaded to the site, resized, and then downloaded again, the image files were degraded. The originals would have had higher resolution and superior visual quality, but they were, of course, long gone.

Personal archivists can find themselves stymied by the roadblocks of obsolescence and potential damage to digital files. Unfortunately, there are still other obstacles that can threaten long-term access. In her article on putting one's electronic affairs in order, *Chicago Tribune* reporter Becky Yerak writes, "Even if a person gives power of attorney to an agent to access digital assets, that doesn't mean a bank, social-media site, or email service will accept that authority."[13] Individuals may take the time to preserve their digital legacy—saving emails, creating online journals, saving photographs to web-based storage services—but without taking steps to ensure access to their surviving loved ones, the information can become irretrievable.

How People Are Archiving

Despite the challenges, people are still finding a way to preserve their memories in both print and digital form. Whether or not individuals consciously define their activities as personal archiving, the efforts generally translate into maintaining pieces of the past—or present—in such a way that they will still be available and usable in the future. Why is this such an ongoing and pervasive concern for so many? Simply put, we as conscious beings do not want to be forgotten. We do not want to disappear from thoughts and memories, nor do we want our loved ones to meet that same fate.

After Sumit Paul-Choudhury's wife passed away, he set out to create a memorial website in her honor in response to her request, "Make sure people remember me."[14] He noted that at the time he initiated the project, it was rather uncommon. Paul-Choudhury created a website and added photographs and text as a tribute to his late wife.

Now, creating a digital memorial is not only more common, but it's easy enough for anyone who has some basic internet skills. Personal websites can now be created easily by novices thanks to templates and WYSIWYG (What You See Is What You Get) editors. Several years ago, before I had learned HTML, I was able to create my first basic website using a blogging platform. These services are made to be user-friendly. Facebook, which allows people across the globe to share the moments of their lives, has taken the desire to memorialize departed loved ones into consideration. If a Facebook account holder passes away, friends and family are invited to contact Facebook to change the deceased person's existing profile into a memorial page.[15] A memorial page allows friends and family to leave messages of remembrance, while at the same time giving them the opportunity to view images of their lost loved one.

These services are better known, however, for chronicling the experiences of the living, rather than creating tributes to the departed. Through widely available—and often free—social media services, people are able to share photographs, life events, and daily musings with their friends, family, or even the general public if they should so desire. A blog, photo stream, or profile page is an easy way to remember the moments of one's own life and keep up-to-date with the activities of others.

As Paul-Choudhury points out, "Facebook and its ilk put a lot of work into keeping your information neatly organized and readily accessible. That's not something most of us are good at."[16] That makes these services highly desirable for the budding personal archivist. They do not require any specialized training or knowledge of the hierarchical structure of files in website development. Users can add photographs, comments, and web links with a click of a mouse (or by pressing a button on a smartphone). He warns, however, that "many preservationists feel that it is not safe to entrust information of sentimental value to companies with fickle agendas and fortunes." Although these sites offer convenience and ease of use, there is an inherent danger in putting all your eggs in one basket—especially when you don't own the basket! If a service goes down or, even worse, goes out of business, the digital archives of countless people could disappear in an instant.

Case Studies

So, aside from social media and other web-based services, how are people preserving, sharing, and organizing their personal memories? How and what are they archiving for posterity?

To answer these questions, I posted a query to my own personal and professional networks. There are many articles available describing how professionals in the field undertake the task of organizing and preserving materials, but far fewer on how individuals and families are engaging in these archiving tasks for their own personal benefit. I conducted informal email interviews with three people who are currently working on their own archiving projects, as well as with the editor of this book. I asked why they decided to initiate their projects and how they started. They shared their obstacles, setbacks, and successes, as well as their plans for the future.

Case Study 1: Claudia Martinez

Claudia Martinez, a former library technician, began a personal archiving project after the passing of her mother in 2011.[17] She said, "When Mom died last year, I inherited four banker's boxes of loose photos, 50- to 100-year-old photo albums, letters, newspaper clippings, 16" x 20" rolled marriage certificates, and 'books' of stories my great-grandfather and great-great-grandmother wrote." For Martinez, the hardest part was deciding where to start. She felt overwhelmed by the size of the collection and the overall lack of organization.

Martinez decided that the best way to approach a project of this magnitude was to just dive in, box by box. She weeded out materials that may have been of interest to the creator of the collection but were of little value in terms of family history or greater historical context. She was mindful of basic preservation as she processed her newly acquired collection. Martinez purchased acid-free sleeves and containers at local office and hobby supply stores and carefully separated and stored delicate items.

Once she had the large inventory pared down and sorted, Martinez began scanning the images using a desktop scanner. At the time of our interview, she estimated that she had completed 140 photo album pages. Having done research ahead of time, she was prepared to employ best practices in her personal archiving project. "I bought an up-to-date edition of Photoshop, which has enabled me to restore faded photos and otherwise illegible letters." She went on to say, "Because I have learned to save most of these as TIFFs, so as to be able to enlarge and edit more exactly, I needed lots of portable file storage. I invested in a 1 TB portable drive that gives me plenty of room to store large files." As additional backup, she created DVDs of the most valuable photos and documents. She shared copies of these DVDs with other family members.

Although most of the images were not labeled, Martinez overcame that obstacle by reaching out to family members to aid in identifications. She has used Ancestry.com (www.ancestry.com) to contact distant relatives to help with her project. This has allowed her to merge her personal archiving and genealogy projects, enabling her to create a richer and more complete picture of her family throughout the generations.

Martinez now has the beginnings of a well-constructed personal archive. She has engaged in basic physical preservation, careful reformatting, identification, storage, and backup. Although she had felt uncertain about how to start, she took admirable measures to follow the standards that would give her the best outcome in the end.

Case Study 2: Rebecca Caldon

Rebecca Caldon, an engineer and mother of three young children, took a different approach to personal archiving. She worked collaboratively with her husband to scan images for a slideshow presentation at his parents' 60th birthday celebration.[18] Together, they scanned photographs and negatives using a scanner capable of handling both formats.

Caldon described their process as follows: "We scan directly into iPhoto. For now they are organized in events based on when they were scanned. Some have been tagged to identify people using Faces in iPhoto. Eventually I will be categorizing them based on a time frame." Although the project is in its early stages, she expressed a solid plan for the continuation of her efforts. At the point of our interview, she was using Time Machine (support.apple.com/kb/HT1427) with an external hard drive as backup. Her intention is to investigate online storage options for the collection.

Caldon's goal in the long run is to use the collection of scanned images to create digital scrapbooks—a way to organize and describe the photographs in an attractive and shareable way. The scrapbooks can be printed and bound, and multiple copies may be ordered to distribute to family. Digital scrapbooking can be a convenient and effective way to organize digital heritage files and store them in both print and electronic forms.

Case Study 3: Anne Hengehold

Anne Hengehold, an independent information professional, started archiving after her parents passed away, and she was tasked with selling their home.[19] She and her sisters were interested in their large photograph collection and wanted to share the very old prints with their extended family. To do so required digitization.

According to Hengehold, there were multiple challenges in the process. The first one was emotion. "It was hard to decide to discard pieces of the family history," but, she went on to say, "Not everything is worth digitizing." Just as a librarian or archivist may do when processing a collection, she made the decision to weed out imperfect and less noteworthy pictures. She also sorted out many duplicates.

Another obstacle that she faced was the volume of the project, which was reportedly overwhelming. She had chosen to scan her own personal photographs concurrently with the ancestral project, and the result was an even greater investment of time, energy, and space within her home. Hengehold made the decision to send some of the materials out for professional scanning. Although time-saving, it added an extra step as she found that she had to manually "marry" the information printed on the backs of individual photographs to the newly scanned image files.

Hengehold estimated that the complete collection consists of approximately 15,000 images. With that many files to organize, she said that "date has been the single most important organizing feature for my purposes." For the images that she sent out for professional scanning, the files were returned with the dates as part of individual file names. To keep the project consistent with the work she had done personally and to bolster the descriptive metadata for the collection, she manually entered dates into the date field in iPhoto.

As an information professional, Hengehold is no stranger to digital storage and backup. She has taken a very thorough and cautious approach to saving her considerable work. She stores all of the digitized images and descriptive data on her iMac and backs up the files in Time Capsule. She even went a step further and saved the project to a removable backup disk, which she has stored off-site.

Looking back on her project and the challenges she faced, Hengehold offered suggestions to emerging personal archivists who may suddenly find themselves in the position of managing a large collection. Her first recommendation was to do some research on organizing such a project before beginning. Like many, she learned as she went, which can add considerable stress to the endeavor. During her project, she wished that she had been able to find a way for others to share the task of labeling and dating the image files. With her home being the base of operations and all the photographs in her possession, there was not a convenient way to do that. Her final recommendation was to expect to spend more than double the time and money originally allotted for such a project. Learning curves and technical issues can arise, making a personal archiving project more of a challenge than anticipated.

Case Study 4: Donald Hawkins

Donald Hawkins, a writer and editor, took over the collection of slides that his father had begun in the 1950s.[20] With decades of accumulation, he estimates that there are now 30,000 slides in the collection. Like many others, Hawkins made the decision to scan the slides to preserve them. Using a Canon 8400F scanner, which scans four slides at a time (Figure 2.1), it takes him about an hour to scan 50 slides, so the project has required a considerable time investment.

Hawkins uses the software (ArcSoft PhotoStudio 6) that came with the scanner to edit the images.[21] It has given him the ability to remove scratches and enhance colors. As a result, the saved images are clearer, brighter, and more visually appealing than the originals, adding value to the digital collection. He is careful to label the files by number. His plan is to make an index when he is finished the scanning and editing phase of his substantial project.

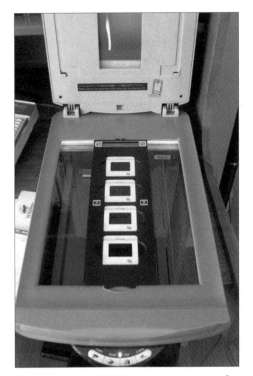

**Figure 2.1 Using a Canon 8400F scanner to scan four slides
at a time**

With such a large number of physical slides, Hawkins had to find a
way to organize and store them. He said, "Early on, I discovered that
cigar boxes make ideal storage containers for the slides—they're just
the right size and height—and about 300 slides fit in the average box"
(Figure 2.2).

He has labeled the boxes with letters (A–Z, AA–ZZ, etc.) and has
numbered the slides in each box. As he works, he creates a directory for
the slides from each box and then copies the directories upon finishing.
To keep track of what images are stored in the individual boxes, he creates a written description of the groups of slides (Family, Trip to
California, etc.). Eventually, he will transfer all of this data to a database.

Digital storage and backup have been primary concerns for
Hawkins. He makes three copies of his scanned files. One copy is

Figure 2.2   Slides organized in a cigar box

stored on an SD card housed in a safe deposit box off-site, a second copy is on a USB drive in his office, and the third is on an external hard drive kept in a different part of his house. Having researched personal archiving practices, he is prepared to take the steps necessary to preserve his collection and safeguard the fruits of his labor.

Real People, Real Applications

When reviewing the experiences of Martinez, Caldon, Hengehold, and Hawkins, it is easy to see the motivations behind personal archiving. The desire to preserve and save a lifetime of memories in a meaningful way is a strong driving force. At the same time, the many challenges, triumphs, and considerations that people face in the course of a personal archiving project are also clear.

The process involves many steps. The first, as seen in all of our examples, is the handling of physical materials. Images and files that are not born digital (i.e., paper- or film-based materials) must be sorted and organized, and basic steps must be taken to ensure their preservation. Then, printed photographs and documents are digitized—a vital step that allows for multiple copies, easier distribution, and the security of additional backup. Digitizing print materials also allows the personal archivist to merge reformatted images and born-digital files into one comprehensive collection.

The finished products for an individual's or family's archive can vary. In Hengehold's project, the archive took the form of an impressively large catalog of digital files that were labeled, stored, and backed up for security. Similarly, Martinez and Hawkins created digital collections and took steps to safeguard their physical materials. Caldon pursued a creative and artistic approach, making a slideshow of images and planning to design digital scrapbooks.

A personal archive can incorporate even more than photographs and important family documents. It may branch out to include personal and professional writing, saved emails, website files, blog posts, downloaded social media history, and more. Genealogy work and related house history research can become part of the ever-expanding collection.

Researching house histories is an interesting subgenre within family history research. The homes in which we and our families have lived are part of the memories we want to preserve. To trace the history of a home, individuals may have to delve into historic documents including deeds, building permits, and insurance records, as well as the usual genealogical sources, such as census records, church records, vital documents, and city directories.[22] Just as photos, letters, and birth certificates—and the digitized copies of each—become part of the cherished collection in a personal archive, the documentation collected in the course researching a house history are part of the story. A completed report with citations and images can become a valuable part of the personal archive.

In her blog, house historian and archaeologist Stacy Kozakavich shares the story of researching her home. She writes, "It certainly didn't qualify for any kind of landmark status or historical designation. But the people who lived there were interesting. ... Finding that story made me feel connected to the history of the place I lived, and the people who inhabited it before me."[23] She went on to share her findings with the new owners when she sold her home. Much like family histories and personal histories, the history of a home lives on thanks to research and the careful gathering and preservation of memories.

Conclusion

Individuals and families want to preserve and recollect the significant moments of their lives. Today, the memories come in the form of copious digital files as well as physical objects. There is a great deal of information to manage and keep accessible, which requires planning and adaptability. Still, people take on personal archiving projects because the information is important in their quest to remember and be remembered. There may be problems along the way, but they find a way to continue toward their goals.

My grandmother who so loved her comparatively small collection of prints would have been reeling over the heritage collections people have now. Nevertheless, I am confident she would have appreciated the new opportunities to save the past. Loved ones are meant to be remembered and memories are meant to be cherished.

Endnotes

1. "Oldest Sound Recording of Christmas Discovered by Museum of London," MuseumofLondon.org, December 20, 2012, accessed May 16, 2013, www.museum oflondon.org.uk/Corporate/Press-media/Press-releases/Earliest+Christmas+ recording.htm.

2. Jeremy Leighton John, "The Future of Saving Our Past," *Nature* 459, no. 7248 (2009): 775–776, accessed May 16, 2013, dcls.idm.oclc.org/login?url=search.ebs cohost.com/login.aspx?direct=true&db=f5h&AN=61029194&site=ehost-live.

3. Bill LeFurgy, "Personal Digital Archiving Outreach at the 2012 National Book Festival," *The Signal: Digital Preservation*, October 3, 2012, accessed May 16, 2013, blogs.loc.gov/digitalpreservation/2012/10/personal-digital-archiving-outreach-at-the-2012-national-book-festival.

4. Sumit Paul-Choudhury, "Digital Legacy: The Fate of Your Online Soul," *New Scientist* 210, no. 2809 (April 23, 2011): 41–43, accessed July 2, 2013, www.newscientist.com/article/mg21028091.400-digital-legacy-the-fate-of-your-online-soul.html.

5. Mike Ashenfelder, "One Family's Personal Digital Archives Project," *The Signal: Digital Preservation*, July 18, 2012, accessed May 16, 2013, blogs.loc.gov/digitalpreservation/2012/07/one-familys-personal-digital-archives-project.

6. Fredric M. Miller, *Arranging and Describing Archives and Manuscripts* (Chicago: The Society of American Archivists, 1990), 5–7.

7. Sumit Paul-Choudhury, "Your Digital Legacy."

8. Wendy M. Grossman, "A Fond Farewell to the Floppy Disk," *The Guardian*, April 27, 2010, accessed May 16, 2013, www.guardian.co.uk/commentisfree/2010/apr/27/farewell-floppy-computer-disk.

9. "History of Kodak," Kodak, accessed May 16, 2013, www.kodak.com/ek/US/en/Our_Company/History_of_Kodak/Imaging-_the_basics.htm.

10. "Chapter I, Digital Reference: Lesson I: Frequently Asked Questions," Kodak Digital Learning Center, January 1999, accessed May 16, 2013, www.kodak.com/country/US/en/digital/dlc/book4/chapter1/index.shtml.

11. Bill LeFurgy, "Floppy Disks Are Dead, Long Live Floppy Disks," *The Signal: Digital Preservation*, April 11, 2012, accessed May 16, 2013, blogs.loc.gov/digitalpreservation/2012/04/floppy-disks-are-dead-long-live-floppy-disks.

12. Elizabeth Leggett, "Digital Storage and Archiving in Today's Libraries," *Kentucky Libraries* 76, no. 3: 30–35 (2012), accessed May 16, 2013, dcls.idm.oclc.org/login?url=search.ebscohost.com/login.aspx?direct=true&db=ofs&AN=78122700&site=ehost-live.

13. Becky Yerak, "Are All Your Electronic Affairs In Order?" Philly.com, September 9, 2012, accessed May 16, 2013, articles.philly.com/2012-09-09/business/33714728_1_digital-assets-accounts-access.

14. Sumit Paul-Choudhury, "Your Digital Legacy."

15. Max Kelly, "Memories of Friends Departed Endure on Facebook," The Facebook Blog, October 26, 2009, accessed May 16, 2013, www.facebook.com/blog/blog.php?post=163091042130.

16. Sumit Paul-Choudhury, "Your Digital Legacy."

17. Claudia Martinez, email message to the author, September 18, 2012.

18. Rebecca Caldon, email message to the author, September 18, 2012.

19. Anne Hengehold, email message to the author, October 11, 2012.

20. Donald Hawkins, email message to the author, December 11, 2012.

21. Donald Hawkins, discussion with the author, December 13, 2012.

22. Kimberly Powell, "House Histories: Tracing the Genealogy of Your Home or Other Building," About.com Genealogy, accessed May 16, 2013, genealogy. about.com/od/basics/a/house_history.htm.

23. Stacy Kozakavich, "About Stacy," House Histories, accessed May 16, 2013, house histories.wordpress.com/about-2.

CHAPTER 3

The Library of Congress and Personal Digital Archiving

Mike Ashenfelder
Library of Congress

Publisher's note: Library of Congress employees do not own a copyright in the works that they create within the scope of their employment because they are U.S. Government personnel. Under the U.S. copyright statute, 17 U.S.C. Section 105, copyright protection is not available in the United States for any work of the U.S. Government. Therefore, this chapter is in the public domain.

Digital preservation is a familiar issue among the world's leading cultural institutions. But despite over a decade of institutional success in preserving digital files and collections, most of the general public—the largest group of digital-file stakeholders in the world—are unaware of what digital preservation or personal digital archiving is or why they should care.

Today, most people, young and old, have some sort of digital files to preserve; digital photographs are the most common. They need to know that their digital stuff is at risk of being lost unless they do something about it. The Library of Congress is trying to remedy that by reaching out to partner with public libraries and other local institutions to teach the public about personal digital archives.

That is a tremendous task. Why should the Library be involved?

The Library is firmly rooted in digital preservation and has been building up its expertise since the mid-1990s with the American Memory Project. But the Library's true digital preservation work began in 2000 when it helped found the National Digital Information Infrastructure and Preservation Program. Its goal was and is to foster digital preservation research, collaboration, and standardization among government agencies, cultural institutions, and other stakeholders.

About 5 years ago, the Library recognized that many people were accumulating digital files (primarily photos, due to the proliferation of cameras on cellphones) but were not aware of the proper way to save these files. Even worse, most people were not aware of the potential threats to digital files: getting stuck on obsolete media, getting lost, or accidentally being deleted. To correct the situation, the Library developed information resources to help raise a general awareness about preserving personal digital material.

On the surface, it seemed like a daunting task to try to communicate everything the Library knows about digital preservation. But it became apparent that its institutional digital preservation knowledge could be distilled and simplified into a few steps and that information would be sufficient to help people get started. "Simplification" is a crucial strategy: Simplifying our information is essential in order to avoid losing an audience due to long-winded explanations with unnecessary technical detail. Too much information can bury a message.

We began narrowing down institutional digital preservation practices to find commonalities with basic consumer practices. Essentially, institutions and individuals use similar equipment (computers and storage media) and have similar stakes (loss of files). Institutions and individuals acquire content (acquisition), and they should organize it and name it in a way that will help them search and find it later (metadata). Finally, the content should be backed up.

Most people already know that they should back up their files. Like flossing or exercising, they know it is a good practice. But despite their good intentions, they may or may not actually do anything about it. It is usually a task put off until "later." The best thing that libraries can do is explain digital archiving, explain how easy it is to safely archive personal digital material, and stress the consequences of inaction and the threat of potential loss of valuable digital possessions.

Potential Loss

Our general explanation of digital loss goes something like this: We can "store and ignore" physical items such as books, paper photos, and documents under optimized conditions for years and expect that we can access them any time. The key word is *expect*. But "store and ignore" does not work with digital files such as audio, video, photos, and email because they are dependent on hardware and software to make them work. If either hardware or software is ignored for a significant length of time, it becomes obsolete, and the digital file will become difficult to access. It essentially becomes trapped.

Software makes the files accessible, and the hardware (the storage medium) is the container in which the files reside. Each storage medium has vulnerabilities and a limited lifespan. The coating on a CD can flake off. Floppy disks require computers built with disk drives that can read them. External hard drives can be dropped and damaged. In general, the life of storage media is cut short by at least three factors:

- Lack of durability

- Obsolescence

- Usage and handling (the more often a storage device is handled, the greater the possibility it will fail)

The whole arrangement is fragile. Not only are files placed at risk just by being transferred around, but the storage device itself needs to be kept in a stable environment with moderate temperature and humidity, and it needs to be protected from harmful elements. Paper books and photos are also fragile; they should not be stored in a damp cellar, for instance, because of the potential damage from mildew and mold. Technology needs similar considerations regarding its own particular vulnerabilities.

Obsolescence is a fact of life in the digital age. As storage technology improves, previous generations of storage containers become obsolete. Even up-to-date computers may not have:

- Drives that can read older media

- Hardware connections that can attach to older media (or media drives)

- Device drivers that can recognize older media hardware

- Software that can read older files on media

And when stuff gets trapped on obsolete media, it is costly to get an expert to rescue it.

Lack of organization can also make finding files difficult. It is easy to lose track of files if they are scattered among websites, floppy disks, thumb drives, and CDs. Leaving content online—whether in the cloud, attached to emails, on social media sites, or on other online services—is risky because commercial services can and do go out of business, at which point the material stored on their sites could get deleted.

Despite these risks, the solution to mitigating the threat of digital loss is deceptively simple: Organize and back up your files. The Library broadened the solution to four best practices for personal digital archiving.

Personal Digital Archiving

The digital preservation steps that the Library delineated for the general public are scaled-down versions of the steps the Library takes with its own digital collections.

For instance, when we take in digital collections, those collections are assigned identifiers and metadata, moved to storage, and backed up. Copies of the backups are kept in geographically different locations. The storage media is replaced every 5 years or so, and the data is transferred (migrated) to new storage media. Files are verified periodically, and their integrity is checked to make sure they are still intact.

So the approach to personal digital archiving that we recommend (and that is described in the sections that follow) is generally the same as for institutional collections: Locate everything to be saved, decide what to keep, organize the files, and save copies in different places and manage the collections.

Locate Everything to Be Saved

Files must be found before they can be backed up. Transfer them off of CDs, old floppy disks and storage media, the camera, and wherever else they might be. Download files from emails and social media sites. Then, gather them all into one place, such as a folder on a computer.

Why transfer files off of cameras? Given a digital camera's large storage capacity, it is common to let photos accumulate on the camera for months. What if the camera gets lost or stolen? And photos can be accidentally deleted from the camera. Get them off the camera or phone and save them with the other digital files to be backed up.

Decide What to Keep

Select the nicest ones, the ones worth keeping, and delete the rest. Does anyone really need 50 photos of clouds or 200 photos of autumn leaves? Blurry, unrecognizable photos? Delete them. Homework from 10 years ago? Delete it. Be decisive and thorough. Whittle the mass of photos down to the best, the "keepers." Toss out document drafts. Clear the clutter.

Organize the Files

There is no set system for organization; it just needs to be consistent and predictable to make it easy to find materials later. Descriptive folder and file names help. The descriptive names could be file types, with photos in a "Photo" folder and documents in a "Document" folder, or by dates, with files named by month or year. Really, any system of organization that makes sense to you is fine.

Save Copies in Different Places and Manage the Collections

Most institutions replicate their digital collections in a separate geographic location far away from the source collection. In the event of a disaster, the distant, replicated collection will be safe, intact, and accessible, backed up on tape or spinning disk drives.

Similarly, personal files should be backed up in separate locations on at least two different types of storage devices. For example, save a copy on a backup drive and a copy on CD or on a flash drive or in online storage (the cloud). Diversity in storage formats is important because no storage device is 100 percent reliable.

Professional photographers who rely on digital files for their income have what they call the "3 - 2 - 1 rule":

- Make 3 copies.

- Save at least 2 onto different types of storage media.

- Save 1 in a different location from where you live.

And there is no set frequency of how often to back up—the more often the better, though.

As time passes and your storage device grows obsolete, the files that reside on that device become difficult to access. To help ensure ongoing access, move your collection to a new storage device every 5–7 years. When you buy a new computer, it is a good opportunity to buy a few new backup devices as well.

Taking an active role with personal digital collections will keep them safely preserved and accessible; ignore them and the collections may become inaccessible. It is that simple. Technology should, in time, automate the archiving process for us and make backing up less tedious. But until the backup and archive process is entirely automated, we need to care for it ourselves.

Another aspect of managing personal digital collections is estate planning. It is important to let a loved one know where important documents reside and supply them with URLs and passwords, if needed. (See Chapter 5 by Evan Carroll for much more on this topic.)

Digital Photos Make Us All Stakeholders

Digital photos rank highest among materials most people want to save. Most cameras come with software and instructions for uploading photos to the computer, but many cellphones do not. Not every cellphone owner is aware of the issues associated with digital photo files, so the Library has created a few different resources and has given several presentations about aspects of preserving digital photographs. Although we try to avoid complicating the explanation with too much technical information, offering a little technical background enables people to better understand the potential threats to their photos and the consequences of their actions.

Beginning at the moment when someone takes a digital photo, three things happen almost immediately:

1. The camera saves the photo as a digital file.

2. The camera assigns a name to the file.

3. The camera inserts some technical information into the photo file about the conditions of the shot.

Most consumer cameras and camera phones save the file in a JPEG format, but the average person should not be concerned about formats unless he or she has an interest in working with a special format. JPEG is the widely accepted standard format, and most websites to which photos can be uploaded only accept JPEGs. When in doubt, we recommend leaving the file format as it is.

Renaming files with descriptive names can help you quickly identify photos later without having to display the contents. Renaming files will not affect the contents, the format, or state of the photo files.

Some photo editing software enables the addition of a description into the photo file, just as you would write a description on the back of a paper photo. This is standard practice for professional photographers who add their copyright and contact information to each of their digital photos. This information can be displayed with the proper software. For a list of metadata resources, visit photometadata.org/META-Resources-Metadata-Links-and-Resources-Guide or search online for *embed description into digital photo.*

> **T**
> **I**
> **P**
>
> *Warning!* Some photo editing and photo management software programs store added descriptions into databases separate from the actual photos. Even though the descriptions are associated with individual photos, they do not actually get inserted into the photo files. This is important to know if you want your digital photos to carry extra identifying information when they are moved or viewed with other software. Also, if descriptions are added to photo files, the process of uploading those photos to social media sites and photo sites and as email attachments may strip out the descriptions. Be aware of the risks when you transfer photos. The Photo Metadata Project did a comparative test of several different social media resources (www.embeddedmetadata.org/social-media-test-procedure.php). For more information about the issues surrounding metadata stripping, see "Social Media Networks Stripping Data from Your Digital Photos" (blogs.loc.gov/digital preservation/2013/04/social-media-networks-stripping-data-from-your-digital-photos).

None of these steps so far has any effect on the state or quality of the photo itself. What if you want to modify a photo? Sharpen it or brighten it or enhance it? The first thing to remember is *never work with the original; always work with a copy.*

When you are ready to modify a copy of the photo, it helps to understand a little about the nature of digital photo files and what effect a modification might have on them. Digital photos are made up of millions of colored and shaded dots or squares called *pixels.* If an image comprises 10 pixels on each horizontal line, and if the image measured 1" wide, the measurement would be stated as 10 dots per inch (dpi) or 10 pixels per inch (ppi).

Resolution is directly related to the density of dpi/ppi. The more dots or pixels per inch a photo has, the higher the potential resolution of the photo, and the fewer the dots or pixels per inch, the lower the potential resolution of the photo. A larger palette of colors or shades of gray generates more pixels per inch on average, so images can be smoother, sharper, and delicately nuanced. A 50,000 dpi/ppi photo will look far nicer, with more subtle gradations, than a 10 dpi/ppi photo.

But the more pixels in a digital photo, the larger the file size will be, just because it has more information. And the larger the file size, the fewer photo files a camera card can hold. A camera menu may offer a choice between saving photos in a high quality (amounting to fewer photos) or lesser quality (amounting to more photos). That is a decision each individual needs to make.

Again, always preserve originals and work only with copies.

TIP

When uploading photos to certain websites, such as photo sharing or social media websites, the photos may get *compressed* to reduce the size of the file and to enable a quicker upload. This compression may be *lossy*, which means that some pixels are discarded in order to reduce the file size. Compression can also lower the quality of the photo. Once a photo is compressed and pixels are discarded, the pixels can never be restored or the original quality regained. However, compression is common, and it is not a bad thing if done right. Often a compressed image looks good enough for most webpages.

Scanning

This chapter so far has been about the challenges of archiving so-called born-digital photos. Scanning paper photographs into digital copies can also be a challenge, mainly due to unclear user manuals and word-of-mouth misinformation.

For pixel density, photography experts at the Library recommend scanning 4″ x 6″, 5″ x 7″, and 8″ x 10″ photos at 300 dpi/ppi. If the scan settings are larger than 300 dpi/ppi for average-size photos, the eye will probably not detect a significant increase in detail.

Photographic slides require a different dpi/ppi setting, due to their physically small size. Referring back to the earlier dpi/ppi explanation, a photographic slide has more photographic information packed into an inch than, say, a 5″ x 7″ paper photo of the same image. Therefore, it is best to scan slides at a higher dpi/ppi setting—about 1,800 dpi/ppi—to capture all of the image "information." The same is true for very small photos.

If the scanning software offers a choice of file formats for saving the scanned photo or slide, the best choices are TIFF or JPEG. TIFF is a lossless format, which means that the scanned image file will be uncompressed and data rich. It will also be a large file size. JPEG is a lossy, compressed format, though if the scanner settings offer a choice of quality (rather than specific dpi/ppi settings), selecting "best" or "highest" will retain the maximum amount of image data. JPEG files, being compressed, will be smaller than TIFFs.

Once the photos are scanned and digitized, treat the files the same as any other digital photos: File names can be changed, descriptions added, originals backed up, and copies modified.

Outreach

To get this digital preservation information out to local libraries and the general public, the Library created a personal digital archiving section on the digitalpreservation.gov website and populated it with instructional videos, downloadable brochures, and topic-oriented pages. We wrote about how to archive the most common digital possessions: audio, video, photographs, email, documents, and websites. (In fact, most of them can be treated the same way: Organize them, back them up, and upgrade to new media about every 5–7 years.)

Some concepts are tricky to explain, so we created a primer to address topics such as scanning, how long storage media will last, how to transfer photos from your camera to your computer (not an uncommon question), and how to archive email.

Our videos (digitalpreservation.gov/multimedia/videos.html) are brief, and they clearly explain the basics of digital preservation and adding descriptions to photos. Podcast interviews (www.loc.gov/pod casts/digital preservation) with leading information technology experts help answer questions like how to get video off of (copyright-free) DVDs. (The Library, home of the U.S. Copyright Office, understandably defends copyright.)

And we learned that to communicate more effectively, we needed to make our terminology less complex and to avoid words and terms like *photometadata*, *digital objects*, *file formats*, *data*, and *records*. These are terminology speed bumps for the general public that only disrupt the flow of explanation. For example, instead of using a word like *metadata*, the word *description* is used instead.

In addition to publishing on our website, we also post digital preservation information to Facebook (www.facebook.com/digitalpreservation), Twitter (@ndiipp), and our blog (blogs.loc.gov/digitalpreservation). The videos and podcasts are added to the Library of Congress channel on iTunes and YouTube (bit.ly/11T9ONf).

Each year, during the American Library Association's (ALA) Preservation Week (usually held in April), we hold a Personal Archiving Day at the Library, a free event to which people can come and talk to the Library staff about preserving digital and physical items. We were also invited to speak about preserving digital photos at several events hosted by the Smithsonian Institute's National Museum of African American History and Culture. We also annually host panels at South by Southwest and staff tables at the National Book Festival.

After Library staff had worked at a few public events for personal archiving, we realized that no matter how much we publish on the web, there is no guarantee that the general public sees or understands any of it. The most effective means of communication is just what we do at the events: answer questions on the spot and directly educate the public.

By far the most effective event, in terms of reaching the most people, is the National Book Festival. For 2 days, we answer questions from a nonstop river of people, and we learn from our interactions with people exactly what we communicate effectively and what we need to clarify. Then we work on the information, create a new brochure, update a webpage or refine our text, and publish it again.

Something else we discovered at our tables at the National Book Festival is that obsolete media are powerful teaching aids. Each time we work the event, we load our table with an array of storage devices, current and obsolete, from punch cards to floppy disks, data tapes to laserdiscs. These artifacts make an impact on everyone who passes by. Older people are gleeful to see something from early in their careers, such as punch cards and zip drives, and parents explain to their fascinated little children what an 8″ floppy disk is. But in handling all of the "museum pieces," the point is driven home: All storage media becomes obsolete. That gives us an opening to talk about good stewardship practices for personal digital collections.

During Preservation Week 2012, staff from the Library partnered with public libraries to give presentations on personal digital archiving. These public library visits were not only outreach events, they were also aimed at establishing an ongoing relationship to provide and improve information resources for the public.

At each public library presentation, the audiences were grateful for the information, and the public library staff was welcoming and pleased to have the Library's involvement. Some of the public library staff came up with ideas of their own, such as asking people to donate copies of their personal files to a community repository at the library;

in that way, the public library could participate in the community's local history efforts.

Based on this success, we expanded our strategy to help local libraries with their outreach efforts by developing Personal Digital Archiving Day Kit (digitalpreservation.gov/personalarchiving), which includes a variety of resources to help users stage their own events.

Reaching a Vast Audience

Each April, the ALA hosts Preservation Week, a week of events—held online around the country—designed to spread awareness about the preservation of personal and shared collections, both physical and digital. Our colleagues asked us to do two webinars for Preservation Week in 2013, and so, on March 20, 2013, we presented a webinar titled, "Hosting a Personal Digital Archiving Day Event," which we designed mainly for library staff, and on April 24, 2013, we presented a webinar titled, "Personal Digital Archiving," which we designed for a general audience.

Both webinars were well-attended, and afterward, the webinar hosts sent us a list of questions the attendees had submitted. We sorted the questions by topic and used the questions and answers to help refine the focus of our information resources. Two-thirds of the questions fell into two topic areas: digital photos and storage media.

After Preservation Week, at the suggestion of the Public Library Association (PLA), we began writing a biweekly blog post for Publiclibrariesonline.org about personal digital archiving. Response to the posts has been overwhelming.

Our goal at the Library is to reach as many people as possible and to make sure that the concepts of digital preservation and personal digital archiving become common knowledge and part of everyday life. We need to communicate on a vast scale if we want to be effective in helping the basic ideas seep into the public consciousness.

Libraries still seem like the optimum place for community outreach. They exist to make information freely available to their communities, and they will be around for many generations to come. Public libraries are increasingly involved in spreading digital literacy—facility with the internet and developing technology skills—into the communities they serve, and the knowledge of digital preservation and personal digital archiving is certainly part of digital literacy.

Until recently, our focus had been for our small team to encourage local libraries to start teaching about personal digital archiving and keep regular educational sessions going on their own, but we realized that was not a practical or realistic approach; at best, we might reach only several dozen people per year.

So, instead of working from the bottom up (i.e., beginning with our local public libraries), we decided to work from the top down. We approached the ALA to explore opportunities for collaboration. Within the ALA, the PLA and ALCTS were excited about collaboration. They were brimming with ideas.

We shared the goal of spreading awareness to local librarians about personal digital archiving and of its importance to individuals and the community in which they live. We brainstormed on ways to work with local public libraries.

There was a suggestion that a library might invite a local archivist or professional photographer to talk about digital photo preservation. They might invite a local oral historian or town historian to talk about personal contributions to local history and offer suggestions on how communities might add their own digital resources. During these events, librarians or library staff could include a PowerPoint presentation from our Library resources, or they could play one of our videos to lay the groundwork.

ALA, with support from the Institute of Museum and Library Services, has formed a partnership with StoryCorps, the organization that drives a mobile recording studio around the country, gathering oral histories from whoever wants to record them. The ALA news release (americanlibrariesmagazine.org/news/ala/ala-storycorps-receive-imls-grant-develop-library-outreach-program) stated: "Pilot libraries will receive equipment, training, promotional materials and other resources to help them implement community documentation projects using the popular StoryCorps interview model. Local libraries will retain copies of all interviews, but preservation copies will also be deposited with the Library. The project team will produce freely shareable training materials to help public libraries better understand strategies for sustaining local oral history programs." This is yet another example of public libraries serving their communities in innovative ways.

We continue to explore collaboration with public libraries on ways to help spread information. We will keep the drumbeat steady and consistent to help ensure that the idea of personal archiving becomes an unremarkable part of life, second nature. We are firm in our conviction that people should have a basic knowledge of how to take care of their digital stuff.

CHAPTER 4

Software and Services for Personal Archiving

Donald T. Hawkins

This chapter reviews some of the software products currently available for those who wish to undertake a personal archiving project. It is important to realize that many systems commonly available on most PCs and Macs or freely available on the web can be used to manage personal archives. For example, documents or photos can be stored in files on electronic media such as CDs, SD cards, or USB flash drives, along with a simple Microsoft Excel spreadsheet listing their metadata. Excel's sorting and searching functions can be used to find the files or the hyperlinks to them.

Other tasks relevant to personal archiving include disk image duplication, remote backup, format conversion, forensics, and reference management. Software programs that accomplish these procedures are readily available and can be found by simple searches in Google or other search engines.

Photo organizing software is popular, and there are many packages available. Typically, one purchases or downloads the software and installs it on a computer, and then the software organizes the photos stored on that computer. One of the most widely known and used is Google's Picasa (picasa.google.com), and like many of Google's offerings, Picasa is a free service. Others include Recollect (www.recollect.com), BR's PhotoArchiver (www.br-software.com/photoarchiver. html), and IMatch (www.photools.com/imatch-3-overview). Most photo organizing services include the capability to add metadata to the photos, and they can also automatically organize them by date using the raw data stored in digital image files. Strictly speaking, they are not archiving services because the organized files are housed on the user's PC or Mac. However, a number of services specifically dedicated to archiving have recently appeared.

Documents and photos are the most common types of objects that can be archived in these systems, but systems for archiving videos and home movies are also appearing on the market. Because of the widespread use of email, several significant email archiving projects are underway as well. For a listing of websites providing digital memorials, posthumous email services, and digital estate services, check out Evan Carroll's The Digital Beyond (www.thedigitalbeyond.com/online-services-list). (Note that many of the services listed there concentrate on estate planning and are therefore outside the scope of this book.) For some helpful tips on preserving archival materials, see the article "Taking Care of Your Own Archives" on the Smithsonian Institution Archive's blog (siarchives.si.edu/blog/you-asked-we-answered-taking-care-your-own-archives). Finally, for an example of how one family's archives were created, read "One Family's Personal Digital Archives Project" (blogs.loc.gov/digitalpreservation/2012/07/one-familys-personal-digital-archives-project).

Gordon Bell and Jim Gemmell at Microsoft Research are the authors of *Total Recall*, a fascinating book published in 2009,[1] in which they discuss various ways that all of the information we come into contact with can be captured and retrieved, either by the original owner or long after the owner's life ends. Bell's MyLifeBits project began as an effort to digitize the books he wrote, but it turned into a much more extensive research project to capture everything he came into contact with and experienced, and from which he developed the concept of Total Recall. Gemmell posts a very useful list of businesses offering software to support "life-logging" on his blog (jimgemmell.word press.com/2012/01/03/your-life-uploaded-2011-report-card-4). Jeff Ubois, author of Chapter 1, makes a valuable comment on Gemmel's list: "Companies are good at building new technologies for recording and for metadata extraction, but they are not trustworthy long-term custodians. ... Preservation needs to evolve in tandem with recording."

MyLifeBits extends many of the ideas first promulgated by Vannevar Bush in his widely cited, landmark 1945 article, "As We May Think" (www.theatlantic.com/doc/194507/bush). Bush envisioned a device called a *memex*, in which a user could store books, documents, and records for later recall as an extension of his own memory. His ideas were a long way ahead of his time, and it is surprising how relevant they continue to be. Bell and his associates recognized that today's computing and storage technologies would permit them to develop a memex-like system. But their goals for MyLifeBits go well beyond Bush's memex. Although their project is strictly for research and has not resulted in its own commercial product, it has formed the basis for many of the products and services now on the market.

A significant component of one personal memory system is an always-on wearable camera, which has been the subject of several research projects. The research conducted by Cathal Gurrin at the Dublin City University in Ireland is typical and was described by Gurrin at the 2011 Personal Archiving Conference. (Gurrin has authored many journal articles about his work; a complete list is available at www.computing.dcu.ie/~cgurrin/styled-4/index.html. His slides from the Personal Archiving Conference can be found at doras.dcu.ie/16241/1/Gurrin_Doherty_CLARITY_Dublin.pdf.)

The rest of this chapter reviews some of the products and services available for organizing and archiving photos and documents, email messages, and videos.

Archiving Photos and Documents

The proliferation of cameras in mobile phones has made it simple to rapidly amass a large number of photos, so it should not come as a surprise that many of today's software systems for archiving were developed primarily to handle photos. Many of these services run on PC and Mac platforms, but because of the explosive growth of mobile technology, they are also being recast as smartphone apps as well.

The growth in consumer photography is remarkable. A widely quoted blog posting by Jonathan Good, one of the co-founders of the 1000memories service (recently acquired by Ancestry.com), presents some fascinating statistics (blog.1000memories.com). Good estimates that more than 3.5 *trillion* photos have been taken in the last 200 years and that we now take four times as many photos each year than we did just 10 years ago (Figure 4.1). Incidentally, the oldest known photograph dates from 1826,[2] and the first photograph showing a living person is a street scene taken in Paris in 1838.[3]

Moreover, every 2 minutes, people take as many photos as the entire world took in the 1800s. According to Good, the largest library of photos is on Facebook, which stores 140 billion photos (Figure 4.2).

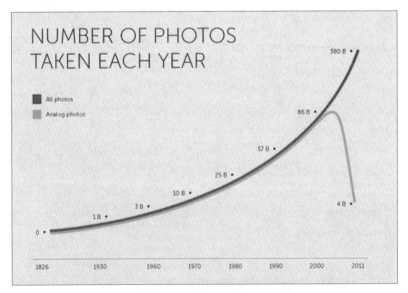

Figure 4.1   Number of photos taken each year (Source: blog.1000memories.com/94-number-of-photos-ever-taken-digital-and-analog-in-shoebox)

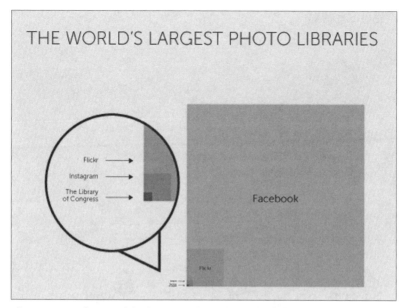

Figure 4.2   The world's largest photo libraries (Source: blog.1000memories.com/94-number-of-photos-ever-taken-digital-and-analog-in-shoebox)

It's no wonder that archiving photos has become a significant endeavor.

1000memories

"Grandma's shoebox" is a very appropriate metaphor for describing old snapshot collections, and 1000memories (www.1000memories.com; Figure 4.3), a pioneer in archiving software for consumers, has adopted the shoebox metaphor in its service.

Users' photo collections are organized in *shoeboxes* around a theme, event, or other subject. Typical subjects for shoeboxes are family history, vacations, weddings, and birthdays. Photos can be added from a user's computer or downloaded from Facebook, Flickr, and similar services. They can also be scanned via a partnership between 1000memories and ScanCafe (www.scancafe.com) at a cost of 22 cents each. (Users owning a smartphone can download a free app from

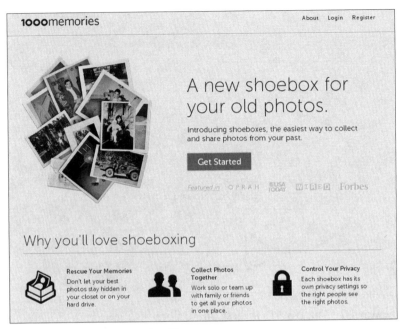

Figure 4.3   1000memories homepage

1000memories and use their phone as a scanner, but the quality of the
resulting scans may be low.)

Photos added to 1000memories shoeboxes can be tagged with dates,
personal names, or other information. During the shoebox creation
process, the user is required to indicate his or her relationship to the
person being tagged (a drop-down menu is provided, but the user can
enter any desired term). Links to video clips or music files can be
embedded in the shoebox. In an excellent outline of the creation
process, including screenshots (web.appstorm.net/reviews/1000memories-
remembering-loved-ones), one reviewer notes that, "1000memories is
as close to a permanent space that you will ever find on the internet—
and it rightly should be." One commenter adds, "It's like Facebook
should be."

A user can create or edit a shoebox individually or collaborate with
others, such as family members. One of the screens during the shoebox

creation process allows users to invite others to contribute to the photo collection. Users have complete control over privacy settings for their shoeboxes. According to the 1000memories website, photos will be stored indefinitely, and precautions against loss, such as multiple backup copies that are stored in several countries, have been implemented.

Lifemap

Lifemap (www.milifemap.com), a service of My Internet Corporation (mi Corp.) located in Toronto, Canada, provides secure private storage for photos, videos, and diaries (documents) that are "archived safely and organized in an intuitive way" from which one can build, enjoy, and archive a life story. Social networking activity, including tweets, Facebook postings, Flickr activity, and Foursquare check-ins, can also be stored on Lifemap, and it is searchable. According to Lifemap's website, while tablets have reinvented the family photo album, their service is "reinventing how to retrieve and display a lifetime of memories." It is important to recognize that, in contrast to Facebook, Lifemap concentrates first on archiving and preservation of photos, then sharing them.

mi Corp. was founded, as many small businesses are, in response to a significant event that exposed an unmet need. According to company founder Denim Smith, the death of a family member's parent was followed by a house fire that damaged memories of that parent. Smith's subsequent investigations revealed that there did not seem to be any services offering an easy way to back up and protect memories. There also didn't seem to be any photo storage services that would allow users to organize their memories into a fluid story and control them with the family over the long term. He also discovered that there was no mechanism to protect and pass memories to succeeding generations. (See Chapter 5 by Evan Carroll for further information.) So he developed the concept of a secure storage facility controlled by the user that focuses primarily on long-term photo storage, but it also provides ancillary services. He postulated that many people would pay a reasonable fee of a few dollars per month (similar to a bank service charge) for the peace of mind that comes from knowing that their precious family memories are preserved over their lifetime, yet readily available. Smith developed Lifemap, which uses the Amazon web service (AWS) for storing and managing users' memories, and designed a user-friendly graphical user interface.

Lifemap was launched in early 2013. Some of the ancillary features currently in development include a retail shopping component for other products based on users' photos (albums, calendars, etc.), facial recognition software for efficient tagging, and scanning services (in partnership with other companies).

In contrast to many social networking services such as Facebook, Lifemap concentrates exclusively on memories and has no plans to add music, commercial videos, or chat. Pricing for the service will be tiered based on the amount of storage required by the user. Each new user will receive an initial allotment for free, and additional free storage will be offered in exchange for new user referrals. The company's business model envisions reselling cloud storage via AWS to users at a very small markup over its wholesale rate, with most of its revenue coming from sales of the ancillary products. Lifemap has several unique features, including:

- *eBeneficiary*: By default, all stored user data is private, but an account owner can invite a trusted person to inherit the content after the owner's death. This unique and important feature removes some of the significant roadblocks imposed by Facebook and other services in accessing and transferring a deceased person's account.

- *Subaccounts*: An owner can create and populate a private subaccount that can be passed on to someone else at a future time. So, for example, parents could create an account with milestones of their child's life and then pass the account to him when he is old enough to maintain it, giving the child a complete record of his life starting from birth.

- *Timelines, milestones, and yearbooks*: All uploaded content is first put on a timeline, where the user can add a title, location, and other tags, or reset the date (Figure 4.4). Once memories are placed on the timeline, the user can easily jump to a specific date or any date range, or use search to recall memories instantly. Milestones can then be created using favorite photos or videos from an event such as a wedding, birthday, or vacation—important life events where one would typically take a lot of photos and build an album. All photos are curated and controlled by the user. Photos may be selected and added to a yearbook to produce a subset of the timelines devoted to special or recurring events each year or to display the photos that illustrate the best moments of the year. This capability also allows the user to choose data and view any event within a yearbook. The timeline also allows searching for specific tags, and search results can be displayed as a slideshow. *Ad hoc* albums can be created on demand from the results.

- *Diaries*: A private searchable diary can be created, tagged, and set to any date in the timeline. The diary feature also allows the user to add other documents such as letters written to young children and family recipes, and to add personal narratives to complement the photos of an event.

- *Batch tagging*: After uploading a batch of photos into Lifemap, a user can tag all of them at once, instead of individually as many other systems require. This can be a significant timesaver, particularly if the volume is large. In addition, Lifemap facial recognition software will add significant efficiencies to uploading and organizing a photo collection.

Lifemap allows users to create a slideshow of selected photos (perhaps using the tags and dates) and share it with those they have connected with on the site. Users can also send the URL of the slideshow, individual photos, groups of photos, or yearbooks to anyone who is not a Lifemap user. Lifemap is also available for the iPhone and iPad, and an Android version is in development.

Lifemap's vision is to become "a family's digital attic box of the 21st century." The company recognizes that typical families cannot be

Figure 4.4   Typical Lifemap timeline

early adopters of every new technology upgrade but would value a "sanctuary" for their memories over which they have control. Lifemap takes away the concern that they are at risk because of a change in business philosophy, because their data might become unreadable due to advances in storage formats, or because data will become inaccessible when someone dies. They can be assured that over the years, the family's emotional assets in analog and digital formats will be transferred from one generation to the next. Lifemap would like to offer the most comprehensive and trusted archive, allowing families to protect and enjoy their priceless memories once and for all. Smith is confident it will gain acceptance in filling this role. A brief video illustration of a typical Lifemap (in this case, one of Smith's) is available at youtube.com/watch?v=tzp9zT6xIFs.

Timebox

Timebox (www.timeboxapp.com) offers a free personal history archive app for the iPhone, iPad, and iPod touch. At present, Timebox is mostly oriented toward photos, but the long-term vision of the company producing it, Pepper Networks, LLC in Kirkland, Washington, is to add functionality for all types of digital materials: videos, documents, email, and so on. The company's CEO, Mary Ellen Heinen, has a master's degree in library and information science and is especially interested in working with libraries as they take a leading role in encouraging personal archiving in their communities.

A robust suite of features is included with Timebox. Photos can be downloaded from iOS devices, iPhoto, or Facebook on a Mac computer. They can then be tagged and organized, using the app's predefined categories or those created by the user. Stories, photo captions, and other additional details can also be added. Timeline, category, or yearbook views are available. Figure 4.5 shows the input screen for a photo, and Figure 4.6 shows the resulting entry in the Timebox database (note the comments that the user has added).

Although photos can be stored on the user's device, Timebox also provides an optional upgrade of 8GB of cloud storage and synchronization to multiple devices for a small fee. Photo collections can be shared by email, Facebook, or Twitter. In addition, PDF pages can be created from either single photos or photo collections, and assembled into an ebook. Version 2.0, recently released, includes several new features:

- A 3D photo selector for browsing photos and adding them to a new or existing collection

- The capability to create physical artifacts from a Timebox account, such as hardcover books, magazines, and laser-etched aluminum cubes

- Dropbox support for photos

Figure 4.5   Timebox photo input screen

Figure 4.6   Completed Timebox entry

Recollect

Recollect (www.recollect.com) backs up tweets, Foursquare check-ins, Flickr photos, and Instagrams from a user's accounts and stores them in a secure archive. A user's archive includes comments, conversations, and anything else related to the stored data. The data is searchable and downloadable at any time. Recollect offers three price plans depending on the number of photos archived, the number of accounts per service, and the frequency of downloads. The service is based in San Francisco and is being managed by three programmers. Its "code blog" (code.recollect.com) has some examples of interesting coding applications developed for the site.

Note Collection Systems

A number of online providers offers free note collection systems, which all feature an easy method for writing notes or capturing information and then storing it for later reuse. They were originally developed as reminder systems to help users remember events and other important information, storing that information on the systems' servers in the cloud so that it is accessible anytime, from anywhere. Not only can users store notes they have created, but they can also capture information from the web using a clipping application. Because they are particularly attractive for mobile users, most of these systems have been developed as apps for popular platforms such as the iPhone, iPad, and Android devices. Most of them also have a desktop application for use with PCs, with extensions for the most popular currently available browsers.

Although note collection services were not originally developed as personal archiving systems, they can be used as such because of their long-term storage functionality. Users must be vigilant, however, because many of these companies are either still in startup mode or have recently entered the marketplace. Although they expect to remain in business due to their long-term secure storage of user data, they are susceptible to rapid market changes and may be acquired by other companies or may even disappear over time.

Evernote

Evernote (www.evernote.com) has experienced significant recent growth and has become a major player in the digital archiving space. With its large number of users, the firm is the market leader for note collection systems. Over time, its eponymous product has been enhanced with additional specialized functions. By the end of 2011, Evernote had grown to 20 million users, up from 6 million at the start of the year; and to 130 employees, up from 40. In an interview, CEO Phil Libin said that Evernote is strongly focused on longevity and that he is building Evernote to be a "100-year company."[4]

Libin's basic business philosophy for Evernote is to build applications that he would want to use himself and then market them. Judging by the marketplace response, this has been a highly successful strategy: The company gains 60,000 new subscribers every day and has 1.5 million paid subscribers.[5] Libin said, "I cannot imagine a possession that in 20 years will be more valuable than my Evernote account."[6]

The Evernote service is a robust and powerful multipurpose archiving system that can capture, store, and organize digital materials in virtually any format. Users can store documents, photos, video clips, or webpages and share them with others. Examples of interesting and unusual uses of Evernote are available on its website and include researching genealogy, planning a vacation, producing a magazine, collaborating with colleagues, and managing the operations of a restaurant. Evernote's logo incorporates the head of an elephant, symbolizing its mission to help users remember everything.

Because the materials are stored on Evernote's servers, they are accessible anywhere. Evernote is built to run on Windows and Mac, smartphones, tablets, or, as its website states, on "nearly every mobile device out there." Items stored on the Evernote service are called *notes* and are collected into *notebooks*. They can be located using an embedded search engine that accepts keywords, tags, or even text from images as input. In addition, the notes are automatically synchronized across all of the user's devices, making access highly convenient. Users can easily share their notebooks with others by email or on common social media platforms, thus enabling collaboration.

Although the main focus of Evernote is on archiving and retrieval, a large suite of related products for special applications has been developed to enhance its main product. These additional applications make Evernote one of the most robust personal archiving and retrieval services currently available:

- *Skitch* allows annotations and notes to be added to an image.

- *Penultimate* is a handwriting app for the iPad that simulates the physical experience of writing on paper.

- *Web Clipper* can save portions of webpages or complete pages to an Evernote notebook (the clips can be tagged or annotated in the process, and pages clipped can also be searched as part of a Google search).

- *Hello* is a mobile phone app that creates a browsable history of people and shared experiences (time of contact, where the contact occurred, and others present), and then stores the information and presents it visually to the user as a series of individual profiles or a timeline.

- *Food* preserves memorable food experiences using photos of meals, people who were there, and the location.

- *Clearly* strips off ads and other extraneous material from webpages, leaving only the content, which can then be read without distractions and stored to a notebook.

- *Peek* is a learning app in which notes are turned into study materials to read on a mobile device, complete with a cover that opens in sections.

- *The Trunk* is a collection of apps for a variety of routine tasks that can be integrated with Evernote.

The basic Evernote service is free for individuals. A premium service (available either monthly or annually) offers increased uploading options (up to 1GB a month), PDF searching, faster image recognition, and other enhanced features. An enterprise version is also available for a monthly fee.

Springpad

Springpad (www.springpad.com) was launched in 2008 and has been compared to Evernote. It offers a web, iPhone, or Android app for creating, saving, sharing, and accessing "smart notebooks" containing information gathered by users.

A unique feature of Springpad is that when information is added, the system can retrieve related information from the web and automatically enhance the notebook, thus providing the opportunity for the user to take immediate action. For example, information on a restaurant can be augmented with a map of its location and reviews, or information on a book can be augmented with purchasing data. Springpad recently added social features such as "explore," which lets users search for information in the public notebooks of other users, and "follow," which allows integration with Facebook so that users can import and share their Facebook Likes. The developers of the service envision that a user's followers and friends will use this information to help them in their own decision-making and discovery activities. These recent additions have also spawned comparisons between Springpad and Pinterest.

According to its website, Springpad currently has 3.5 million users, who have saved more than 50 million notes. It obtains revenue by taking a small fee if a user makes a purchase based on data stored in notebooks, which is a business model similar in some respects to Google's.

Diigo

Diigo (www.diigo.com), whose acronym stands for "Digest of Internet Information, Groups and Other stuff," originally began as a replacement for the Delicious.com bookmark organizing and sharing service (now operated by AVOS Systems, Inc.). Now in version 5.0, Diigo has added functionality similar to the other systems of this type and supports storage of documents, notes, screenshots, and photos. Diigo claims to be different from competing services due to its emphasis on ereading. According to its website, Diigo views itself as "a research and collaborative research tool on the one hand, and a knowledge-sharing community and social content site on the other."

Diigo's web clipper permits users to add notes to a clipping, which are saved along with the original webpage and appear when the user returns to that page. Building on its social bookmarking origins, Diigo allows tags added to notes to be publicly shared, creating a social knowledge community. Users can even search the tags to find "people like me" with similar interests and communicate with them through the Diigo service.

Diigo offers a free plan that provides limited search capabilities and a limited number of notes and stored pages, but its reasonably priced basic plan will probably appeal to users wishing to use the system for more serious purposes.

OneNote

OneNote (office.microsoft.com/en-us/onenote) has been part of the Microsoft Office suite since 2003 and could possibly be used as a personal archiving system. However, the data is stored on the user's PC or Windows phone (which is probably not a secure location), and given the well-established reluctance of users to systematically back up their computers, OneNote is not likely to be a strong contender in the personal archiving market. A comparison of Evernote and OneNote is available at www.techhive.com/article/248992/evernote_vs_onenote_ note_taking_apps_showdown.html. While both services have their strengths, the article favors Evernote by a small margin.

Email Archiving

Why archive emails? After all, don't the email providers do that? Some do, particularly web-based ones like Gmail or Yahoo!, provided the user sets up a special folder to hold them. (Gmail's Trash folder is not reliable for archival storage because emails are permanently deleted after they have been in there for 30 days.) Storage on these systems is virtually unlimited; many people simply allow the messages to accumulate, with the result that many email collections now number in the tens of thousands of messages.

But disasters can happen. For example, Google lost about 40,000 Gmail accounts in February 2011 because of a software bug in an update. Even though Google makes several copies of its data, the loss affected the copies as well. Fortunately, Google also makes a copy on tape that is stored offline, so it was eventually able to restore the lost accounts (Google's official blog provides the details at gmailblog. blogspot.com/2011/02/gmail-back-soon-for-everyone.html). In light of such vulnerability, it is important for users who wish to archive their emails to create backups and store them offline.

Reasons for archiving email are similar to those for archiving other types of information:

- To preserve a record or recapture memories

- For legal reasons, such as proof of an event or conversation

- To analyze the messages and find patterns in them

- To leave a legacy for succeeding generations

Because searching and analysis of large email archives is difficult and time consuming, interest in dedicated email archiving systems is growing. Archive systems also guard against the dangers of malicious hacking or computer malfunction, particularly with systems such as Microsoft Outlook, which stores deleted email on the user's computer. And when a user's email is lost, generally the address book and contacts list go with it. A Google search for *personal email loss* brings up horror stories about how an email user's entire personal digital life was deleted by hackers. Gmail archives are not safe from these problems, either. A story in a recent issue of *The Atlantic*[7] describes how someone hacked into the author's wife's Gmail account and deleted her entire archive. (Fortunately, through the writer's acquaintance with a Google executive, he was able to restore the archive.) For more reasons on why archiving emails is important, check out ask.metafilter.com/191128/Should-I-be-keeping-over-a-decade-of-personal-email and blogs.loc.gov/digitalpreservation/2011/09/why-should-we-save-our-email.

Libraries are now being asked to serve as repositories for the email collections of prominent people, and some of these collections have significant value because they provide a unique window into the owner's thought processes, moods, and beliefs in a way that other methods of communication cannot. For example, The British Library paid £32,000 (approximately $51,000) for an archive of more than 40,000 email messages of the poet Wendy Cope. At the time of the acquisition, that was the largest email collection that the library had acquired. According to Rachel Foss, one of the Library's curators:

> In Wendy Cope's archive, there is a massive volume of email material and a lot of it is ephemeral. But even something like an Amazon receipt is very rich data when you are talking about an author. It gives us a sense of what they were reading and what may have influenced them. The fact that every digital object comes with a date stamp is incredibly useful … The big benefit of acquiring the email correspondence is the email chains. With paper, you often only get part of the dialogue. Emails give us a really good way to map literary and personal networks—you can easily forward emails and copy someone else into them.[8]

Foss also noted that it is now the library's practice to include an author's email correspondence in discussions of the acquisition of its archives. The library is working with professional authors' organizations to spread the message that their emails have value because they form an important part of their legacy.

In an article on the Library of Congress's digital preservation blog, Susan Manus, digital project coordinator, says that email should be saved and offers some suggestions for doing so, as well as a link to the Library's Digital Preservation page on email archiving (www.digital preservation.gov/personalarchiving/email.html).[9] In a posting on email preservation that appeared on his blog, Chris Prom, assistant university archivist at the University of Illinois, says that archivists must "help people save email in a way that makes it likely that email records will one day become research collections, openly accessible for their historical value."[10] As good systems for personal use, Prom suggests MailStore Home (discussed in the next section in this chapter), and Stanford's Project MUSE. Project MUSE (Memories USing Email; mobisocial.stanford.edu/muse) is a research project at Stanford University's Mobile and Social (MobiSocial) Computing Research Group that is studying the analysis of long-term email archives. It has a number of unique features. Peter Chan, digital librarian at Stanford University Library, describes MUSE in detail in Chapter 12.

Email Backup With Manual Archiving

As already mentioned, just because you use a web-based email service with the data stored in the cloud does not necessarily mean that it is safely archived. Copying a large number of email messages stored in a number of folders can be a long and tedious task, but fortunately, systems are now available that handle the job easily and with little user effort.

MailStore Home

MailStore Software GmbH, based in Germany, a leading provider of email management and archiving services for businesses and other enterprises, also offers MailStore Home (www.mailstore.com/en/mail

store-home.aspx), a free version for personal use that is designed for a single computer.

MailStore can process messages from most of today's popular email clients. The user creates an archive profile for each source; the profiles can be different from each other, if desired. (The free Home version has a limit on the number of profiles that can be created for a single account, and no scheduling feature is available.)

MailStore supports emails handled by a wide variety of platforms, including Outlook, Thunderbird, Gmail, and Yahoo! Mail. Despite being a free system, MailStore Home is robust and can handle up to 100,000 messages without degradation of performance. It can be launched from a USB drive, and the messages can be hosted there if desired (Figure 4.7). An article published in *PCWorld* in October 2008 was highly complimentary of MailStore:

> MailStore Home promises to solve two of the biggest problems facing those with email overload: How to find information fast, and how to back up your email data. This centralized email archive does an excellent job of both. It imports mail from many different email systems and software, and offers lightning-fast search. That way, you can search through all of your email, even if you use multiple services and software. Once you've imported your email, you can easily search through it all, using sophisticated tools, such as searching by subject, message body, folder, attachments and so on.[11]

Data archived by MailStore resides on the user's PC and must be archived by exporting it to other media such as a USB drive, CD-ROM, and so on. Once the messages are archived (the archive process can be run in the background for a large email collection), the search functionality is rapid—much faster than the native email client's search function. A significant advantage of MailStore is the ability to interface with a variety of email systems, so it provides an easy method

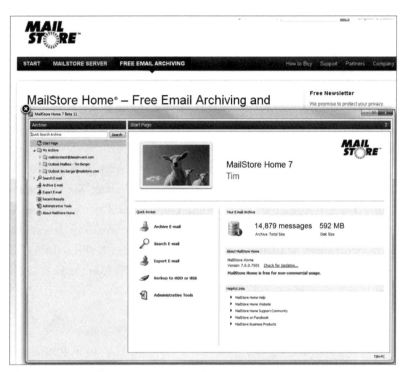

Figure 4.7   MailStore Home opening page

of converting messages from one format to another. Messages can be imported from one client and then exported to another.

Gmail Backup

Like MailStore, Gmail Backup provides the capability to archive all of your Gmail messages in a single backup file on your hard drive. The process requires you to download the backup software and to enable IMAP access to the Gmail account. Messages can be restored to any Gmail account, which is a simple way to transfer a large number of messages from one account to another. It is not possible to search the backup file.

Archiving Home Movies and Videos

There appear to be few software packages especially designed for archiving home movies and videos, but there are many commercial services that will convert 8mm home movies to DVDs, which can easily be found with a Google search for *photo archiving, archiving home movies,* or *archiving home videos*. A discussion of the various video formats available can become very technical and is outside the scope of this chapter. To learn more about the possibilities, check out www.larry jordan.biz/picking-the-right-video-format-for-storage.

Center for Home Movies

The mission of the Center for Home Movies (www.centerforhome movies.org) is "to provide the means to discover, celebrate, and preserve them as cultural heritage." Its foremost project is the sponsorship of Home Movie Days (HMDs; www.homemovieday.com/index.html), which were launched 10 years ago by a group of film archivists. HMDs occur annually at many locations globally. Most of them occur on the same day (e.g., in 2012, it was October 20) and provide a venue for home movie owners to meet local film archivists, receive advice on storage of their movies, and learn about the advantages of preservation in various formats (the original films are generally regarded as more stable than DVDs).

The HMD website has an extensive review of the various options for those who wish to transfer their movies to another format (www.homemovieday.com/transfer.html). Projectors are frequently available for HMD attendees to use and view their old movies. A DVD titled "Living Room Cinema" contains 22 films screened at HMDs in 2003 and 2004 and can be purchased from Amazon.com. HMDs are all hosted by volunteers.

The Center for Home Movies has also transferred several home movie collections to the Internet Archive and welcomes donations from anyone who wishes to support its work. (Those who wish to contribute their movies to the Internet Archive should read the conditions and procedures at archive.org/about/faqs.php#224.)

Home Movie Depot

Home Movie Depot (HMD; www.homemoviedepot.com) provides a service to transfer film, videos, and images to DVDs. It also offers a transfer from the DVD to a customer's Facebook page, from where it can be shared with anyone the customer wishes. When a movie is shared on Facebook, any of the customer's Facebook friends can order a copy of the DVD for only the shipping cost.

HMD also offers an archiving service, My Online Memories, which will archive a user's movie files on a secure server for an annual subscription fee. Users can download their movie files from the server at any time and as often as they wish.

Vimeo

Vimeo (www.vimeo.com), founded in 2004 by a group of filmmakers, has created a video archiving community that currently consists of 5,880 publicly available videos and 83,500 subscribers. Vimeo is owned by the internet media and advertising company IAC (www.iac.com) and has won several prestigious awards. It has more than 8.5 million registered users.

Community members can create groups and upload their videos, which then become available for sharing. A robust array of privacy settings allows the owner of the video to control who can view it. Many features of the Vimeo community platform resemble those of Facebook, including "like" and "follow" options. The Vimeo support FAQs are unusually comprehensive and cover a wide range of topics about the service and how to use it.

Videos are archived in perpetuity as long as a member logs in to the service periodically. A free basic account gives the user up to 10 uploads per day and 500 megabytes of upload space. Premium accounts are available as well, and they give the user more space and many advanced functions. There is also a Pro service for business and commercial uses. Users can show their appreciation for a video by making a small donation with the "Tip Jar" service, and video owners will soon be able to charge others for viewing with a pay-to-view feature.

Texas Archive of the Moving Image

The Texas Archive of the Moving Image (TAMI; www.texasarchive. org/library) provides free digitization of films and videos so long as the material is Texas-related (i.e., was shot in Texas, is by a Texan, or is about Texas) and the owner is willing to contribute the work to the archive (i.e., the owner is the rightsholder and is willing to make the material public). Up to 50 films and/or 10 videos can be contributed every 2 years. The archive is freely available on the TAMI website, as is a Home Media Preservation Guide.

Conclusion

This chapter has reviewed a number of software packages and services for archiving and preservation of personal materials in a number of formats. Research on personal archiving systems continues unabated. See Chapter 12 for a description of other interesting and promising projects that are especially relevant.

Acknowledgment

Special thanks to Jeff Ubois for reviewing this chapter and suggesting several services to add.

Endnotes

1. Gordon Bell and Jim Gemmell, *Total Recall: How the E-Memory Revolution Will Change Everything* (New York: Dutton, 2009).

2. "History of Photography," Wikipedia, accessed April 10, 2013, en.wikipedia.org/ wiki/History_of_photography.

3. "Boulevard du Temple by Daguerre," Wikipedia, accessed April 10, 2013, en.wikipedia.org/wiki/File:Boulevard_du_Temple_by_Daguerre.jpg.

4. Colleen Taylor, "For Evernote, 2011 Was a Year to Remember," *GigaOM*, December 27, 2011, accessed April 10, 2013, gigaom.com/2011/12/27/evernote-2011-growth-users.

5. Ibid.

6. Cristina Rouvalis, "Remembers Only," *United Hemispheres*, accessed April 10, 2013, www.hemispheresmagazine.com/2012/12/01/remembers-only.

7. James Fallows, "Hacked!" *The Atlantic*, October 3, 2011, accessed April 10, 2013, www.theatlantic.com/magazine/archive/2011/11/hacked/308673.

8. Mic Wright, "Why the British Library Archived 40,000 Emails From Poet Wendy Pope," *Wired*, May 10, 2011, accessed April 10, 2013, www.wired.co.uk/news/archive/2011-05/10/british-library-digital-archives?page=all.

9. Susan Manus, "Why Should We Save Our Emails?" *The Signal*, September 8, 2011, accessed April 10, 2013, blogs.loc.gov/digitalpreservation/2011/09/why-should-we-save-our-email.

10. Chris Prom, "Email Preservation Options," *Practical E-Records*, November 17, 2011, accessed April 10, 2013, e-records.chrisprom.com/email-preservation-options.

11. Preston Gralla, "MailStore Home," *PCWorld*, October 10, 2008, accessed April 10, 2013, www.pcworld.com/article/232768/mailstore_home.html.

CHAPTER **5**

Digital Inheritance: Tackling the Legal and Practical Issues

Evan Carroll
The Digital Beyond

Publisher's note: The material presented in this chapter is for informational purposes only and not for the purpose of providing legal advice. You should contact an attorney to obtain advice with respect to any particular issue or problem.

Outside of an institutional setting, individuals do not often consider personal digital archiving. As a matter of normal practice, institutions do often choose to archive the digital materials of those who retire or depart. While departure is often a suitable milestone to trigger archiving for institutions, personal digital collections containing family mementos, correspondence, and other similar materials lack a natural milestone at which they are archived. In fact, such collections are subject to benign neglect, leaving the curation of an individual's digital content unaddressed.[1] Yet as social media and other cloud-based services have flourished, some individuals have considered what will happen to their content at another milestone: death. This topic, often referred to as the "digital afterlife" or leaving a "digital legacy," has received an increasing amount of attention in recent years.[2]

Why Now?

Before the proliferation of social media websites and cloud-based services, the vast majority of personal digital content was stored locally on computers and storage devices belonging to the owner of the content and located in the owner's home or office. For institutions with archival procedures in place, considerations of personal digital archiving became apparent as they began ingesting digital media such as disks, CDs, and hard disks. But for the individual, digital content was treated largely the same as tangible property. Most, if not all, digital content belonging to individuals existed on some tangible media, which was often located among other tangible items in their home. When a person died, the media, along with the other tangible assets, were disposed of in some way, largely because the family or other executor needed to settle the affairs of the decedent.

In contrast, social media websites and cloud-based services have caused personal digital content to spread beyond the tangible media in the possession of the individual. Today, people commonly store digital content on numerous computer systems that they themselves do not own and that are not physically located with the remainder of their estate. Realizing the sentimental and perhaps cultural importance of this information, along with its fragile and distributed nature, individuals have begun to consider how these assets should be handled when they die. This heightened social awareness has brought attention to various issues of digital inheritance from both legal and practical standpoints.

Awareness

The primary issue of inheritance is practical, not legal. With the infinite number of cloud-based services an individual can use, there is only a small chance that an heir, lacking any documentation, will know all of the accounts the person had with those services. In fact, many individuals cannot even remember all of the accounts they have created. While many of those digital accounts may not contain important information, the chance remains that important content will be lost at death due to a lack of awareness. From a personal archiving standpoint, an unknown account is effectively lost, even if the contents of the account are preserved in some other way. One effort by Entrustet offered consumers a "digital property report" service, which searched for an individual's name across multiple social media and cloud providers and provided a one-time report of the matches.[3] This service was eliminated when Entrustet was acquired by SecureSafe (www.securesafe.com), leaving the task of finding accounts to heirs. Despite these efforts to discover accounts, both automated and manual, the chances of finding all accounts belonging to an individual is reduced once that person has passed away.

Access

Assuming that an heir knows the various services an individual used to store his or her content, the next challenge is gaining access to that content. Access is primarily a legal issue, which has practical workarounds. By far, the easiest way to solve the access problem is for an individual to leave behind a list of user names and passwords. Such an inventory will allow an heir to access an account and manage, archive, or delete that account on behalf of the decedent. Due to the largely anonymous nature of the web, a password list is an effective solution in practice, despite some of the legal issues discussed later in this chapter.

Another effective solution involves resetting passwords. With access to key information, such as answers to security questions, and access to the decedent's email account, an heir can often reset the passwords of various online accounts, effectively positioning email as a "master key" to the decedent's accounts. In fact, many email accounts not only offer the ability to reset passwords, but they also contain a detailed record of the various online accounts the decedent might have held, as evidenced by account confirmations or other marketing emails that may be stored within the account.

While gaining access to an account may solve the initial practical issues in archiving its contents, it creates a legal issue with regard to an heir's right to access the contents of the account.

Rights and Ownership

As fundamental concepts of copyright law, ownership and usage rights are significant issues in personal digital archiving. For any single object, there is an individual, group, or corporation that holds the exclusive legal right to possess that object. The copyright owner for any intellectual property, which usually includes personal digital content, has the ability to grant usage rights to another party and can place any number of restrictions on that right. For example, the copyright owner of a book manuscript may grant publication rights to a publisher. The owner and publisher could agree to restrict those rights to a specific medium such as print or digital, a specific timeframe, a specific geographic region, or within other mutually agreed parameters.

In an institutional setting, usage rights and ownership of materials are fairly straightforward. Generally speaking, under the provisions of fair use, educational institutions have the right to archive materials, including those under copyright, to ensure future access. In some situations, the copyright owner may have donated the materials, along with the rights, to the institution. An institution often has its employees sign a contract that grants either ownership or certain usage rights to the institution. Thus, archiving personal digital content within an institution is usually acceptable and straightforward from a legal standpoint.

By contrast, ownership of personal content outside of the institutional setting is not as straightforward. Rights to use any intellectual property, such as photos, videos, or writing, are usually granted through a contract. In the case of book publishing, these contracts are usually negotiated and executed on paper, but in the case of social media websites and other cloud-based services, users enter into contracts called "terms of use" when they register.

The terms of use document is a legally binding contract between the company offering the online service and the user, which, generally speaking, outlines the expectations that one party has of the other. In practice, these contracts usually contain limited protections for the user and significant protections for the online service. In almost all cases, the user cannot negotiate the terms of the contract and must agree to them as-is in order to use the service. While many of the provisions in those contracts are not of direct interest to archivists, the portions that cover the ownership of the content uploaded, the rights to use that content, and who is authorized to access the account are particularly important.

In many cases, the terms prohibit the transfer of an account to another party and restrict users from allowing other individuals to use their username and password to access the service. From a legal standpoint, these restrictions cause an issue with using a list of passwords or changing a password to access the account of a decedent. In other, rarer, cases, the terms state that the account is subject to termination should the account holder pass away, although some attorneys believe that a legal executor acting as the fiduciary of the decedent has the right to access those accounts, despite any terms to the contrary. Even though another individual is accessing the account, the attorneys argue that the executor is acting on behalf of the decedent and not on their own accord; therefore, legally it is as if the decedent were accessing the account, which is within the terms of service. This belief, however, is a gray area and has not been substantiated by case law. In light of this problem, many legal experts have called for changes to the typical terms of service, changes to estate law, and procedures for specifically authorizing this type of access in a will or other testamentary document.

Solutions

From a legal standpoint, the disposition of an individual's possessions following his or her death generally follows a legally enforced and socially accepted process. An executor (often named in a will) is appointed by the estate and handles the affairs of the deceased until the estate is settled. In cases when a will is not in place, estate laws, which differ from state to state, provide the rules for handling the estate.

For the most part, estate laws in the United States do not specifically address digital information as an asset of value to the estate. In the event that a will does not exist, or does not mention digital assets, this creates a situation where the disposition of digital assets is unclear.

State Laws

Presently, five states have estate laws that pertain to digital information. The oldest of these laws, in Connecticut (2005) and Rhode Island (2007), specifically grant executors access to the email accounts of the deceased. While ideally these laws would apply to digital assets more broadly, in practically all situations, access to an email account will afford access to a broader set of accounts, as mentioned previously. Indiana (2007) specifically grants executors access to the "electronically stored documents" belonging to the deceased. More recently, Oklahoma (2010) and Idaho (2011) enacted similar laws that specifically name email accounts and social networking websites as property that the estate must be able to access.

With increasing attention on this issue, lawmakers in other states, including Maryland, Massachusetts, Michigan, Nebraska, Nevada, New Hampshire, New Jersey, New York, North Carolina, North Dakota, Oregon, Pennsylvania, and Virginia, have considered or are considering similar legislation (Figure 5.1).[4] Additionally, the Uniform Laws Commission (ULC), a national organization that suggests laws to U.S. states, has formed a committee to prepare a sample law that addresses digital assets.[5] In some states, including Oregon[6] and Massachusetts,[7] online service providers have lobbied against laws of this type. The ULC committee includes representatives from various companies to address their concerns.

While the efforts of these activists and lawmakers are important, there is a potential gap between the state laws and the terms of service to which users agree when they sign up for an online service. In estate

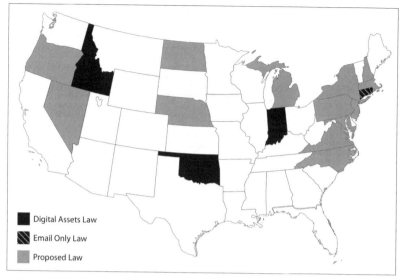

Figure 5.1   Status of state legislation

law, the estate of an individual is executed under the laws of the state where he or she was domiciled. A terms of service contract, however, has a provision referred to as "choice of laws," which allows the author of the contract to specify the laws and courts under which the contract is interpreted. Due to the prevalence of technology companies in California's Silicon Valley, many of these terms specify the laws of California and choose the courts of Santa Clara County as the venue for any litigation. While this issue has not been challenged, it is doubtful that an estate law in any state other than California would affect a contractual agreement in California. This situation will likely become the subject of future litigation and may place pressure on service providers to provide access to executors.

Estate Planning

In the absence of applicable laws in every state, attorneys have suggested sample language and processes for incorporating digital assets into wills and powers of attorney.[8] While these documents may also be subject to the same law and venue conflicts as the state laws, they provide executors, service providers, and courts with the documented intent of the decedent, which is generally regarded as the correct course of action when settling an estate. By expressing their wishes in testamentary documents, individuals can rest assured that their digital assets are likely to be disposed of in a way that is satisfactory to them.

To add these powers to a will, an individual simply needs to include language that empowers the executor to handle both their digital assets and digital accounts, which usually necessitates a definition of both.[9] This type of statement will provide blanket powers over digital assets. Moreover, anyone who wants to provide more specific instructions regarding each digital asset can prepare a memorandum (often referred to as a "digital will") that lists digital assets, the login information to access them, and his or her wishes for each line item. This document should be separate from the will itself but can be referenced in the will, giving the executor specific instructions for how these assets should be handled. Some individuals have also considered the idea of a separate digital executor, an individual whose technical expertise makes him or her a better choice to handle digital assets than the legal executor of the estate. An individual can appoint a digital executor by adding language to the will similar to the following: "I authorize my executor to engage _____ to assist in accessing, handling, distributing and disposing of my digital assets."

To aid in the preparation of a digital will, numerous online services exist to help individuals provide executors with access information for online accounts.[10] These types of services, which include Legacy Locker (legacylocker.com) and SecureSafe, generally ask users to input a list of their digital assets, including the username and password for each, and to specify instructions for each asset. They then provide safekeeping for this information and have some form of "trigger" that releases the information to a specified executor upon the death of the account holder. Triggers take various forms, from secure codes to a share in testamentary documents to manual verification, which requires the executor to submit a copy of the death certificate to the service before the information is released.

In Practice

At the present time, different considerations are involved in accessing and ultimately archiving the various types of digital assets.

Email

Among popular web-based email providers, there is no standard procedure for handling the accounts of the deceased. Google provides executors access to email accounts, provided that they meet certain requirements and make a formal request.[11] Microsoft will allow family members to access the account but recognizes that the process may take up to 6 months. It offers a way to request that the account be preserved while the executor prepares documentation and waits for the company to provide access.[12] In contrast, Yahoo! refuses to allow anyone access to a Yahoo! email account, even in event of the account holder's death.[13] Lack of standardization across providers is not only inconvenient to executors but is also a barrier to preservation. Ideally, there should be one standard process for accessing accounts, and archivists could educate the public about these standards. In lieu of standardization, more education is required to inform users of these issues before they pass away.

Social Networking

As previously stated, nearly every social media or social networking website is governed by a terms of service document, which is essentially a binding contract between the company that operates the site and the registered user. For instance, Facebook's policy is to allow deletion or memorialization of accounts after the account holder passes away, but it generally does not permit executors to access the account.[14] Naturally, the workaround is to gain access to the password, either via estate planning or by resetting the password. In the event that an executor can access the account, Facebook does provide account holders with the ability to download all of the information they have posted to the site in a compressed format.[15] This standalone archive provides a view of the entire Facebook account as the account holder would have seen it. From an archival standpoint, a Facebook export can be a valuable part of a personal archive, and those planning ahead might wish to consider downloading their information periodically. Twitter will provide the next-of-kin a means to deactivate the account.[16] Due to the nature of Twitter's technology, archivists will have a difficult time creating a full archive of a user's tweets unless an account with a third-party archiving service is established ahead of time.

Future Considerations

As the concerns of personal digital archiving become more salient in the minds of everyday consumers, additional advancements in law and technology will undoubtedly change the state of digital inheritance. For instance, designers and researchers such as Richard Banks are presently developing interfaces that will allow future generations to more naturally interact with the large amount of digital information that individuals will likely leave behind in the future (see Chapter 11). These digital heirlooms will likely shape the way that we remember and reflect upon the past.

Archivists and technologists have also predicted that future technology for archiving cloud-based content will be automated, providing secure storage and adding necessary metadata so that individuals do not have to plan ahead, thus eliminating the issues of benign neglect.[17] In fact, the EXIF metadata schema for digital photographs already includes date and location fields, and smartphones such as Apple's iPhone include functionality to automatically record this metadata and upload photos to the cloud for storage. On other fronts, services like 1000memories and Recollect have created compelling interfaces for interacting with personal digital memories (see Chapter 4). In time, these disparate efforts will likely give rise to a more integrated and automated system for archiving and organizing personal digital content from the cloud.

As technology develops, the law will also develop, probably giving consumers more control over their digital information. As consumers become more educated, services will feel direct pressure to build archival hooks into their services. The net result will be more portable information that can be more easily ingested into personal and institutional archives. As Chuck Palahniuk wrote in *Diary*, "We all die. The goal isn't to live forever; the goal is to create something that will."[18] Perhaps our personal digital archives will both fulfill that goal and contribute to our greater digital heritage.

Endnotes

1. Cathy Marshall, "Rethinking Personal Digital Archiving, Part 1," *D-Lib Magazine*, March/April 2008, accessed April 11, 2013, www.dlib.org/dlib/march 08/marshall/03marshall-pt1.html.

2. Evan Carroll and John Romano, *Your Digital Afterlife: When Facebook, Flickr and Twitter Are Your Estate, What's Your Legacy?* (Berkeley, CA: New Riders, 2011).

3. "Entrustet Launches Digital Property Reports for Recently Deceased," *PRWeb*, April 28, 2011, accessed April 11, 2013, www.prweb.com/releases/2011/4/prweb 8345804.htm.

4. "Law," *Digital Estate Resource*, 2011, accessed April 11, 2013, www.digitalestate resource.com/law.

5. "Fiduciary Access to Digital Assets," *Uniform Laws Commission*, 2012, accessed May 11, 2013, www.uniformlaws.org/Committee.aspx?title=Fiduciary%20 Access%20to%20Digital%20Assets.

6. Lauren Gambino, "In Death, Facebook Photos Could Fade Away Forever," *Associated Press*, March 1, 2013, accessed April 11, 2013, bigstory.ap.org/article/ death-facebook-photos-could-fade-away-forever.

7. Katy Steinmetz, "Your Digital Legacy: States Grapple With Protecting Our Data After We Die," *Time*, November 29, 2012, accessed April 11, 2013, techland.time.com/2012/11/29/digital-legacy-law.

8. Evan Carroll, John Romano and Jean Gordon Carter, "Helping Clients Reach Their Great Digital Beyond," *Trusts & Estates*, September 1, 2011, 66–70.

9. "Sample Language," *Digital Estate Resource*, 2011, accessed April 11, 2013, www.digitalestateresource.com/sample-language.

10. Evan Carroll and John Romano, "Digital Death and Afterlife Online Services List," *The Digital Beyond*, 2013, accessed April 11, 2013, www.thedigitalbeyond.com/online-services-list.

11. "Accessing a Deceased Person's Mail," *Google*, December 7, 2012, accessed April 11, 2013, support.google.com/mail/bin/answer.py?hl=en&answer=14300.

12. "My Family Member Died Recently/Is In Coma, What Do I Need To Do To Access Their Hotmail Account?" *Microsoft*, March 15 2012, accessed May 11, 2013, answers.microsoft.com/en-us/windowslive/forum/hotmail-profile/my-family-member-died-recently-is-in-coma-what-do/308cedce-5444-4185-82e8-0623ecc1d3d6.

13. "Yahoo! Terms of Service," *Yahoo!*, November 24, 2008, accessed April 11, 2013, info.yahoo.com/legal/us/yahoo/utos/utos-173.html.

14. "Deactivating, Deleting & Memorializing Accounts," *Facebook*, 2013, accessed April 11, 2013, www.facebook.com/help/359046244166395.

15. "Downloading Your Info," *Facebook*, 2013, accessed April 11, 2013, www.facebook.com/help/131112897028467.

16. "How to Contact Twitter about a Deceased User," *Twitter*, 2013, accessed April 11, 2013, support.twitter.com/groups/33-report-a-violation/topics/148-policy-information/articles/87894-how-to-contact-twitter-about-a-deceased-user.

17. Evan Carroll et al. *"Digital Immortals: Preserving Life Beyond Death"* (Presentation at SXSW Interactive, Austin, TX, March 11 2012), accessed, May 11, 2013, schedule.sxsw.com/2012/events/event_IAP9715.

18. Chuck Palahniuk, *Diary: A Novel* (New York: Anchor Books, 2004), 109.

CHAPTER 6

Social Media, Personal Data, and Reusing Our Digital Legacy

Catherine C. Marshall
Microsoft Research, Silicon Valley

I remember what the web was like in 1994. That's when I put up my personal homepage and when many of my colleagues published theirs, too. The initial rush of personal homepages joined the physics preprints, the websites constructed with a hobbyist's fervor (for example, documenting the Klingon language, early music, or San Francisco graffiti), and the first few web-based businesses (such as the online wine retailer Virtual Vineyards and the online magazine *Hotwired*). The fight for readers' attention had not yet reached a fever pitch, although scholars such as Richard Lanham (1993) and David Levy (2001) anticipated that it would, picking up on a recurring century-old leitmotif of attention as the scarcest resource (James 1890; Thorngate 1987). In short, it was still a human-scale handmade web populated at least in part by navigable user-contributed content. Even official content (e.g., the city homepage for Bremond, Texas, "Home of Friendly People & Polish Sausage"[1]) was often the product of a single enthusiast who had hand-edited the HTML.

Local storage was tractable as well. Most of us had a work computer and a home computer. Digital cameras were new to the market. Doing anything significant with video required an Avid editing bay, a proposition too expensive and too technically difficult for the average consumer. Computer science graduate students played Doom, a shoot-em-up video game that was laughably primitive by today's production-heavy standards; there were no characters to level, no voice-over actors doing the vocal sound effects (the oofs and grunts of effort and pain), and no long-term investment in the game. Email was largely a simple affair; the occasional MIME-type attachment was regarded as a nuisance and a challenge to open. In short, you probably had a manageable number of files you cared about, which were stored in a fairly small number of places.

At that time, many of our personal information management problems—and hence, our personal archiving problems—stemmed from the mix of digital and paper files in our lives (Sellen and Harper 2001). Writing this chapter, for example, might mean crossing from digital to paper and back again many times; maintaining a history of the chapter's versions would involve coordinating between alternating print documents and digital files.

Soon corporations and commercial concerns seized upon the web. Bureaucracy moved online. And for a while, the web became the province of professional designers and media creators. Creative types moved to places like New York and San Francisco, where tiny startups and giant corporations hustled and competed to enlist what came to be called content creators. Much of what we used on the web wasn't ours, and we had little apparent interest in keeping it safe.

But soon thereafter, user-contributed content again came to play a significant role in life online. Naturally, this shift did not go unnoticed; writing was framed in terms of addressing the interests of a long tail of readers (Anderson 2004), and curation was put into the hands of the crowd, who would ultimately be wiser than editors (Surowiecki 2004). Social networking sites like Myspace and then Facebook picked up momentum. At the same time, everyone had more ways to record things, more ways to edit things, and more venues to share what they had.

Thus, we have arrived in 2013 with three puzzling pieces of baggage left over from an earlier era of computing. These issues are essential to the way we think about personal digital archiving.

The first is long-term protection under the guise of *backup*. We have long thought it advisable and necessary to back up the precious digital files on our computers to keep them safe, so why is it so hard to get people (including me) to back up their files?

The second extends the concept of backup to our stuff *in the cloud and on social media*. Should we think of our stuff in the cloud and on social media as an extension of our local stuff, and does this mean we should have a plan for keeping it safe, too?

Finally, the third challenge stems from the complexities of *ownership and control* that accompany storing stuff on social media services. Is that online stuff still under our control? What do we own and what can we use? Does it have value to other people?

All three of these issues represent rational practices and ideas: Who really wants to lose stuff? Why would the stuff on social media be different from the stuff we store locally? Who wants to shrug off the protections afforded by existing notions of ownership and control? But at the same time, none of the old ways of doing business make sense the way they once did.

Sometimes I log on to my old account at Texas A&M University, where I was a research faculty member in the mid-1990s. Besides the files that I use for my personal website, everything else is just as I left it. And compared with the files I've created since, there's almost nothing there. In 1995, these files (largely research data and publications) plus some short stories and personal email that I had stored at home made up the whole of my digital belongings. That it now seems so spare and so localized speaks volumes.

The locus of personal information and people's associated management practices have shifted dramatically over the past decade. I have seen this not only through reflecting on my own practices (which is dangerously limited, as I will demonstrate, as is reflecting on the practices of our own social network—you must get out there to see what is going on) but also through the window of a series of studies that I have conducted along with various colleagues. The studies use a variety of methods; some focus on detailed snapshots of individual use, and others take a broader (but necessarily shallower) perspective. They are all looking at personal information from the vantage point of the technologies we use to keep it and the practices that we use to control it.

One way I like to look at the study results is to single out what surprised me at the time. I often walk into a study thinking one thing, and I come away from data collection and analysis thinking something entirely different. In this chapter, I'll quickly discuss three studies performed over about 7 years and tell you what surprised me in each. Don't think of them as studies for their own sake but rather as signifiers of larger changes that were afoot. Even the questions that once made sense to ask have changed.

Study 1: Stumbling on Curation via Benign Neglect

Study 1 was performed in 2005 with my colleagues Sara Bly and Francoise Brun-Cottan, and it was the first one we had done that specifically took on the question of digital archiving (Marshall, Bly, and Brun-Cottan 2006). We wondered how people were trying to keep their digital stuff safe over the long haul and whether they were bringing physical metaphors to the problem. We used a professional recruiter to find study participants in three West Coast cities, reasoning that if we stuck to the San Francisco Bay Area, we might get too many technology-oriented people. We required that participants use a computer and a varying number of other devices such as digital cameras and recorders, iPods, and PDAs. (Smartphones had not yet been introduced.) The people we interviewed for the study were diverse: a performance artist; a few high school and college students; a young auteur; a woman who ran a daycare center; an urban beekeeper; a real estate broker and mom;

a young, single professional guy; a blue-collar worker in a lumberyard who was a NASCAR fan; and a psychotherapist. Indeed, at first blush, they seemed to have little in common.

But when we analyzed our interviews with them, it turned out they did have something in common: They had islands of deep understanding (for example, several could use Photoshop in sophisticated ways), but these islands existed amid roiling seas of confusion. In particular, I had started with the bad initial assumption that everybody who can create content of any type can write heterogeneous files to removable media. It's a simple assumption, but it has its roots in a clear understanding of the basic premise of the Windows or Mac hierarchical file system. Oddly enough, only a few of the participants could do this, which meant that, for the rest, saving significant portions of their digital possessions (without ongoing help) was unlikely.

Perhaps the biggest surprise that came out of the first study was a profound sense of digital benign neglect, as indicated by cycles of accumulation and loss. The majority of the study participants were struggling with computer viruses, half-installed software, and an impenetrable forest of digital content (some their own, some downloaded, some shared with others), along with partially implemented strategies for taking care of it. It wasn't that the participants in the study didn't want to keep their stuff; it was more that they had neither the time nor expertise to do so. Using eerily similar metaphors, when asked about digital loss (either real or hypothetical), many of them said things like, "I mean, if we would've had a fire, you just move on" (Marshall, Bly, and Brun-Cottan 2006; Marshall 2011).

It appeared that the long-term disposition of participants' digital belongings would be left to fate.

Study 2: Personal Data Begins to Lead a Life of Its Own

The second study that I think of as a bellwether of larger trends in personal digital archiving took place about 2007 and was done in collaboration with Michael Nelson from Old Dominion University and his then-grad student Frank McCown (Marshall, McCown, and Nelson 2007). They were interested in reconstructing webpages and websites using what they called web infrastructure, a collection of caches and archives that span many web resources (Nelson et al. 2007; McCown, Nelson, and Van de Sompel 2009). So what we were looking at together was online loss; we were interviewing and surveying people who had lost stuff they had stored on the web.

What was surprising was the way this loss came about. The study participants had lost their online content largely by losing track of it, by not understanding the terms and conditions of the services they used, and by storing it in proximity to illegally stored stuff, but not by what we generally think of as the most immediate path to loss: hardware failure.

The British Library conducted a study with similar findings: "Nearly 70 percent of [reported data loss in the home] manifested itself in an inability to find information; by comparison ... [only] 8 percent [of loss was] due to hard drive failure" (John et al. 2010). But if you ask people about backing up online content, they will invariably tell you that there's no need to do that: Everything online that matters has gone through local storage. Photos are taken off the digital camera and stored on the hard drive; video is produced locally, using local tools, as are documents. And these local copies are usually considered the digital originals: They are the highest fidelity and the most complete.

In fact, something else was happening when we first saw this result: A certain amount of circular reasoning was inherent to this personal information management strategy. Yes, the local copies were of the highest resolution, but a certain amount of curation had taken place when this material was moved online: A service (and implied audience) was chosen; items were selected; metadata was added; and collections were organized. Furthermore, the online content was subject to ongoing stewardship as the items began to have lives of their own in the context of the larger digital resource. For example, photos in Flickr were selected by others to be part of thematic collections, comments were added, and views were accumulated that reflected a picture's popularity. Meanwhile, the local originals languished, their actual location forgotten.

We concluded that study participants had lost important online assets through a variation on the theme of benign neglect.

Study 3: Ownership and Control of Online Assets Is Messy Business

Frank Shipman and I began the third series of studies in early 2010. We began the study series because we had a suspicion that ownership and control of online user-contributed material was different than it had been in a heterogeneous print/digital era, which would have an effect on both personal archives and institutional archives of personal content.

For example, I remember using stills from the movie *True Stories* in a talk I was giving in 1994. It took considerable effort to appropriate these images: I found a book about the movie; I scanned the pages containing the images I wanted to use; I did some primitive manipulation to get the pictures I wanted; I created a floppy disk with the image files on it; and I shuttled the media over to a local business so it could print the images as 35mm slides. Once they came back (several days later), I put them in my slide carousel. It was sufficiently painful that only a few of the images I used in talks were not my own to begin with. Today, I do the same thing by doing a quick image search and a copy-paste into a PowerPoint deck. So does everyone else (as I have verified in recent interviews). Our personal archives have overlapping elements as well as casually appropriated and repurposed content.

Frank and I were convinced when we started that implicit social norms around saving, reusing, and archiving other people's content are coalescing. Surely people were curating content that wasn't their own, and they were expecting others, both individuals and institutions, to be doing so as well. But what surprised us was how a broad range of study participants were able to articulate their own rules and expected social norms.

For example, in data we gathered in mid-2010 about photo reuse (Marshall and Shipman 2011a), we saw participant reactions like this: "[Reusing photos from the web] is okay most of the time. The only time I would think it isn't would be when the main focus is of someone you don't know. Like when people email out the People of Walmart photos. Those are taken by people who don't know the person in the photo and posted." This heuristic was far more specific, thought-out, and interesting than we had anticipated.

The remainder of this chapter focuses on these results, and what they mean when they are taken together with the results of the earlier studies.

Why the emphasis on reuse? Why would it matter that content we harbor in personal archives originated from online sources? We tend to think of personal archives as having crisp boundaries and that we own everything we keep. But because people are such facile users of digital material (and keepers of appropriated stuff), the boundaries can be blurry. Some stuff is intentionally gathered to be part of an archive (e.g., photos of oneself, one's friends, one's family, or important events); these photos may have been taken by someone else. Other stuff becomes an accidental part of a personal archive (e.g., a funny video clip that's circulating or a movie still appropriated to use in a talk).

Of course, we can identify purely technical problems associated with reuse; for example, single-instance storage may be more efficient than storing copies. But that's not really why we're looking at reuse and the social norms that surround it. Rather, it helps to think about personal archives as something *live*, as resources, as material we (and others) might draw on in both the near future and long-term. In other words, personal archives (and archives in general) will become sources for future creative efforts. Reuse is an important motivation for maintaining a personal archive.

It is also likely that at least some of our personal online content will be part of an institutional archive (such as the Library of Congress's Twitter archive). Once such archives have been assembled, they will become a broader resource, and material in the archive is likely to be reused. Who will reuse the material and how it will be reused is part of an ongoing social negotiation. Certainly reuse is at the heart of the uproar around the Library of Congress's Twitter effort—if preservation were the only consideration and no access was planned, objections would be harder to justify.

Of course, use has always been a factor in the construction of archives. But digital archives are fundamentally different than their physical predecessors. Not only is access far less constrained and rarified, but the use of digital materials can be as extensive and imaginative as is permitted. In other words, reuse of materials—possibly re-reuse—will go far beyond historical research or social science analysis. This marks a distinct change from a time when you'd have to physically go to the archive, use a finding aid to establish what you wanted, and access the personal materials through the keeper of the archive.

If reuse is commonplace and, as legal scholar Larry Lessig (2008) suggests, it is the basis for modern creative efforts, our personal archives and—more importantly—institutional archives of personal material will be replete with "lightly owned" content. An understanding of social norms will help inform both policy and design.

Emerging Social Norms

In his book *Code, Version 2.0* (2006), Lessig noted that people's behavior is governed through interaction among market forces, law, constraints imposed by technology (as well as affordances offered by technology), and social norms. While there's no denying that the first three factors have a pronounced effect, it is clear that the fourth, social norms, dominates most people's sensibilities when they decide whether or not they should save or reuse a photo turned up by a search engine.

"Will I get caught?" "Will the photographer mind?" "Are the subjects in a compromising position?" "Do I really need this photo?" All of these questions seem to float through the user's mind; in an instant—the amount of time it takes to copy-paste the image into a PowerPoint file—the doubts have been dispelled and possibly forgotten. They only resurface if a take-down email appears, and, even then, they only seem to have an effect if legal action is imminent. "Will I get caught?" Probably not: Most audiences are small, and most photographers only detect reuse if a photo credit is already given. If the photo becomes part of the user's personal archive—and any potential reuse is deferred—no second thought is usually given.

As of May 2010, 70 percent of the world's digital content was user-contributed; needless to say, that proportion has probably risen since. In other words, reuse is not limited to formally published content. Furthermore, reuse itself should be broadly construed: As Lessig has pointed out, much reuse may fall under the rubric of *remix*, a practice which results in derivative works that substantively change the intent and context of the appropriated material. Thus, content creators are reusing less formal efforts and more narrowly shared material, and they are using this material in ways the original owner is not likely to have imagined. And even if content creators seek permission before reusing user-contributed material, they are likely to engage in additional reuse without ever asking again.

Unfortunately, although Creative Commons labeling is a great system, designed for exactly this set of circumstances (Boyle 2008), it is used and understood less frequently than it might be. For example, some participants in the study I'm about to describe think Creative Commons simply means that the labeled content is "in the commons" and may be reused without further thought.

Thus, for most purposes, social norms are emerging through successive cycles of use, reuse, modification, repurposing, and take-down notices. And although I'm about to tell you that many people in our studies adopt the aspirational attitude that permission should be granted prior to reuse, if we examine actual instances of reuse, the same participants would rather ask for forgiveness if they are caught rather than going through the potentially time-consuming and frustrating process of asking for permission beforehand.

A Series of Studies of Ownership and Control

Almost 3 years ago, Frank Shipman and I decided to look into these social norms by performing a series of studies. In particular, we wanted to characterize what these social norms were, discover when they break down, find out whether and how they vary across media types, and reveal what people's concerns were when archival institutions absorbed personal content from online sources. By doing this, we hoped to better understand people's attitudes and behaviors about content ownership and control; we also wanted to find out what people thought about archives as a source for repurposed content. So far we have looked at six media types: microblog posts, specifically tweets (Marshall and Shipman 2011b); personal photos (Marshall and Shipman 2011a); book reviews; educational videos; comedy podcasts; and recorded videoconferences.

The other studies I have discussed took an ethnographic approach to answering their central research questions: We conducted lengthy interviews with a relatively small number of participants in an effort to reveal what they actually did with their personal digital belongings; we engaged with them over their own computers, storage media, and files. In this case, we wanted to reach out more broadly in order to recruit a greater number of people (even if it meant we couldn't delve as deeply into what individuals did), to investigate attitudes as well as practices, and to compare answers across media types and specific user actions in a more structured way. Our publications about the studies describe the approach in greater detail.

To explore this notion of digital ownership, we used a technique familiar to legal scholars: hypotheticals that systematically vary a situation's fact pattern (Rissland and Ashley 1986). The technique relies on a description of the basic case or scenario, followed by a series of "what ifs." In our application of the technique, participants rated the hypothetical propositions using a 7-point Likert scale (a 1 rating means *disagree strongly*; a 7 rating means *agree strongly*) as a single aspect of the fact pattern changed.

Let's say the central scenario posits a candid photo of a Halloween party-goer dressed up like Wonder Woman. A photographer who attended the Halloween party posts this photo to his Flickr account and tags it *Wonder Woman*. This tag enables a comic book fan who is looking for pictures of Wonder Woman to find the photo. Now we can vary aspects of the fan's subsequent actions to reveal the edges of what the participant finds acceptable. For example, the first hypothetical might say that, after the comic book fan downloads the photo, he stores it on his local disk in his Superheroes folder. The next variation might say he stores the photo in his public directory on Dropbox. Two subsequent hypotheticals might explore the difference between the fan reusing the photo by posting it to Facebook and reusing it to illustrate his blog. Varying facts this way enabled us to explore the ethical edges of the situation and to see where participants agreed and disagreed as well as investigating what they thought was acceptable behavior. We focused the questions on common actions such as storing, sharing, publishing, and removing different types of content.

Besides using the scenarios and hypotheticals, we also asked the participants to report on their own behavior. Of course, self-reported behavior is tricky; we applied various tactics to keep participants from answering in a strictly aspirational way (by describing what they would do rather than what they have actually done). We kept these questions simple and neutral. At the end of each study, we also asked one or two questions about belief: For example, is it OK to reuse photos that you find online? Why or why not?

The participants in these studies were young (in their 20s and 30s), but younger and older people were also part of the study population. About one-third of the population were students, and over 90 percent had gone to college (about 60 percent had college degrees). Thus, the study population was young, well-educated, and probably underemployed. Many were freelance workers or office workers who spent much of their day in front of a computer screen. These are the people who are likely to be in the vanguard of content creation and reuse—*exactly* who we wanted to reach in these studies.

Although they were social media-savvy, participants were also remarkably diverse. Some claimed to spend most of their time reading and watching; others participated more actively by blogging, tweeting, Facebooking, and gaming. What we discovered was that although almost all of the participants reported that they shared and published online content, they had a broad definition of content in their minds. Profiles for social media, dating, and shopping, for example, all counted to participants as published content.

When we asked about sharing content, the participants exhibited nonchalance about reusing other people's material, and this was particularly true if something was funny or informative: "[I share] music, interesting, or funny pictures I come across, videos, jokes." Others passed on material they regarded as helpful, including coupons and good deals: "[I share] information about ... deals I find or interesting articles I come across." Some even admitted to passing on explicitly copyrighted material. "[I share] movies and videos. [I share] pornography and video games." As we might expect, participants feel relatively comfortable saving anything they encounter online, regardless of the media type involved and their relationship to the content. Anyone can save any user-contributed content they find. But do they?

Here, practice is divorced from attitude. While downloading photos belonging to others is relatively common (72 percent of the study participants say they do so at least sometimes), saving reviews locally is far less so; participants rarely even save their own reviews. These join the other online ephemera, useful and used, but they are not saved or extensively curated. In fact, the only non-positive reaction we elicited from participants was when we proposed hypotheticals that limited the ability to save content locally. For example, allowing a review's author to save her own review but not the comments that had accrued on it elicited a largely negative reaction. Similarly, limiting a tweet's author to save only his or her side of a Twitter conversation garnered a far more negative reaction than other hypothetical situations.

With this in mind, we can look at reuse, which is bound to be controversial and to have a more nuanced sense of where the boundaries are. The following table shows four responses to a question about the last time a participant remembers reusing a photo:

Boundary	Quote
Of me	"Someone tagged a picture of me on Facebook and I saved the picture and put it into my album because it was a nice picture."
Of friends and family	"My friend took a picture of my son and her son. I reposted so everyone can view from my family."
Of an event I plan to attend	"Earlier this week I downloaded a picture of a dog wearing a party hat for a story I was doing on my pet blog about an event coming up. It was a photo included in a press release by the store holding the event."
Of a place I've been to	"I couldn't find a photo I'd taken on a trip, which I wanted to use in a Facebook album, so I found a photo of the same landmark on someone's blog and republished it in my album."

What we see is a slippery slope of acceptability. In agreement with what we saw in the hypotheticals, social distance matters: *Even though I didn't take the photo, it's a picture of me. Or it's a picture of my son. Or it's an event I've attended. Or it's an event that I plan to attend. Or*—and here's where distance begins to increase, perhaps to a breaking point— *it's a place I've been, and it's a picture of a landmark, not a person.*

People navigate a complex moral and ethical terrain when they reuse pictures. They may apply what they know of the law—or what they think they know of the law—and come up with a notion of the public web as a place that is conceptually in the public domain. There has been ample discussion of limiting risk by simply not posting content; participants echo this discourse by saying things like, "If you don't want your picture or face to possibly end up being seen by future bosses, kids, friends, parents whatever, then don't post it." In this regimen, Creative Commons is literally that, a commons, a place where content is offered for reuse without restriction, rather than a labeling system.

Although participants occasionally take their cues from the technology, using Share With buttons as a signal that it's OK to reuse the content, more commonly they try to reason from the creation context or the photo's intended genre as a means to intuit the implied permission to reuse. As we saw earlier, there is more sensitivity around personal photos than there is around landscapes, particularly photos that are not intended as artistic statements but rather are simple evocations of vacation memories. If you've gone to Paphos and I've gone to Paphos, and you've taken a picture at the restaurant with the live pelican, and I eat there too but forget my camera in my hotel room, there would seem to be no reason why I can't use your photo in Facebook to illustrate my travel story. It's probably just as out-of-focus as mine would be, and with my small audience of friends, it's unlikely I would be caught.

The closest that participants come to echoing a fair use proposition is when they reason from a reuse context. They intuitively know that commercial reuse is more controversial than non-commercial reuse, that derivative works may be a legitimate type of reuse, and that the particular motivations of the reuser matter. In practice, it seems that reuse may be mediated in a large part by need: When the participant actually needs a photo (instead of being handed a hypothetical situation), he or she is apt to rationalize reuse. Furthermore, the content's history (i.e., has it been around much?) plays into the equation.

Most interesting are factors that arise from participants' experience of life online. Will the reuse alter subsequent perceptions of the content's veracity or importance? After all, if it is reused, it will appear in more places and may seem truer or more significant because of its ubiquity. Is the reuse mean or malicious? There seems to be a fine line between "funny" and "making fun of." Several participants cited PeopleOfWalmart.com as a website that crosses that boundary. Is the reuse misuse in the sense that it perpetrates fraud? When participants think about this type of reuse, they are more apt to think of a Photoshop job in which they're made to look 20 pounds heavier than they are of phishing or other more blatantly illegal deceptions.

A Case for Institutional Archiving

When I argue that most people seem to approach the curation of their digital belongings with a mixture of benign neglect and unrealized plans to do better, I am in no way maligning them. We all are interested in keeping at least some of our digital stuff for the foreseeable future. In fact, my colleagues at the Library of Congress report that people have shown considerable interest in the Library's outreach efforts and classes (see Chapter 3), and the Internet Archive has customers for its new personal archiving service. I regularly hear of new internet startups with either long-term backup or archiving as part of their core mission; they have all perceived a need and detected an interest.

Why don't I believe that, with this instruction and guidance, people can and will do it themselves? There are three reasons I'm skeptical.

First is the *disaggregation of necessary skills.* To be good personal archivists (even amateur ones), people need to perform curatorial duties (creating viable metadata, assessing long-term value). They need to perform the regular and extraordinary IT tasks that come with personal information management, everything from normal maintenance including installing software to heroic rescues such as recovering from malware or device driver failures. On occasion, they may need to be media type experts, too (e.g., is it better to store personal photos in RAW format or JPEG?). To make matters more complicated, the family member who knows how to use Photoshop may not be the same family member who has an abiding interest in personal archiving, and neither of them may be the family member who has the IT expertise to perform everyday system maintenance. Add in the occasional duplication of roles and consultations with outside experts, and the result is an extensive roster of stakeholders and potential conflicts between them.

Second is *trends in personal data storage.* The storage picture is increasingly complex, but it's complex in a good way. We have more capable devices (our phones are all we need some days) and more special-purpose devices (think of Apple's ecosystem of pads, pods, minis, and desktop-filling devices). There are more places in the cloud to store things and more things to store. Content that was once transient now may be kept indefinitely (for example, we can store everything from Skype conversations to screen captures of our latest raid in World of Warcraft), and content that was once personal is now shared via a growing array of social media services (at one time, Flickr was the dominant venue for photo sharing; now Instagram is the place-of-the-moment). There are more ways to publish the fruits of any creative effort that might cross our minds (some communities such as deviantART have been going strong for over a decade; YouTube is a place where one can waste whole afternoons or seek emergency instruction for peeling a pomegranate; and Pinterest changes the focus from creation to curation). The ecology of on- and offline storage is complicated and unstable (Odom et al. 2012). I have interviewed people who pay for services they no longer actively use, simply because (like a physical storage locker) they don't know what to do with what they've stored there.

Third, and final, is the *overwhelming tendency toward benign neglect.* Digital possessions accumulate rapidly. To properly curate them, we would probably need to drop everything we were doing and just devote ourselves to our legacy. At this point, it is important to recall the difference between personal archiving and archiving personal material: In the first instance, the owner of the material must set aside time and marshal other resources (the technical and curatorial skills I referred to previously) to address digital belongings that may be of uncertain personal value; in the second instance, an archivist's considerable skills and an institution's resources can be brought to bear on the task and the material's value is seen from a broader cultural perspective. The poet's email acquired by The British Library that Donald Hawkins discusses in Chapter 4 is a perfect example of this distinction. Although over the last few decades, there has been considerable hand-wringing in some quarters about the disappearance of the literary letter (Arnold 1999; Geoghegan 2010), efforts by institutions like The British Library to preserve the email of important literary figures belie this fear. Yet for an individual, preserving his or her own email is onerous; email is often stored in a way that is opaque and figuring out a way to keep it safe is not offset by its overall personal value. The alternative (finding and saving specific high-value messages) is also time-consuming and usually seen as not worth the trouble. So usually personal email is simply left in place, and its owner just hopes for the best: benign neglect at work. And certainly, in the end, for the individual archiving his or her own stuff, creation is just more rewarding than stewardship.

These three trends suggest that public institutions have a role to play in archiving personal digital belongings: If they don't intervene, there is no way to predict what will survive and what won't. But recent efforts, for example, the Library of Congress's initiative to archive the public Twitter feed, have been met with skepticism and even a certain amount of resistance. The skepticism stems from the feed's perceived lack of long-term value. To quote a study participant, "Things like Facebook, Twitter, Google+ [should not be archived]. Some contain personal data that has no historical or archival significance." The resistance arises from privacy advocates, for certainly institutional archiving of social media violates an expectation of privacy through obscurity.[2] On the other hand, this initiative is consistent with Twitter's terms and conditions, and we must ask ourselves: How much control do we have over data we have contributed to a site that stores it for free? If we examine people's concerns, it's not that the Library of Congress is storing social media. Instead, it's the potential for access and reuse. But it is that potential—the value of yesterday's social media for research, for art or everyday use—that may be the best justification for the cost and invasiveness of institutional archiving.

Frank Shipman and I have been interested in probing these attitudes as part of the series of studies I described earlier. In the six studies to date, we always included a media-specific set of three hypotheticals based on this scenario: "The Library of Congress is acquiring the public portion of the Twitter feed | Flickr | Amazon's book reviews | YouTube | iTunes educational recordings | popular iTunes podcasts, dating back to the site's origins. They are planning to provide access to the archive." (We used the Library of Congress as a proxy for any public institution that would undertake a large-scale archiving effort because we felt that participants were likely to be familiar with the Library of Congress as an institution.) Then we posed three standard hypotheticals about how the archive might be accessed: by researchers now, by everyone now, or by everyone in 50 years. The results of these cross-media comparisons are described in Marshall and Shipman (2012). We also probed concepts such as anonymity, satire, attribution, before-recording consent, creator permission, and removal from archives, many of which are analogous to those in models of fair use (Sag 2012). We wanted to see how sensitive our participants were to immediate public access (which is not that far from the initial situation; presumably the same works are available to the public through the services in which they were originally shared) and what kinds of limitations would ease any concerns they had.

If we look at the data for the immediate access scenario, participant opinion falls into two clusters. Tweets, photos, and reviews form the first cluster; participants seem less sanguine about immediate access to these collections. For tweets, in particular, the distribution is notably bimodal: Some participants are very much opposed to immediate access, while others are mildly favorable. Educational recordings, podcasts, and YouTube videos form the second cluster; these are far less controversial. Most participants feel that immediate access would be acceptable. The reason for this seems straightforward, especially in the light of open-ended responses that are included in some of the questionnaires: The more personal the medium, the less acceptable public access is.

What would happen if we limited the access to the collection to researchers? For simplicity's sake, we did not define researchers, preferring to let participants use their intuitions. This limitation apparently eases risk in the participants' eyes, since most of the negative reactions have been attenuated. Tweets and photos have the most negative responses; educational recordings, the most positive.

Finally, we looked at the element of time. What would happen if we deferred access for 50 years? Twitter and reviews summon the least enthusiasm, possibly because users rely on privacy through obscurity or perhaps because they are textual and most readily subject to retrieval and analysis. Time seemed to assuage some of the privacy concerns for visual media.

Open-ended questions about what should be excluded from this type of institutionally curated collection revealed that participants assumed four perspectives that were similar to those we found for reuse by individuals. Figure 6.1 shows these four perspectives.

Unsurprisingly, it seems that participants were most concerned with the potential effects of public access to these hypothetical collections. The prevailing concerns from the creator's perspective were permission and privacy. If participants took the content's perspective, they seemed to consider the content's value, weighed against the countervailing costs (supposing the content was, say, untrue or harmful). I was happy to see that a considerable number of responses brought up the overarching social good of such a collection. Only a few participants assumed the position that there were already technology-based mechanisms in place to handle these problems (e.g., Facebook's privacy settings). Figure 6.2 shows examples of the participants' responses to an open-ended question about institutional archiving of social media content.

Although we suspected that ownership boundaries are fuzzy and that social norms are evolving, we also saw that content type and genre mattered. How personal the content is perceived to be has a substantial effect on how sensitive participants are to institutional acquisition. Furthermore, participants' familiarity with the media type in question and how much experience they have with it in their everyday lives seems to make a profound difference in how they react to the hypotheticals we pose. Most importantly, we saw that collection building

Creator	Content/media
• *permission*	• *inherent value*
• *credit*	• *veracity*
• *privacy*	• *harm/bias/malice*
Technology	**Legal/social**
• *authorization*	• *public record*
• *settings*	• *public domain*
	• *social good*

Figure 6.1　Four participant perspectives on institutional archiving

Permission/Privacy	Value/Veracity/Harm
"Everything created deserves to have proper credit by its creator, and if the creator doesn't want it archived that should be an available choice."	*"No one cares what status updates someone in Colorado writes about the sandwich they ate for lunch."*
"Facebook pages, Twitter accounts, and any other social media ... It is that person's private account and should not be messed with."	*"I think the Library of Congress is more useful by keeping information that has reasonably been researched to know is true, as some of these things out there are not real."*
"Videos are a lot more personal than anything written on paper so they should be treated more cautiously."	*"I think social media that contains racial bias or any kind of prejudiced based content shouldn't be archived."*
Existing Mechanisms	**Law/Social Good**
"Profiles indicate the user's express wish not to have their information accessible to everyone."	*"Once something is on the web, it belongs to the web users."*
	"We are creating culture and history. No matter how some people feel about a certain subject or genre, nothing should be excluded."

Figure 6.2   Examples that illustrate dominant concepts of each of the four perspectives

and access need to be teased apart; people aren't making this distinction on their own.

It is clear that public institutions have an important role to play in archiving social media. Between personal benign neglect and the onerous nature of the curatorial effort, it is unlikely that individuals will be able to do it themselves. Participants in our studies readily acknowledged the role of public institutions in this immense stewardship effort; one participant said, "The Library of Congress should really keep at least a sample of everything. We are creating culture and history. No matter how some people feel about a certain subject or genre, nothing should be excluded." It is also evident that considerable effort still awaits us as archival institutions set the public's expectations about what should be in these collections; who should be able to use them and for what; and whether creators should expect long-term plans to maintain their identity and to enforce attribution. As the Preserving Virtual Worlds project reminds us, even conservative approaches to obtaining permission have an associated cost. In that effort, they tried to obtain in-world permission to archive content, and their overtures were met with hostility. In the end, they only achieved a 10 percent permission rate (McDonough et al. 2010), one that is heartbreaking for those of us who have set out on these missions with the best of intentions.

In the end, it is important for us to acknowledge and accommodate the enormous changes to personal archiving wrought by the emergence of digital content and modern personal information management practices. Physical metaphors (think of cardboard boxes in the attic or the office file cabinets) have broken down as digital content is stored in many forms, in an increasing number of venues, and under the control of many stakeholders. Just as digital content has evolved, so too have digital practices. The ease and primacy of sharing, publication, and reuse has changed the nature and scope of personal archives.

Over the course of the studies I have described in this chapter, I have undergone a sea change myself. I started out naively believing that addressing the "personal archiving problem" was simply a matter of understanding individual practices and developing a system or a service for people to use to archive their own files. Over time, I have come to appreciate the complexity of the problem: Personal digital archiving will require more than well-designed technology to become a force that is more powerful than benign neglect. Policy, education, and public and private efforts are necessary to realize the inherent sociality and reach of today's personal archives.

Endnotes

1. This page (www.rtis.com/reg/bremond; version February 13, 1997) can be retrieved from the Wayback Machine. This version of the page from 1997 agrees with my memory of what the city's homepage was like in late 1994, when I first encountered it.

2. In 2010, Fred Stutzman wrote the following in his post, Twitter and the Library of Congress (fstutzman.com/2010/04/14/twitter-and-the-library-of-congress; this website is no longer available): "This is what makes Twitter's 'gift' troubling. It assumes that all content shared publicly is truly public and for posterity. ...

[Consider this scenario:] Bob wants to be practically obscure—private in public—without going to all the trouble of setting up complicated privacy controls. So what happens, 2 years from now, when Bob accidentally discloses his handle in the wrong context, and he needs to remove some Tweets?"

References

Anderson, Chris. 2004. "The Long Tail." *Wired* 12.10. www.wired.com/wired/archive/12.10/tail.html.

Arnold, Martin. 1999. "Making Books; Pen in Hand? Maybe No More." *New York Times*, January 21. www.nytimes.com/1999/01/21/books/making-books-pen-in-hand-maybe-no-more.html.

Boyle, James. 2008. *The Public Domain: Enclosing the Commons of the Mind*. New York: Yale University Press.

Geoghegan, Peter. 2010. "Epistles at Dawn: The Dying Art of Letter Writing." *The Guardian*, June 23. www.guardian.co.uk/books/booksblog/2010/jun/23/epistles-letters-writing-saul-bellow.

James, William. 1890. *The Principles of Psychology*. New York: Holt.

John, Jeremy Leighton with Ian Rowlands, Peter Williams, and Katrina Dean. *Personal Digital Archives for the 21st Century: An Initial Synthesis* (Digital Lives Research Paper, Beta Version 0.2). March 3, 2010. britishlibrary.typepad.co.uk/files/digital-lives-synthesis02-1.pdf.

Lanham, Richard A. 1993. *The Electronic Word: Democracy, Technology, and the Arts*. Chicago: University of Chicago Press.

Lessig, Lawrence. 2006. *Code: And Other Laws of Cyberspace, Version 2.0*. Tucson, AZ: Basic Books.

———. 2008. *Remix: Making Art and Commerce Thrive in the Hybrid Economy*. New York: Penguin.

Levy, David M. 2001. *Scrolling Forward: Making Sense of Documents in the Digital Age*. New York: Arcade Publishing.

Marshall, Catherine C. 2011. "Challenges and Opportunities for Personal Digital Archiving." In *I, Digital: Personal Collections in the Digital Era*, edited by Cal Lee, 90–114. Chicago: Society of American Archivists.

Marshall, Catherine C., Sara Bly, and Françoise Brun-Cottan. 2006. "The Long Term Fate of Our Personal Digital Belongings: Toward a Shared Model for Personal Archives." In *Proc. Archiving 2006*, 25–30.

Marshall, Catherine C., Frank McCown, and Michael L.Nelson. 2007. "Evaluating Personal Archiving Strategies for Internet-Based Information." In *Proc. Archiving 2007*, 151–156.

Marshall, Catherine C., and Frank M. Shipman. 2011a. "The Ownership and Reuse of Visual Media." In *Proceedings of JCDL 2011*, 157–166. New York: ACM Press.

———. 2011b. "Social Media Ownership: Using Twitter as a Window onto Current Attitudes and Beliefs." In *Proceedings of CHI'11*, Vancouver, BC, May 7–12.

———. 2012. "On the Institutional Archiving of Social Media." In *Proceedings of JCDL 2012*, 157–166. New York.

McCown, Frank, Michael L. Nelson, and Herbert Van de Sompel. 2009. "Everyone Is a Curator: Human-Assisted Preservation for ORE Aggregations." In *Proc. DigCCurr 2009*.

McDonough, Jerome P., Robert Olendorf, Matthew Kirschenbaum, Kari Kraus, Doug Reside, Rachel Donahue, Andrew Phelps, Christopher Egert, Henry Lowood, and Susan Rojo. 2010. *Preserving Virtual Worlds Final Report.* hdl.handle.net/2142/17097.

Nelson, Michael L., Frank McCown, Joan A. Smith, and Martin Klein. 2007. "Using the Web Infrastructure to Preserve Web Pages." *International Journal on Digital Libraries, Special Issue on Digital Preservation* 6 (4): 327–349.

Odom, William, Abigail Sellen, Richard Harper, and Eno Thereska. 2012. "Lost in Translation: Understanding The Possession of Digital Things in the Cloud." In *Proc. CHI 2012*, 781–790.

Rissland, Edwina L., and Kevin D. Ashley. 1986. "Hypotheticals as Heuristic Device." In *Proc. Strategic Computing Natural Language*, Marina del Rey, California, May 1–2, 165–178.

Sag, Matthew. 2012. "Predicting Fair Use." *Ohio State Law Journal* 73 (1): 47–91.

Sellen, Abigail, and Richard Harper. 2001. *The Myth of the Paperless Office.* Cambridge, MA: MIT Press.

Surowiecki, James. 2004. *The Wisdom of Crowds.* New York: Little, Brown.

Thorngate, Warren. 1987. "On Paying Attention." In *Recent Trends in Theoretical Psychology*, edited by William Baker et al., 247–263. New York: Springer-Verlag.

CHAPTER 7

Reading Ben Shneiderman's Email: Identifying Narrative Elements in Email Archives

Jason Zalinger, University of South Florida,
Nathan G. Freier, Microsoft Corporation, and
Ben Shneiderman, University of Maryland

When you don't know what you are looking for, how do you find it? This question was the initial motivation for this research. Specifically, the goal was to test a narrative approach to searching through an email archive accumulated by Professor Ben Shneiderman from 1984–1998 that contained 44,971 messages with over 4,000 relationships. Shneiderman—like any careful professional—was "always aware that my emails could become public or fall into some unexpected recipient's hands, so I was fairly careful in self-censoring, or at least cautious in sending notes that could be problematic."[1] Regardless, the archive contained fascinating and often highly personal and emotional exchanges. Here, we focus on the professional when possible, but it is often the personal that seems to yield the "best" results using narrative search techniques.

We define *narrative search* as both a set of search techniques and a way of thinking as a writer or storyteller. The goal is not to find complete narratives (although many do exist) but to search for critical narrative clues, like the right jigsaw puzzle piece, that will lead users to find rich, rewarding information about someone else's life in email— especially when they do not know much about that person's life. We found that searching for these narrative elements is a promising search technique that can be productively applied to other email archives. Narrative search is not just a technique but a way of approaching or thinking about what to search for and why.

Personal digital archives have become significant enough in breadth and depth to stand as a reflection of a lifetime's worth of work and lived experience. In 2012, the world sent 144 billion emails every day.[2] (This number is estimated to reach 192 billion by 2016.) In 2011, in the U.S., we sent 6 billion text messages per day,[3] which does not include instant messages, Facebook email, Twitter updates, and so on. Although the historical record has never been more complete and potentially offers historians and others a rich record of a person's life, the question that remains to be answered is how best to make some kind of narrative sense out of all this "data." Specifically, how should we design effective archival systems to help users explore a vast email archive of, in this case, the life of a scholar?

An Academic's Request

In April 2009, at the ACM SIGCHI Conference on Human Factors in Computing Systems Conference in Boston, I [*Authors' note:* In this chapter, "I" refers to Zalinger] was in a workshop with Professor Ben Shneiderman, who has been an influential and prolific academic for 30 years. The workshop began with introductions, and we had 30 seconds to say something about ourselves. I rambled on for 28 then blurted out the word *narrative*. I didn't realize it at the time, but when I said that word, Shneiderman's antenna went up. At the lunch break, he approached me. He pointed his finger at me: "You!" he said, and then told me he had a substantial email archive of nearly 45,000 messages that he would give to me.

"You are going to let me read 15 years of your email?" I asked in amazement.

"Yes," he replied.

A few weeks later, I received a DVD containing the email archive and a search program. Shneiderman's archive was well-curated; he had saved only key emails, no junk mail, and very little of the daily traffic of announcements and so on. In addition, he had saved them in folders organized by name and year from 1984–1998. So, this chapter is really the story of trying to find and piece together the narrative elements about an academic's life.

Shneiderman was interested to see what an outsider thought about his archive. After spending about 80 hours reading or searching through well over 1,000 emails, how would I interpret 15 years of professional and even some very personal material? This chapter is organized around my descriptions of what I searched for and why I searched for it. Along the way, I offer a variety of design suggestions for creating an interface to help users (from professional historians to interested novices) make narrative sense of an overwhelming mass of emails.

Related Work

Ironically, we must search hard to discover new ways of thinking about exploratory search tools to help people make sense of large email archives. These new tools and techniques for exploratory search will require novel research and collaboration.[4] The narrative search strategies described here seem closely related to Gary Marchionini's notion of interactive information retrieval,[5] which looks at the search problem from the perspective of "an active human with information needs" and "information skills." To characterize this exploratory narrative searching, we can simply change the word *information* to *narrative*. (Of course, the perfect interface would not require narrative skills from users but would help them to think like storytellers.) Although we believe our approach is unique, some previous work relates to our main themes of narrative discovery in email archives. For example, Anton

Leuski[6] argued that it is possible to detect someone's role by analyzing "speech acts" in email. Victor Carvalho and William Cohen[7] showed how to improve on the classification of "email acts." Jon Kleinberg[8] explored how to model "bursts" of email activity in order to more efficiently identify and organize the underlying content of the messages. A recent successful meme-tracking approach followed short, "distinctive phrases" as they traveled through the internet, revealing a "coherent representation" of the temporal patterns in the news cycle.[9]

Others have taken a more visual approach to gaining insight from email archives. For example, the first attempt to analyze and understand Shneiderman's archive was documented by Shneiderman along with Adam Perer and Douglas Oard,[10] who argued that to understand email conversations in an archive, context is needed. They provided methods for "constructing meaningful rhythms from the email headers by identifying relationships and interpreting their attributes." Their visualizations of rhythms showed that important relationships became evident, and they discovered insights "that may have been otherwise hidden."

Fernanda Viégas, Scott Golder, and Judith Donath[11] created Themail, a "visualization that portrays relationships using the interaction histories preserved in email archives." Themail was built "with the working hypothesis that a visualization of email content constituted meaningful portraits of people's relationships." PostHistory and Social Network Fragments are visualization tools that allowed users to see the "higher-level" patterns of their email habits.[12] PostHistory focused on email relationships between two people, and Social Network Fragments explored the social groups that emerge within email exchanges. Another research project, CrystalChat, used a 3D-representational model of personal instant messenger history to "reveal the patterns and to support self-exploration of one's personal chat history."[13]

Lifelogging technology is also related to our work. Probably the best-known example of a lifelogging project is the Microsoft-funded MyLifeBits, which its creators call "a lifetime store of everything." It is the fulfillment of Vannevar Bush's 1945 memex vision including "full-text search, text and audio annotations, and hyperlinks."[14] The creators describe themselves as being on "a quest to digitally chronicle every aspect of a person's life."[15] Of course, it is an open research question as to whether or not this is even a good idea. Other lifelog researchers have argued, "Given the volume of content contained within a lifelog collection, we cannot expect a user to manually locate and construct individual stories from its contents. As such we must make the process of constructing a narrative retelling as automatic as possible."[16]

There have also been attempts to design narrative interfaces. For example, Daniel Gonçalves and Joaquim Jorge showed that "narratives can be successfully used as a way to help users recall important autobiographic information about their documents and convey that information to the computer."[17] In another study, David Elsweiler, Mark Baillie, and Ian Ruthven "investigated what people tend to remember when looking for their old email messages.[18] The study showed that people tend to remember quite a lot regarding their emails, but there are situations where they remember less. These last two approaches were autobiographic: Our perspective here is outsider-looking-in, whereas they took an insider-looking-in perspective (OLI vs. ILI).

All these studies provide potential answers to the vexing problem of finding meaning in vast amounts of personal data, especially email. However, none has yet focused on finding narrative elements. Our approach is narrative, and we believe a well-designed interface can help users find the narrative clues that lead to stories. And all those stories can add up to a robust characterization of a person's life—in this case, Shneiderman's life.

Why Narrative?

In his book *On Stories*,[19] Richard Kearney explores some of the reasons why telling and sharing stories are such critical elements of human behavior. The fundamental question he asks is, why are stories important? He offers some trenchant insights. For example, he writes that it is "only when haphazard happenings are transformed into a story, and thus made memorable over time, that we become full agents of our history." Stories are not just about some things that happened. They are a transformation of events placed into a particular sequence using particular words that renders them into art: something that we want to tell and retell. Kearney also wrote that:

> When someone asks you who you are, you tell your story. That is, you recount your present condition in the light of past memories and future anticipations. You interpret where you are now in terms of where you have come from and where you are going to. And in so doing you give a sense of yourself as a narrative identity that perdures and coheres over a lifetime. Storytelling may be said to humanize time by transforming it from an impersonal passing of fragmented moments into a pattern, a plot, a mythos.[20]

Kearney's interpretation of the transformative power of storytelling endows it with the ability to control time. Humans need to organize, classify, and understand (i.e., control). We search for order amid chaos. We crave logical patterns, yet we also crave emotional patterns, which is what stories seem to provide. Stories organize emotions, moments, and life into meaningful patterns that we can then share with each other. We need stories. How else can we make sense of such bizarre things as love and death and birth? Logic resonates with one part of the human mind because it is an organizing agent. Stories are just as powerful as logic. They are the other organizing agent in our lives. Logic cannot make sense of love lost, but a story might be able to. A story about love lost is something we can understand and share.

If Kearney is right, then it is only when the seemingly haphazard happenings of an email archive are transformed into story that they will be made memorable over time. Our approach does not look for complete stories but the narrative elements that make up stories. The question is: How do we find these elements in someone else's archive?

Where to Begin?

What makes a story interesting if you don't know much about the life of Shneiderman or the people surrounding his life? In what narrative systematic ways might an outsider explore someone's email archive? One possibility was to use a timeline to try and visualize the messages more clearly. Timelines are an excellent technique for placing events in time and giving users an overview of results. I asked a colleague to build a timeline into the existing interface, which made it much easier to see conversations. Unfortunately, I found it difficult to gain insight or find narrative elements using a timeline approach (Figure 7.1). In this particular case, a timeline was not as useful as I had hoped; however, more work needs to be done merging timelines with a narrative search. Shneiderman suggested identifying influential people with whom he had been in touch with over the years, doing Google searches on all his correspondents to see who had the top 10 highest number of hits, or searching for people at key companies (e.g., Apple or Microsoft), in other countries, or at major universities. Other ideas included locating co-authors from Shneiderman's list of publications or finding his most frequent correspondents and then reading through the history of a single relationship.

These were all interesting starting points, yet, feeling overwhelmed, I decided to search the archive for mentions of Shneiderman's book *Leonardo's Laptop*[21] to see what came up. At the time, I was a PhD candidate and hoped to write a book someday, so I was curious to know what sort of messages surrounded the creation of this book. Searching for *Leonardo's Laptop* returned 15 messages. The first thing I realized is that the book was likely not referred to exactly that way when Shneiderman began work on it. In fact, maybe the last thing Shneiderman did was give it a title. So, without asking Shneiderman, how could I locate the beginnings of a book project in all of these messages? What are similar keywords? Should I have tried *book project*, *Ben's book*, or *Leonardo*? Surely, a book project for which Shneiderman, or anyone for that matter, is the sole author must have generated more than 15 email messages.

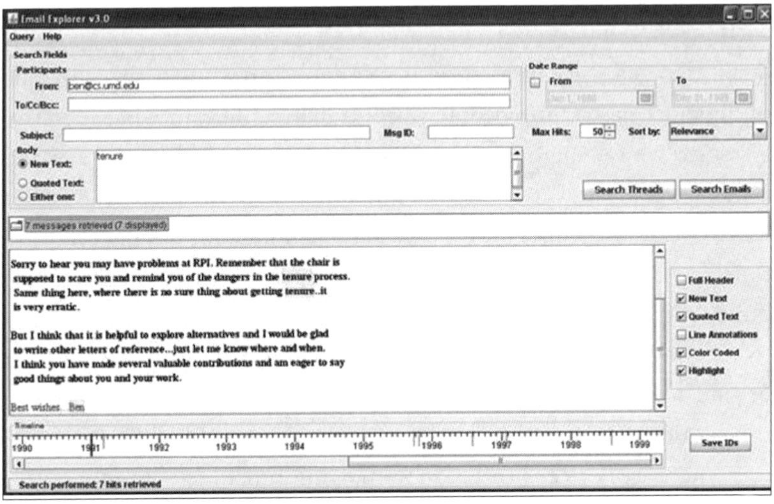

Figure 7.1   A search for _tenure_ in Shneiderman's archive using Elsayed's Email Explorer interface with Manuel Freire's timeline addition. Short ticks on the timeline indicate retrieved messages; long ticks mark the currently selected one.

The design of the current interface to the email archive is somewhat limited because it was not designed for finding narrative elements. That is not the interface designer's fault. The interface simply was not created to answer the potential range of questions that a historian or biographer or writer might have nor was it designed to answer narrative questions. The same questions we were asked in high school English class have only become more important as we continue to accumulate decades of life "data." Who is the protagonist? Who is the antagonist? What is the plot? What is the dramatic want of the character? What is the obstacle the protagonist faces? Maybe these questions are wrong, or maybe there is no interface that can answer them. However, a good interface, like a flashlight in a dark room, might allow us to explore and see interesting things for ourselves. We do not want a computer to tell us the complete story of Shneiderman's life. Instead, we want a program to help us find and put together the narrative pieces of the jigsaw puzzle in a way that makes sense. Humans will write the final story.

The Mysterious Bill

The first message I looked at was from January 22, 1998. I knew that *Leonardo's Laptop* was published in 2002, so the first thing that came to mind was that I was reading the seeds of what would eventually become an influential book. The email is from someone named Bill. [*Authors' note:* Bill is a false name. Because of privacy concerns, at certain points we quote directly from Shneiderman's archive without identifying any information about the sender or date.] Bill appears to be from the University of Victoria, according to the "from" address. Bill tells Shneiderman that they met at ACM MM'97. Wondering who Bill is (or was), my first reaction was to do a Google search for *ACM MM'97*. Of course, I was now presented with two options. Searching with quote marks gave me 33 results, while searching without retrieved 1,050,000. Without quotes, the first link Google offered suggested that Shneiderman and Bill most likely met at the Fifth ACM International Conference on Multimedia held November 9–13, 1997. That conference does not seem to have a permanent web presence but exists as proceedings published by the ACM. Bill goes on to say that "you impressed all of us with the [*sic*] Leonardo's Laptop." Obviously, whatever presentation Shneiderman gave left a very positive impression. How did this make Shneiderman feel? Was this public confirmation that his *Leonardo* project was on the right path, or did he still have many doubts? As an outsider, I could not know. However, there was a clue in the next sentence. Bill writes, "Since you wanted to see your pictures. I have posted two of them in the web." This is interesting because, first, Shneiderman clearly asked to see pictures. Lots of people want to see pictures of themselves and their experiences. However, I also happened to know that Shneiderman has a serious interest in photography, and I wondered if he downloaded those pictures and added them to his archive, which is exactly why we are able to look through these emails in the first place—because Shneiderman is an archiver and always has been. Obviously, I went to the URL for the pictures, but they were long gone. So from this email we have learned some things about Shneiderman the person and the scholar, yet we are left with many questions, too: Who is the mysterious Bill? How would I find him?

I put Bill's name into the database that came with the archive, and the only return was the email already in question. Can we use a program to seek him out based on the little data we have, or would we have to simply do the old-school detective work of calling up the University of Victoria and find out where he might be? Luckily, another option existed: I could ask Shneiderman. Thus, can we create an accessible archive that would allow Shneiderman to go through and comment on his own email archive? Would that be remarkable bias, or would it shed light on these little moments of a person's life that were stepping stones on the way toward a larger accomplishment, in this case *Leonardo's Laptop*? Not all historians have the ability to simply ask the person who created the archive what they think, but we must use all available resources, and Shneiderman is the best resource on his own life. Finally, would Shneiderman, or any scholar with a vast archive, even want to do this? We know that Shneiderman actually seems to enjoy tagging his photos, but would it be tedious to go through 44,971 messages and add notes? There is yet another option here, too, which is technically easy to do but ethically a bit challenging. What if we could find Bill and ask him to comment on the email? In fact, what if we were to send an email to everyone in Shneiderman's address book and ask them if they would be willing to comment upon any thread of which they were a part? This would turn Shneiderman's email archive into a closed wiki in which only those who had access to the original emails could add their notes. In this case, Bill could only comment on his one email. There was nothing in that message that was sensitive, but what if there were something personal?

Where are the pictures that Bill posted? Are they gone forever, or did Shneiderman happen to grab and tag them years ago? Clearly, any mention of pictures should be linked to Shneiderman's other substantial archive of about 12,000 well-curated photographs.[22]

Was ACM MM'97 a significant moment in the history of the human–computer interaction field? Shneiderman's email archive may not tell us the whole story, but it is most likely the largest, most significant piece of the puzzle. Furthermore, how could we provide context for users? The most obvious design solution is to link or somehow provide data from the conference: How many people attended? How many papers were published in the proceedings? Critically, what did Shneiderman publish, if anything, and how many times has that paper been cited? Is there any documentation of Shneiderman's presentation? All of these elements and all of this context should be provided to the users in a way that helps them make some kind of narrative sense.

Finally, it is always important to remember that narratives contain action. People do things in a narrative. In this particular email, Bill wrote "you wanted" the pictures. Perhaps this is a semantic computation problem, but it seems that we could somewhat easily find narrative elements by defining them and then searching for them. We could define narrative action as "Ben + verb." For example, I searched for *Ben decided* in the email archive, but it returned only five results. Still, we imagine that Shneiderman and the word *decision* (or some variant of that word) came up more often in this archive. The point here is to look for moments when Shneiderman takes some kind of action. (In addition, the interface could use a "Google Suggests" feature and suggest words as they are typed, thus helping users narrow down their search before they even begin.) I never did find the mysterious Bill, but my explorations turned up both new questions and some answers about how to design narrative systems.

The Big "However"

The first time I explored Shneiderman's archive I came across what I considered to be a very interesting email exchange between

Shneiderman and a long-time collaborator. However, after a few weeks had gone by, although I could still search and find the thread, I had forgotten what keyword I had used in my original query. What word or phrase did I use to find this message? The program clearly needed a way to save searches so that users could go back and follow their tracks, much like browsers save a session and restore it once you reopen the program. Regardless, as a PhD candidate, I found this particular email very revealing. The message is dated Monday, August 26, 1996. Shneiderman begins by describing a recent trip to his colleague, "traveling in Israel with my daughters, mostly relaxing, beaching, dealing with the needs of my parents ..." He goes on to write, in an almost literary style, of the "nice hiking days in the Golan Heights—hot days, but the narrow gorges were filled with cool streams, waterfalls, and some places to swim—and the always inspiring walks through old Jerusalem."

The "cool streams" and "waterfalls" sound soothing and calm and function as a strong introduction to the next two paragraphs, in which Shneiderman characterizes his message as a "sensitive issue so I think we should discuss this carefully." After the "cool streams" and almost whispery, gentle way he begins the message, in the third paragraph, we get a big "however." This paragraph, again, begins positively and cordially:

> I think it's great that you wrote the history (of HCI) and put forward the university role. I also like the positive tone and attention to universal access; **however**, after reflection, I am troubled by the thin mention of my role in this history. My two main points in my note to you were about direct manipulation and hypertext. I was pleased that you referred to my direct manipulation article, but you gave it such a shallow treatment that it was uncomfortable for me. This paper is probably the most referenced paper in HCI.

Shneiderman continues this paragraph and the next four in the same polite and professional yet focused and unwavering tone. He finishes the email by writing, "We've been colleagues and professional friends for a long time, so I hope I can ask directly for better treatment of my role. Sincerely, Ben." Shneiderman then helpfully includes a list of eight of his publications.

This email is revealing for a number of reasons. First, for aspiring academics, it is fascinating and instructive to see how another scholar handled a difficult, even awkward situation with a long-time colleague. Additionally, this email tells us a lot about Shneiderman and how he was able to have such a successful career. In short, he had confidence in his work and was not afraid to speak up for his accomplishments when he felt it was necessary. This email reveals a lot about what it takes to be a successful scholar: You cannot be afraid to politely but firmly tell a colleague or "professional friend," as Shneiderman puts it, that you are unhappy with their description of your role in a particular situation.

Furthermore, this email is filled with narrative and contextual data. In a narrative, *however* is a key transitional word. In this particular email, the word *however* plays a major role in the narrative arc of the main character's dramatic want (Shneiderman's desire to have his historical role more prominently detailed), conflict (his colleague's thin mention of Shneiderman and the trickiness of politely standing one's ground), and the resolution of this scene, which is not clear to the reader because Shneiderman's colleague only responded by saying he would consider his comments and put the project aside for awhile.

The point here is that we can search for these kinds of transitional phrases, but we need a database of common transitional phrases from which to select. Would it be possible to create or pull from an existing database to help explorers find key moments like this one, where an academic stands up for his work? By searching for transition phrases, we might be able to locate revealing scenes such as this one.

Finally, this email is full of contextual data that could help explorers get a better sense of the world in which Shneiderman worked, professionally and personally, during 1996. For example, here is a short list of some of the places, concepts, people, and literature mentioned: Golan Heights,

Jerusalem, Israel, Direct Manipulation, Hypertext, Alan Kay, (Vannevar) Bush, ZOG, Apple, Hypercard, CACM, ACM, IEEE Software, FilmFinder, and the SIGDOC Award. Also noted are a number of Shneiderman's publications, all of which are clues as to what the Shneiderman world looked like at that particular moment in time. Linking to many of these things would be useful.

Bearded Professional Vision

In a fascinating story-within-a-story, on October 21, 1993, Shneiderman wrote an email to three friends in which he tells the story of his train ride after a conference: "I wrote this to record what happened for my own memories, but thought it made for a good story." He calls his train story, "An Encounter on the Metroliner" and begins by discussing his opening keynote address at the 4th International Stein Conference. On the second day, Shneiderman writes, Ed Fitzsimmons of the President's Office of Science and Technology gave a speech that "turned off most of the people in the room." Fitzsimmons was hoping to push technology into education. But Shneiderman's complaint was that Fitzsimmons paid little attention to teachers or equipment: "There was barely any attention to teachers or students, and no mention of educational philosophies, encouragement of teamwork, and so on."

At this point, Fitzsimmons, as a character in this story, seems to be a very stiff Washington bureaucrat who seems out of touch with what schools and teachers actually need. Shneiderman writes, "One person who didn't quite know what to do with her anger settled for pointing out how embarrassing it was that such a high federal official had several typos in his presentation." This sentence was how I actually found the entire message. I searched for the word *anger* because I was looking for points of tension, moments when anger, disappointment, confusion, or pain might have entered into Shneiderman's life. I did this not because I hoped to find such things but because in a narrative, tension is what makes for a good story. Without tension and conflict, we have no drama, and we have no story. Searching for what we will call tension words helped me find an amazing story-within-a-story. Thus, narrative search interfaces should include word suggestions, for example, a list of 1,000 words that might convey tension, such as *sadness*, *hate*, *love*, and so forth. In addition, a list of interesting or unusual words such as *guitar* or *ninja* (or, at Shneiderman's suggestion, *tibia*) retrieved interesting results.

Next, Shneiderman describes sitting next to Fitzsimmons on the way home, "His six foot stature and healthy fifty-ish military style were quite foreign to me." Fitzsimmons listened "openly to my ideas about education. ... We tried some scenarios and I think he liked the fresh perspective that I offered." So it turns out that the Fitzsimmons character is slightly more complex than we might have first thought. Next, Shneiderman invites him to discuss his military experience. Although it is a little lengthy, we believe it is worth including the rest of Shneiderman's story:

> He started talking about flying helicopters in Vietnam. I invited his further stories by saying that he must have had some scary experiences. He responded by telling about a volunteer mission at the time of the Tet Offensive in early 1968. He and another captain volunteered to fly in to rescue the remnants of an American company that had been "hammered" by the North Vietnamese. The first chopper took off uneventfully with many dead soldiers and his chopper was loaded with wounded, plus eight survivors. As he rose slowly above the trees he saw two soldiers step out firing AK-47s. Forty-seven bullets hit all around him, ripping up the windshield and floor, cutting his microphone cord, and leaving two bullets in his chest protector, but he was untouched. ...
>
> At this point the guy in the seat in front of us on the train, stood up and apologized for interrupting. He was fifty-ish, with a large white mustache and cowboy hat. He

introduced himself as Tom Carhart and said that he was one of the eight guys who was picked up from that terrible killing field on January 24, 1968. Fitzsimmons couldn't confirm the date, but the story was close enough that the two of them could not dismiss the possibility. As our visitor related that he was finishing a PhD in military history at Princeton, he unbuttoned his shirt to reveal an aging dark blue t-shirt with the shield of the 101st Airborne Strike Force. The eagle with its menacing claw made an impact on me, but when Fitzsimmons pulled down his suit jacket and showed the same shield on his lapel, amazement thundered through the train. He and Carhart quickly exchanged life histories (Purple Hearts, Silver Stars, etc.) and found dozens of common companions. Their easy discussion of death and war shook me, but I was grateful for the chance to witness this encounter. As an opponent to the Vietnam War, I remain troubled about that national tragedy and saddened that so many died, but I can respect what Carhart and Fitzsimmons did a quarter of a century ago. Is there any chance that Fitzsimmons could accept my bearded professorial vision about how students might collaborate?

First, as for Shneiderman, he ends the email with a brutally honest, personal, and yet a suitable question for all academics to consider: Why would a war hero listen to a scholar? Why would someone, *anyone* care about the work we do? Thus, one way to read the Metroliner story is as a self-reflective call to all academics to think hard about the relevance of their work as well as their ability to communicate their ideas to a wide variety of people not just to friends and colleagues. Furthermore, this story suggests something very interesting about Shneiderman's character: He is clearly aware that his "bearded" academic life could be seen as a stereotype and dismissed by men and women who have seen war or similarly horrible situations. Thus, he seems truly sensitive to having his ideas taken seriously by people who have experienced life-changing events.

Unlike the previous exchange in which Shneiderman stands firm on his body of work and disagrees with a colleague, here we see another side of Shneiderman—that of a listener, in awe, quietly recording a fascinating scene on a train. His interest in people and their stories seems to be in harmony with (or is a clear reflection of) his larger body of work dealing with the human side of computing. In addition, this email story reminds us of how our lives magically intersect with the lives of others. Of course, after reading this, I immediately searched for any information on Ed Fitzsimmons and Tom Carhart. I did not find much useful data on Fitzsimmons; however, a simple Google search on *Tom Carhart* provided the following information:

> Tom Carhart has been a lawyer and a historian for the Department of the Army in Washington, D.C. He is a graduate of West Point, a twice-wounded Vietnam veteran, and has earned a law degree from University of Michigan and a PhD in American and military history from Princeton University. He is the author of five books of military history and adjunct professor of history at University of Mary Washington in Fredericksburg, Virginia.[23]

Clearly, this must be the same man. Therefore, should Shneiderman email Carhart or Fitzsimmons? Could Carhart, a military historian, verify that he was, indeed, one of the soldiers picked up by Fitzsimmons? Have the two of them been in contact since the train ride? What would the two men think of Shneiderman's telling of this story? This email and the other two we have analyzed offered us a fertile, rich set of stories from which we can learn a lot about Shneiderman, personally and professionally.

What Is "Flemington"?

Another exploratory option, as we previously mentioned, is to use Shneiderman as a resource. In an email, Shneiderman suggested I search a range of possibilities for how to locate narrative elements in his archive. At the end of his list, he suggested that I could look for place names: "Try Flemington for some personal history allusions," he wrote. The word *Flemington* struck me as interesting. Places are powerful in our memories. Was Flemington the narrative setting for some particularly emotional period in Shneiderman's life? Was he trying to lead me to something? Was Flemington the spot for some sort of traumatic event? Had he witnessed a murder?!

As it turns out, Shneiderman wrote in a subsequent email to me, "I was not quite sure what Flemington would bring up." So what was Flemington? "It was," Shneiderman wrote, "our childhood weekend chicken farm … with five families sharing an 1880 farmhouse with 20,000 chickens and 26 acres in Flemington, New Jersey."[24] At first, I struggled to find any illuminating narrative elements related to Flemington; however, after much digging, I came across one fascinating message dated January 15, 1994, that just happened, in passing, to mention Flemington. In it, Shneiderman describes a range of challenges, both emotional and professional. Having just returned from giving lectures in Florida and Georgia, he writes to an old friend that "the brochures are meant to make me look like a 'big muckamuck.'" This seems to indicate a level of modesty that has probably helped Shneiderman—or any academic—keep his balance as a career begins to take flight. Shneiderman writes that he is gratified that "within the narrow community of user interface design and human–computer interaction, people value what I have done. Of course, you also acquire strong opposition as you go along, so there are often battles to fight. Also, by my pressing forward on these human-oriented issues, I have become an outsider to many people in the broader computer science community."

Here we find an academic struggling to assert his ideas and gain the respect of his peers—in fact, it seems the most challenging fight was closest to him. "My hardest struggle," Shneiderman continues, "is, of course, within my own department where I have relatively few supporters, and must fight for my students, financial support, room space, etc." In this same email, Shneiderman also discusses some very interesting personal details regarding his divorce, financial issues to iron out, scheduling time with his kids, and so forth. He writes, "I am very much the kind of person who hangs on loyally to current relationships, but I think it is time for me to move on ..."

Again, we find another side of Shneiderman: Frustrated but self-aware enough to feel that the time has come to move on. It is not important here to detail the personal nature of this message in its entirety. What is important is that I found it because Shneiderman mentioned Flemington. And that is the lesson. Shneiderman gave me a narrative clue that led to another rich message. The lesson is to listen for narrative clues when the creator of the archive gives them to you—provided they are there to help. I keyed into Flemington because it was a setting, and setting is powerful in stories and life.

However, the owner of an archive might sometimes have a fuzzy memory about what happened and when. Shneiderman suggested that I look for Flemington, and it produced interesting results. However, the aforementioned *tibia* was actually not what Shneiderman meant for me to look for. He meant to say *talus*, which brought up an interesting story of Shneiderman's daughter falling while hiking and ending up with titanium pins in her ankle—the talus bone. The lesson that I learned was that medical/anatomical words can lead to moments of emergency and thus narrative tension. A list of 1,000 common medical/anatomical words or phrases could help produce more such results.

Do Email Characters Change Over Time?

Characters change over time. Think of any good story you have ever read. The main character must go through some kind of metamorphosis, either physical or psychological. Think of the classic example of Scrooge in *A Christmas Story*. Scrooge starts off as a mean and selfish man only to end up warm and giving. Therefore, how can we discover character change in email archives? Although our keyword interface is not optimal, it does allow us to search by contact. If we define each conversation with a contact as a small scene, we can at least begin to look for what we will call "change phrases"—similar to how Shneiderman seems to have come to a changed state in the previous section when he decides to move on emotionally. Possible change phrases could be: *I have changed, he has changed, she is different, you are different*, and so forth. However, those strings yielded few results in my initial searches. I then chose to look for threads from the same long-time friend in the previous section on Flemington. My hope was that this person might reference changes in Shneiderman's character.

My initial searches yielded few results. However, inspired by the brilliant software art project We Feel Fine, which collects millions of human emotions from blogs,[24] I searched for the phrase *I feel*, which produced some very interesting results. Although the goal is to focus on the professional side of Shneiderman's archive, exploring this one contact for change phrases yielded results that can be applied, I believe, to other systems and archives more broadly. For example, in January 1994, Shneiderman's friend wrote, "I feel hopeful." In May, his friend wrote back and said, "I feel less anxious and more excited about my new status." By late August, his friend was now describing how "the stuff with the divorce has felt hard" yet also wrote that "I feel much less captive." In September, the friend wrote, "I feel very uncommitable [*sic*]."

These email exchanges between Shneiderman and his friend from 1994 are highly personal, inspiring, and fascinating. I followed the trail of exchanges and found Shneiderman's friend writing 2 years later in 1996 that she was "still with Rob, [*Authors' note:* This name has been changed] the man I have been with for two years almost. We are doing real well." Although she did not use the specific phrase *I feel*, the initial query led me to this obvious character change. Again, although my goal was to focus on the professional, these exchanges suggest that change phrases can be very effective in discovering how characters in email change emotionally over time.

Suspense

H. Porter Abbott writes, "Narrative is marked almost everywhere by its lack of closure. Commonly called suspense, this lack is one of the two things that above everything else give narrative its life."[25] Email is useful and stressful, and it is, we argue, suspenseful. It seems we are always waiting to hear back from someone about something of importance. Academics seem especially prone to being left with lots of email cliffhangers. Unlike the postal system, the answer—good or bad—can come any time of the day or night, increasing, we argue, the sense of suspense, this lack of closure. Therefore, how would one search for suspense in the email archives of an academic? The key to suspense is that the characters must have a "dramatic want," which is different from a normal want. A normal want is, "I hope our paper is accepted," while a dramatic want is, "If this paper is not accepted, my career is over—I will be ruined." Characters must care deeply about something and must have something at stake. They must want something so badly that it will either cause great harm or death or at least *feel* that way.

What would a professor of human–computer interaction care deeply about professionally? Among the many possibilities, I decided to start with grant money. I searched for *National Science Foundation*, *NSF*, and *grant* in various combinations, looking for scenes where Shneiderman was waiting to hear back about funding. These types of narrative searches can be called suspense phrases. On April 29, 1996, Shneiderman emailed a contact at NASA to ask if she would pitch in some grant money to bring Richard Beigel, at the time a Yale computer scientist, down to his lab for the year. Shneiderman included Beigel's biography, which stated that he studied things like "fault diagnosis" and "complexity theory." Having no idea what complexity theory was, as an outsider, I was intrigued to learn more and to find out if Beigel was able to get the money and spend his sabbatical at Maryland. The NASA contact wrote back to say, "Ben, this sounds very promising. I'll get back to you shortly."

Did he get the money? Did Beigel spend a year in Maryland? Did he and Shneiderman work on complexity theory with NASA? To a former

English major, it all sounded incredibly impressive and fascinating, but I was unable to find the next thread, so I had to search outside the database. Searching for the last name *Beigel* brought up enough results to suggest that he did get the grant. However, I wanted more proof, and a quick search on Google Scholar found what I needed. In a co-authored article by Egemen Tanin, Beigel, and Shneiderman,[26] a footnote reads: "beigel@cs.umd.edu, partially supported by NSF grants ... and by NASA grant NAG 52895, on sabbatical from Yale University until 8/1/97." I found what I wanted to know, and it also led me to think about another narrative query: What do academics do? They write articles and books. Just like grants, they submit and wait. Thus, I searched for *your submission*, which seems to be a standard phrase for confirming with potential authors that their work has been received. This query found many interesting messages regarding the acceptance and sometimes rejection of various projects Shneiderman worked on. This particular query seems to get at the heart of academic life. The results returned lots of scenes of acceptance ("Our paper has been accepted. It is exciting.") and rejection ("The UIST '95 Program Committee regrets to inform you ..."). Other words that might be useful for searching through a scholar's archive include *tenure, promotion, failure, success, citation,* and *keynote.*

"Suddenly, Shneiderman Pulled Out a Gun!"

As far as we know, Shneiderman has never pulled a gun on anyone. However, the point of this final section is to again illustrate the power of a simple transition word. Unlike the word *however*, which suggests a more subtle contrast and transition, the word *suddenly* indicates a dramatic transition. It is a word used constantly in literature or any kind of storytelling to indicate a dramatic change. Read any compelling book, and you will almost certainly find the word *suddenly* in abundance. For example, on the first page of *Alice's Adventures in Wonderland*, Lewis Carroll writes, "Suddenly a White Rabbit with pink eyes ran close by her."[27]

Searching for *suddenly* in Shneiderman's archives pulled up a rich variety of results, sometimes happy, at other times sad, but mostly very compelling, filled with drama: suddenly struck [by an idea]; "suddenly discovered, to my extreme embarrassment"; "he died suddenly"; "father died suddenly"; "Suddenly, lots of little problems make our daily living quite colorful"; and "Then suddenly your laughter sounds hollow as if it stemmed from your mouth and not your stomach. And the sun's rays feel hot like needles stabbing your back. You can no longer breathe, you feel choked."

Sometimes the query found miscommunications: "I replied, 'so I hear,' and suddenly I'm 'issuing a critique.'" It found epiphanies: "We are actually quite excited about the data visualization ideas. When you added color to the model, suddenly it made a whole lot more sense." It found a robbery: "In the brief time we were away from the car, we had been robbed! I was blind-sided by the realization and suddenly felt very weak." It found people quitting: "called to tell me you had quit suddenly." It found refreshing honesty: "About keynote speakers: I suddenly decided to speak my mind." There were travel stories from others: "When I still did not have the money 6 weeks later I was starting to wonder … but here suddenly Dieter stood in my office, with the money, some fruits from the island and all smiles."

The search found breakthroughs: "It suddenly hit me and was clearly the right idea … we've been stuck on how to overcome this limitation for a few years and there it was." It found a powerful story from a friend describing life before and after a 6-hour, open-heart, triple-bypass operation: "Suddenly, I had no alternative; I was out of the picture." And, of course, it found money problems: "Now suddenly, we are running a $25,000 'deficit' when we were told not to worry about the budget." In fact, *suddenly* seemed to suddenly turn up some of the longest, story-driven messages in the archive, and we believe that it is clearly a promising technique for finding even more interesting messages, especially if the archive is more personal as opposed to professional.

Lessons Learned

For designers of archival systems, we believe this research provides a variety of useful lessons learned:

- Think like a storyteller and encourage your users to do the same.

- Simple timelines do not seem to work well with a narrative approach; they do not provide enough context.

- As others have noted, context is important. Find links to important events/places/people mentioned in the archive.

- Create a list of place names to define the setting.

- Listen to the creator of the archive for narrative clues and treat them as clues that lead you to narrative elements because the creator may have a fuzzy memory of what happened and when.

- Create a list of transition words or phrases.

- Search for tension. Searching for emotional or medical words found moments of stress or emergency, moments when people felt tense. Narratives pivot on moments of conflict and tension.

- Search for unusual words (*ninja* brought up interesting results). Also look for swear words, which can help locate moments of tension and conflict.

- Look for email "characters" to change over time. Common phrases such as *I feel* produce fascinating results.

- Understand what the creator of the archive did for a living. An academic's email is surely different from the personal email of a jazz musician.

- Find suspense. Challenging though it is, finding these moments led to some of the richest and most compelling messages in the archive. Words like *suddenly* indicate these dramatic transitions.

Conclusion

This study produced some interesting results and suggests fruitful areas for further research. When I began to explore, I wondered, what will I find interesting? Will it be interesting to others? Will Shneiderman regret letting me read his email? The first two questions depend on the explorer and his purpose. At the time, my interest in narratives and personal digital archives was beginning to take shape. These factors influenced what and how I searched. What was interesting to me might not be interesting to an undergraduate library science major. As for Shneiderman and the idea of regrets, I cannot say there are any because we focused on the professional side of his archive. There were times, however, when I found personal details, and I would ask him if he was comfortable with what I found. Sometimes he was, sometimes not. Regardless of the nature of the messages, we believe narrative search can be productively applied, whether the archive is professional or personal.

Gary Marchionini wrote, "Exploratory search makes us all pioneers and adventurers in a new world of information riches awaiting discovery, along with new pitfalls and costs."[28] We believe that our strategies will help users find the narrative riches awaiting discovery in email archives. By thinking like a maker of narratives and thinking about narrative elements, system designers can create robust interfaces that help users—with or without the archive creator's help. Someday, we will find ourselves and our hard drives so packed with data that we will be at a loss to make any sense from it. Thus, if designers think about narrative elements now, we can build systems that help users find the often revealing exchanges such as those I found in Shneiderman's archive. Personal digital archives are stories waiting for a narrator, and narrative elements exist in all email archives: We just need to help users find them. Nathan, Ben, and I hope this chapter helps to lay the groundwork for narrative system designers.

Acknowledgments

Jason Zalinger and his contributors would like to thank Manuel Freire and Douglas Oard for their assistance in the development of this work.

Endnotes

1. Ben Shneiderman, personal communication, 2009.

2. Sara Radicati, *Email Market 2012–2016* (Palo Alto, CA: The Radicati Group, Inc., 2012), 5, accessed May 11, 2013, www.radicati.com/wp/wp-content/ uploads/2012/10/Email-Market-2012-2016-Executive-Summary.pdf.

3. Michael O'Grady, "SMS Usage Remains Strong in the US: 6 Billion SMS Messages Are Sent Each Day," *Forrester Blog*, June 19, 2012, accessed April 15, 2013, blogs.forrester.com/michael_ogrady/12-06-19-sms_usage_remains_strong_ in_the_us_6_billion_sms_messages_are_sent_each_day.

4. Ryen White, Bill Kules, Steven Drucker, and M. C. Schraefel, "Introduction," *Communications of the ACM* 49, no. 4 (2006): 36–39.

5. Gary Marchionini, "Exploratory Search: From Finding to Understanding," *Communications of the ACM* 49, no. 4 (2006): 41–46.

6. Anton Leuski, "Email Is a Stage: Discovering Peoples' Roles from Email Archives," in *Proceedings of the 27th Annual International ACM SIGIR Conference on Research and Development in Information Retrieval*, Sheffield, U.K., ACM Press, New York, 2004, 502–503.

7. Victor R. Carvalho and William Cohen, "On the Collective Classification of Email 'Speech Acts' in *Proceedings of the 28th Annual International ACM SIGIR Conference on Research and Development in Information Retrieval*, Salvador, Brazil, ACM Press, New York, 2005, 345–352.

8. Jon Kleinberg, "Bursty and Hierarchical Structure in Streams, " in *Proceedings of the Eighth ACM SIGKDD International Conference on Knowledge Discovery and Data Mining*, Edmonton, Canada, ACM Press, New York, 2002, 91–101.

9. Jure Leskovec, Lars Backstrom, and Kleinberg, Jon, "Meme-tracking and the Dynamics of the News Cycle," in *Proceedings of the 15th ACM SIGKDD International Conference on Knowledge Discovery and Data Mining*, Paris, France, 2009, ACM Press, New York. 497–506.

10. Adam Perer, Ben Shneiderman, and Douglas W. Oard, "Using Rhythms of Relationships to Understand E-mail Archives," *Journal of the American Society for Information Science and Technology* 57, no. 14 (2006): 1936–1948.

11. Fernanda Viégas, Scott B. Golder, and Judith Donath, "Visualizing Email Content: Portraying Relationships from Conversational Histories," in *Proceedings*

of SIGCHI Conference on Human Factors in Computing Systems, Montreal, Canada, ACM Press, New York, 2006, 979–988.

12. Fernanda Viégas, danah boyd, David H. Nguyen, Jeffrey Potter, and Judith Donath, "Digital Artifacts for Remembering and Storytelling: PostHistory and Social Network Fragments," in *Proceedings of the 37th Annual Hawaii International Conference on System Sciences*, Waikoloa, HI, IEEE Press, 2004.

13. Annie Tat and Sheelagh Carpendale, "CrystalChat: Visualizing Personal Chat History," in *Proceedings of the 39th Annual Hawaii International Conference on System Sciences*, Kauai, HI, IEEE Press, 2006.

14. "MyLifeBits," Microsoft Research, accessed April 15, 2013, research.microsoft.com/en-us/projects/mylifebits/default.aspx.

15. Gordon Bell and Jim Gemmell, "A Digital Life," *Scientific American*, May 4, 2011, accessed April 15, 2013, www.sciam.com/article.cfm?id=a-digital-life.

16. Daragh Byrne and Gareth Jones, "Towards Computational Autobiographical Narratives Through Human Digital Memories," in *Proceedings of the Second ACM International Workshop on Story Representation, Mechanism and Context*, Vancouver, BC, 2008, ACM Press, New York, 9–12.

17. Daniel Gonçalves and Joaquim A. Jorge, "In Search of Personal Information: Narrative-based Interfaces," in *Proceedings of the 13th International Conference on Intelligent User Interfaces*, Gran Canaria, Spain, 2008, ACM Press, 179–188.

18. David Elsweiler, Mark Baillie, and Ian Ruthven, "Exploring Memory in Email Refinding," *ACM Transactions on Information Systems* 26, no. 4 (2008): 1–36.

19. Richard Kearney, *On Stories* (New York: Routledge, 2001).

20. Ibid, 4.

21. Ben Shneiderman, *Leonardo's Laptop: Human Needs and the New Computing Technologies* (Cambridge, MA: MIT Press, 2002).

22. URL available upon request to ben@cs.umd.edu.

23. "About Tom Carhart," *Tom Carhart* (blog), accessed April 15, 2013, tomcarhart.net.

24. "Mission," *We Feel Fine*, accessed April 15, 2013, wefeelfine.org/mission.html.

25. H. Porter Abbott, *The Cambridge Introduction to Narrative*, 2nd ed. (New York: Cambridge University Press, 2008).

26. Egemen Tanin, Richard Beigel, and Ben Shneiderman, "Design and Evaluation of Incremental Data Structures and Algorithms for Dynamic Query Interfaces," in *Proceedings of the IEEE Symposium on Information Visualization*, Phoenix, AZ, IEEE Computer Society, New York, 1997, 81–86.

27. Lewis Carroll, *Alice's Adventures in Wonderland*, 1865. Retrieved from Project Gutenberg, www.gutenberg.org/files/11/11-h/11-h.htm.

28. Marchionini, "Exploratory Search."

CHAPTER **8**

Faculty Members as Archivists: Personal Archiving Practices in the Academic Environment

Ellysa Stern Cahoy
The Pennsylvania State University Libraries

In an era of increasingly cloud-based distributed computing and storage, the creation, management, and archiving of scholars' personal libraries merits increased attention in the college and university environment. Faculty find, organize, share, save, and make searchable a wide range of print and online intellectual assets, including scholarly output, collections of research materials, and more informally created web-based social content. Personal scholarly archiving has become a dynamic process rather than a rote exercise at the end of a faculty member's career.

Microsoft researcher Catherine C. Marshall with colleagues Sara Bly and Francoise Brun-Cottan identified user challenges relevant to personal archiving: accumulation (a weighty issue in the current online/offline environment), distribution (storage of items both online and offline, on a variety of media, and on different devices and computers), curation (managing and organizing files effectively and consistently

137

migrating important files to "maintainable formats"), and long-term access.[1] These challenges provide a structure for emerging personal archiving literacies for faculty and outline an imperative for instructional work for archivists and public services librarians working with faculty members.

This chapter outlines the personal archiving issues currently confronting scholars and will identify critical personal archiving literacies and instructional principles for helping scholars effectively manage, maximize, curate, and archive their scholarly materials throughout their academic career. Examples of current initiatives supporting and exploring personal archiving in the scholarly environment will be shared, as well as recommended practices for integrating personal archiving support within higher education.

Literature Review

Several existing studies have looked closely at personal archiving by faculty. The most significant of these studies are "Understanding Faculty to Improve Content Recruitment for Institutional Repositories," by Nancy Fried Foster and Susan Gibbons, and the Andrew W. Mellon Foundation-funded "A Multi-Dimensional Framework for Academic Support."[2] These valuable projects provide an excellent foundation for research on faculty needs regarding personal archiving and the use of institutional repositories (IRs). While of great value, the most recent of these studies is now nearly 5 years old, and the landscape for information creation and storage has changed drastically with the widespread usage of cloud-based tools including Google Docs, Dropbox, Zotero, and Mendeley. Social media as well, including Facebook, Twitter, LinkedIn, and other personal data-driven platforms, have also become repositories for scholarly content, and scholars' social data should be considered in parallel with their more formal scholarly output.

Foster and Gibbons' article details an ethnographic, work-practice study of how faculty members at the University of Rochester conduct their research and writing.[3] Participants in Foster and Gibbons' study reinforced Dorothea Salo's assertion that faculty's primary needs with regard to IRs are sharing capabilities while versioning and building capacity for storing in-process (and eventually final) versions of materials.[4] That study also identifies educational needs for faculty, including devising user-centered strategies for digital preservation and helping faculty build a basic understanding of the functions and benefits of utilizing IRs. A later work by Foster and David Lindahl also uses a work-practice study methodology to identify necessary features for an IR, utilizing participatory design and mapping of user needs.[5] The authors reinforce the importance of ethnographic research in human computer interaction and interface design to uncover unanticipated solutions and limitations of current tools.

Institutional Repository Infrastructure and Educational Services

The literature on faculty use of IR services confirms that the existing model of an IR as a one-way, static archive must change, broaden, and become more flexible in order to attract a sustained depth of faculty users. In "Innkeeper at the Roach Motel," Salo, discussing faculty needs, asserts that "Repository software serves observed and stated faculty needs surrounding content creation and dissemination *hardly at all*"(author's emphasis).[6] She continues, "'Roach motel' repositories, in which materials fixed in their final form are the only acceptable content, hold no value for many faculty." Salo emphasizes the need for IRs that assist faculty with document versioning and sharing materials (and data) in process with other faculty collaborators at the institution or elsewhere. Emphasis on actively collecting draft content (rather than passively storing finished content) is essential.

Marshall's article, "From Writing and Analysis to the Repository: Taking the Scholars' Perspective on Scholarly Archiving" brings forward recommendations that back up Salo's assertion that an IR must support collaborative, in-process authoring.[7] Marshall takes this idea further, pushing for filtered IR synchronization with scholars' local (desktop) collections. She notes that a good IR infrastructure "must beat email along all of these dimensions if it is to be adopted in email's stead." Marshall's article was written nearly 4 years ago; we could now also substitute "Dropbox" (a synchronized cloud/desktop file storage service) for "email" in her assertion.

In "Structure, Features, and Faculty Content in ARL Member Repositories," Holly Mercer and colleagues survey the structure and features of 72 IRs hosted by ARL libraries.[8] The authors conclude, "Institutional repositories can, and should, continue the dual goals of preservation and access, but emphasis should be placed on the benefits of increased access to scholarship, and the repository as a destination for research information."[9] Two software packages are highlighted as possible facilitators for faculty collaboration and individual information management within an IR: VIVO (www.vivoweb.org) and BibApp (www.bibapp.org). These services exist outside of the repository and seek to draw together faculty research and publications for wider impact and availability.

Matthew Kirschenbaum's report on "Approaches to Managing and Collecting Born-Digital Literary Materials for Scholarly Use" provides an exciting view into the grand future scope of scholarly archiving, where not only are texts collected, but physical computers are archived and online interfaces are preserved.[10] At the Maryland Institute for Technology in the Humanities (MITH), the Deena Larsen Collection (mith.umd.edu/larsen) pushes the boundaries of traditional scholarly archives, with more than a dozen Macintosh Classic computers and an expansive collection of creative electronic writing. Similarly, Emory Libraries makes available Salman Rushdie's computer desktop and files in preserved form for online browsing and exploration (findingaids.library.emory.edu/documents/rushdie1000). These creative projects cast a path for future archiving of electronic, computer-created works. Viewed together with Salo's and Marshall's research, the resonating concept of an IR as a dynamic, user-centered, collaborative tool preserving a wide scope of digitally created objects is obvious and apparent.

Critical Digital Literacies for Faculty

As mentioned earlier, Marshall, Bly, and Brun-Cottan identify critical user challenges relevant to personal archiving: accumulation, distribution, curation, and long-term access.[11] These challenges provide the backbone for exploration of emerging digital literacies in this area and may become the instructional lifework for future academic librarians. Marshall et al. also highlight environmental factors that must be considered in tandem with personal archiving needs: malware, availability of IT support, and attitudes of users. Attitude, the affective behaviors of users, is an important factor to consider in helping faculty learn effective personal library management skills. Prior research has noted the significance of affect on learning.[12]

"The Academic Library in a 2.0 World" stresses that the future role of the library does not reside in collection development and stewardship, but instead in supporting and enriching teaching, learning, and research. The report states:

> The institution as a whole will need to embrace new critical literacies and core skills required for the teacher, learner, and researcher of the digital age. Among other things, these will encompass multimedia creation skills, conventions of behavior in new communication media, computer-aided searching and data analysis skills, new ways to develop scholarly communication, and new ways of assessing student learning. Most significantly, intensive new curricular support programs will be needed to train not only students but also faculty and staff in these skills, and the library should be a leader in this area.[13]

The report's focus on a user-empowered environment where the librarian's primary role is as teacher and facilitator confirms the importance of the dual focus of our proposed study. Salo asserts that librarians "must prepare themselves to help faculty with data management throughout the research cycle."[14]

Building a user-centered repository that will be actively utilized by faculty requires a close connection to faculty needs and established scholarly behaviors. In "Content In, Content Out: The Dual Roles of the Reference Librarian in Institutional Repositories," Barbara Jenkins, Elizabeth Breakstone, and Carol Hixson explore the importance of the subject specialist in connecting faculty with an IR, describing how reference librarians can help faculty understand not only what is in the IR, but how to easily access, search, and add to the IR.[15] Library instruction, perhaps often on a more individual level tailored to faculty's needs, is an essential element of rolling out an IR university-wide. Suzanne Bell, Foster, and Gibbons also reinforce the centrality of the reference librarian in recruiting and assisting in the process of bringing new scholarly content into the IR.[16]

Model Academic Programs/Archiving Initiatives

Higher education and academic libraries in general are in a nascent phase of recognizing personal archiving as an imperative for proactively retaining a diversity of faculty work. A variety of universities have begun exploratory projects that explore the scope of scholars' collections, as well as strategies for saving, annotating, and preserving a wide swath of faculty works.

SALT (Self Archiving Legacy Toolkit; sites.google.com/site/stanford luminaryarchives) was an effort by Stanford University in 2007 to create a web-based service for faculty self-archiving.[17] Described as offering "Stanford luminaries including prominent faculty, alumni, and associates a web-based personal archive for depositing, organizing, and annotating their life-work collections," SALT's primary purpose was to add narrative to collections. Faculty were offered the option of labeling and annotating folders and digital documents, offering users the ability to "create a narrative or thematic structure for their own work." SALT worked collaboratively with Zotero, enabling faculty to pull directly from their own personal libraries into the archival management interface. While SALT is not currently active for a public audience, selected principles upon which it was designed are embedded in other current Stanford digital library initiatives.

A variety of higher education institutions are innovatively developing the process of collecting both print and born-digital materials from prominent faculty members. As the lifespan of technology gets shorter and shorter with each year (and with each new technology), faculty education on the migration and maintenance of core files is truly significant. In just one prominent example, the author John Updike sent 50 5½" floppy disks to Harvard's Houghton Library just prior to his death.[18] While the library has yet to place these files online, they are being kept in climate-controlled storage as the library awaits a static process for intake and digitization of born-digital materials. This challenging situation is not unique. Faculty education on file preservation and management along with development and continued revisiting of processes for managing born-digital materials are critical to the longevity of scholarly information collections.

The best-known example of online archiving of born-digital materials may be the previously mentioned Salman Rushdie Papers, a project undertaken at Emory University. For this collection, Emory archivists took the visionary step of allowing visitors to browse Rushdie's files on his original computers, with the computer desktop, software, and file organization preserved. The computers and hardware available to visitors include one Macintosh Performa 5400/180, one Macintosh PowerBook 5300c, two Macintosh PowerBook G3 models, and one external hard drive,[19] which provides a layered browsing experience that gives the user a depth of understanding of the technology in use by Rushdie as he created his works. Erika Farr, director of Born-Digital Archives at Emory, noted in an interview on the Rushdie Archive with the *New York Times*: "If you're interested in primary materials, you're interested in the context as well as the content, the authentic artifact. … Fifty years from now, people may be researching how the impact of word processing affected literary output, which would require seeing the original computer images."[20]

In addition to the Rushdie archive, Emory hosts several other born-digital archives, including the collections of Lucille Clifton, Eamon Grennan, and Turner Cassity (marbl.library.emory.edu/collection-overview/digital-archives). The university's Manuscripts, Archives, and Rare Book Library (MARBL) also has a sample "Pre-Acquisition Digital Assets Survey" for donors of born-digital collections (marbl.library.emory.edu/sites/marbl.library.emory.edu/files/preacq_digiassets_ind_donor_survey.pdf). This tool is an excellent example of how archivists can walk donors through born-digital collections and help them understand the scope and distribution of their collections. Emory archivist Laura Carroll and her colleagues discuss the intricacies and challenges of dealing with a print and born-digital collection (such as the Rushdie archive) in their article, "A Comprehensive Approach to Born-Digital Archives," and provide additional information on how MARBL has developed its born-digital archival services and collections.[21]

The Stanford University Libraries have invested significant energy into acquiring and processing digital archival material and handheld media material. The Born-Digital Program is focused on these efforts and includes a Digital Forensics Lab (lib.stanford.edu/digital-forensics/home) designed to rescue and retrieve information stored on outdated technology. The Digital Forensics Lab is currently undertaking a number of born-digital projects, including the Xanadu Project collection, founded in 1960 by the father of hypertext, Ted Nelson, and the Stephen Jay Gould collection, which includes data from floppy disks and computer tapes central to the paleontologist's seminal research. The Digital Forensics Lab is a model for peer libraries facing an increasing influx of born-digital materials in the years to come. Such a facility allows for easier retrieval and preservation of data on outdated file formats, while also providing a valuable physical presence that helps promote the importance of born-digital file migration and conservancy.

Colleges and universities are also very active in bringing increased access to prominent faculty members' print-based personal archives.

MIT has created the Edgerton Digital Collections projects (edgerton-digital-collections.org), centered on the life and work of inventor and professor emeritus Harold 'Doc' Edgerton. While the collection is focused on digitization of primarily print material from Edgerton's academic career, there is a social and interactive element to the online collection. Collection users are invited to contribute stories or remembrances of Edgerton, and the collection is also crowdsourcing the transcription and identification of items in the collection in collaboration with the userbase. This is a unique way to bring a dynamic and engaging online dimension to a primarily print-based online collection.

Educational Initiatives

Colleges and universities are teaching users how to archive and preserve important information. The University of Illinois at Urbana-Champaign (UIUC) Libraries hold workshops on personal information management, as part of the Savvy Researcher series (www.library.illinois.edu/sc/services/savvy_researcher.html) offered by the libraries' Scholarly Commons. The workshops cover the basics of information management and encourage attendees to begin thinking critically about the span, composition, and lifespan of their personal information collections. UIUC's Scholarly Commons also offers data service walk-in hours where users can consult with an expert on how to manage their individual collections with an eye toward future data longevity.

In 2012, Columbia University held its inaugural Born Digital: Personal Digital Archiving Week.[22] This series of educational events was organized by the libraries and covered several topics on archiving, including emerging technologies and support in the Columbia University Libraries for personal and research archiving. Similarly, in 2012, the University of California San Diego's Personal Digital Archiving Day held an intensive 1-day workshop on preservation related topics, including archiving photos and creating metadata, saving email messages, and preserving web-based content.[23]

While the topic of personal archiving is always worthy of a special event, there are also ways to weave preservation concepts into more traditional instruction on finding and using information. Most academic libraries provide support for, and workshops on, the use of citation management tools, including (but not limited to) Zotero, Mendeley, and EndNote.[24] These software packages help users manage their own personal libraries. Every time a student or faculty member learns how to use citation management software, there is an opportunity to embed instruction on personal information management and preservation. With Zotero, Mendeley, and EndNote, libraries save and organize only one type of information—scholarly resources—but they present a structure to help users think more broadly about their information collections, how (and where) they are accessed, as well as where they are saved (and archived). As citation management tools become even more robust and comprehensive, there will likely be opportunities for enhanced and expanded personal information management. This is the lifework of librarians now and in the relative future—helping users understand, manage, and maximize the entire scope of their individual information collections.

Future Development of Services and Resources

A next step will be for colleges and universities to begin connecting their institutional repositories to the scholarly workflow. A body of research exists documenting the low use of IRs, and reasons why faculty are (or more frequently, are not) archiving materials there.[25] While it is important to teach faculty and other academic users how to look expansively at their information collections and cull and curate the important pieces for future access, it is also imperative that academic institutions connect their archival tools in a manner that is seamless and effortless for even the novice user. Several services in development provide promise in this area for higher education, including VIVO and BibApp. Both of these tools work in conjunction with IRs to highlight faculty research. Mercer and colleagues observed, "If repositories are marketed less for their preservation capabilities and more as platforms for experimentation in scholarly communication, additional new tools and new structures may emerge."[26] Similarly, the COAR (Confederation of Open Access Repositories) report, "The Current State of Open Access Repository Interoperability," asserts that easy information exchange with other research management systems is essential. The report asks, "How can we support repository integration with information systems that support research and scholarly communication, from journal publishing platforms to Current Research Information Systems (CRIS)?"[27]

This is, arguably, the direction of the future for IRs and the faculty workflow. Bringing personal archiving onto the scholar's desktop, making IRs malleable and collaborative, and continuing educational initiatives that help faculty learn how to store, organize, cite, share, and archive their works throughout their academic careers is essential to this process.

At The Pennsylvania State University, a Mellon-funded project is exploring the information workflow of disciplinary faculty and faculty needs regarding the acquisition of the digital literacies essential to effective research management, robust scholarly creation, and continued navigation of the archiving process. Led by Penn State Libraries faculty, the author of this chapter, and Scott McDonald, a Penn State college of education professor, the project seeks to define the following:

- A set of design principles for archivists and librarians on how archival interfaces can be created that support not just archiving and archival access but sustained easy integration of archival practices into the online scholarly workflow

- Identification of critical digital literacies for faculty management of online scholarly workflow, and a set of recommendations for librarians on best practices for supporting faculty in developing critical digital literacies[28]

This project focuses on information management needs at earlier stages of the research lifecycle, with the goal of developing architecture that supports the entire online scholarly workflow, and facilitates the development of critical literacies for faculty's personal information management needs. Figure 8.1 shows the researcher's phases of information management, creation, sharing, and archiving. With this figure as a guiding model, the study aims to unify the all stages of the research life cycle. This study will inform the work of user-focused librarians, both at Penn State and beyond, as they help faculty learn how to maximize and mine their personal collections.

Librarians are increasingly relied upon to help faculty members develop strategies that address their personal information management

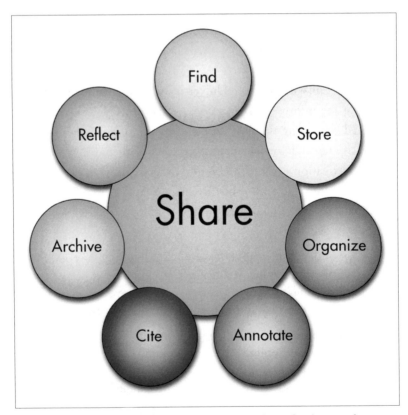

Figure 8.1   Information management, creation, sharing, and archiving model

needs. Indeed, subject librarians, with their close connections to discipline-based faculty, colleges, and departments, are on the front line of scholarly communications and are integral players in building faculty's understanding and acceptance of the online archiving process.[29]

Documenting existing practices and needs, this proposed project will highlight gaps in existing library services and technology infrastructures. While the initial project aims to gain a general understanding of needs central to personal scholarly archiving, the proposed next phase will begin to look at how research management software (such as Mendeley or Zotero) can better integrate into the faculty member's workflow. Specifically, the primary investigators hope to design a manner for institutional repositories to connect seamlessly with research management software, allowing faculty to deposit into and draw from IRs in a manner that is complementary, and not disruptive to the flow of a scholar's online work.

Conclusion

As information moves increasingly online and into the cloud, the time is ripe for academic libraries (and colleges and universities in general) to begin formalizing self-archiving strategies for faculty and students. While technology-based solutions (such as institutional repositories) are significant in the academic environment, attention must also be paid to developing educational initiatives for users. The scholar's workbench is crowded with many disparate tools, devices, and information collections. In order for intentional, sustained self-archiving to occur, users must learn how to draw together, assess, manage, and archive the most important scholarly materials in their dispersed collections. Helping faculty and students understand the impermanence of online information and the importance of duplicate data archives is a significant challenge. Even more challenging is the goal of creating a centrally located, institutionally relevant place where scholars can store, share, and self-archive.

In "The Next Generation of Academics: A Report on a Study Conducted at the University of Rochester," Ryan Randall and colleagues describe the need for an institutional repository platform that allows users to write, collaborate, self-archive, and self-publish.[30] We are on the verge of developing such a tool that draws together the various phases of the scholarly workflow. With more study of our users' needs, increased attention to faculty education on importance of self-archiving, and a willingness to experiment with software, we will hopefully soon achieve a more unified pathway for robust and sustained self-preservation of scholarly works.

Endnotes

1. Catherine C. Marshall, Sara Bly, and Françoise Brun-Cottan, "The Long Term Fate of Our Digital Belongings: Toward a Service Model for Personal Archives," *Arxiv Preprint arXiv:0704.3653* (2007), arxiv.org/abs/0704.3653.

2. Nancy Fried Foster and Susan Gibbons, "Understanding Faculty to Improve Content Recruitment for Institutional Repositories," *D-Lib Magazine* 11, no. April 2004 (January 2005): 283–290, doi:10.1045/january2005-foster; University of Minnesota Libraries, "A Multi-Dimensional Framework for Academic Support: A Final Report," *Social Sciences* (2006).

3. Foster and Gibbons, "Understanding Faculty to Improve Content Recruitment for Institutional Repositories."

4. Dorothea Salo, "Innkeeper at the Roach Motel," *Library Trends* 57, no. 2 (2009): 98–123.

5. Nancy Fried Foster and David Lindahl, "Enhancing E-Resources by Studying Users: The University of Rochester's Analysis of Faculty Perspectives on an Institutional Repository" (2008): 1–14.

6. Salo, "Innkeeper at the Roach Motel," 11.

7. Catherine C. Marshall, "From Writing and Analysis to the Repository: Taking the Scholars' Perspective on Scholarly Archiving," *Human Factors* (2008): 251–260.

8. Holly Mercer, Jay Koenig, Robert B. McGeachin, and Sandra L. Tucker, "Structure, Features, and Faculty Content in ARL Member Repositories," *Journal of Academic Librarianship* 37, no. 4 (July 2011): 333–342, doi:10.1016/j.acalib.2011.04.008.

9. Mercer et al., "Structure, Features, and Faculty Content in ARL Member Repositories," 342.

10. Matthew Kirschenbaum et al., *Approaches to Managing and Collecting Born-Digital Literary Materials for Scholarly Use*, 2009, drum.lib.umd.edu/handle/1903/9787.

11. Marshall, Bly, and Brun-Cottan, "The Long Term Fate of Our Digital Belongings: Toward a Service Model for Personal Archives."

12. Diane Nahl and Dania Bilal, *Information and Emotion: The Emergent Affective Paradigm in Information Behavior Research and Theory* (Medford, NJ: Information Today, Inc., 2007).

13. Susan V. Wawrzaszek and David G. Wedaman, "The Academic Library in a 2.0 World," *ECAR Research Bulletin* 2008, no. 19 (2008).

14. Salo, "Innkeeper at the Roach Motel."

15. Barbara Jenkins, Elizabeth Breakstone, and Carol G. Hixson, "Content in, Content Out: The Dual Roles of the Reference Librarian in Institutional Repositories," *Reference Services Review* 33, no. 3 (2005): 312–324.

16. Suzanne Bell, Nancy Fried Foster, and Susan Gibbons, "Reference Librarians and the Success of Institutional Repositories," *Reference Services Review* 33, no. 3 (2005): 283–290.

17. Stanford Luminary Archives, *Self Archiving Legacy Toolkit* (Stanford University, 2007), sites.google.com/site/stanfordluminaryarchives/StanfordSALTWhitePaper 081027.1.pdf.

18. Patricia Cohen, "Fending Off Digital Decay, Bit by Bit," *New York Times*, March 16, 2010, www.nytimes.com/2010/03/16/books/16archive.html.

19. Emory University Libraries, "Series 11: Computers and Related Devices," *EmoryFindingAids: Salman Rushdie Papers, 1947–2008*, accessed April 17, 2013, findingaids.library.emory.edu/documents/rushdie1000/series11.

20. Cohen, "Fending Off Digital Decay, Bit by Bit."

21. Laura Carroll, Erika Farr, Peter Hornsby, and Ben Ranker. "A Comprehensive Approach to Born-Digital Archives," *Archivaria* 72, no. Fall 2011 (2011): 61–92.

22. Columbia University Libraries, "Born Digital: Personal Digital Archiving Week at Columbia," April 19, 2012, accessed April 17, 2013, library.columbia.edu/content/ libraryweb/news/libraries/2012/20120419_personal_archiving_week.html.

23. University of California, San Diego, "Personal Digital Archiving Day Event to Provide Tips on Preserving Your 'Stuff'," April 16, 2012, accessed April 17, 2013, ucsdnews.ucsd.edu/pressreleases/personal_digital_archiving_day_event_to_ provide_tips_on_reserving_your_stuf.

24. Dawn Childress, "Citation Tools in Academic Libraries," *Reference & User Services Quarterly* 51, no. 2 (2011): 143–152.

25. Jihyun Kim, "Motivating and Impeding Factors Affecting Faculty Contribution to Institutional Repositories," *Response* 8, no. 2 (2006), journals.tdl.org/jodi/article/ viewarticle/193/177; Foster and Gibbons, "Understanding Faculty to Improve

Content Recruitment for Institutional Repositories"; Amanda J. Grundmann, "Increasing Self-Archiving of Faculty Publications in Institutional Repositories," *Open and Libraries Class Journal* 1, no. 2 (2009); David Seaman, "Discovering the Information Needs of Humanists When Planning an Institutional Repository," *D-Lib Magazine* (2011): 1–15, doi:10.1045/march2011; Jingfeng Xia and Li Sun, "Assessment of Self-Archiving in Institutional Repositories: Depositorship and Full-Text Availability1," *Serials Review* 33, no. 1 (March 2007): 14–21, doi:10.1016/j.serrev.2006.12.003.

26. Mercer et al., "Structure, Features, and Faculty Content in ARL Member Repositories," 342.

27. Confederation of Open Access Repositories, *The Current State of Open Access Repository Interoperability*, 2012, accessed April 17, 2013, www.coar-repositories. org/files/COAR-Current-State-of-Open-Access-Repository-Interoperability-26-10-2012.pdf.

28. Ellysa Stern Cahoy and Scott McDonald, "A Proposal to the Andrew W. Mellon Foundation from The Pennsylvania State University Libraries and The Pennsylvania State University College of Education," January 2012.

29. Bell, Foster, and Gibbons, "Reference Librarians and the Success of Institutional Repositories."

30. Ryan Randall, Katie Clark, Jane Smith, and Nancy Fried Foster, *The Next Generation of Academics: A Report on a Study Conducted at the University of Rochester* (Rochester, NY: University of Rochester, 2008).

Landscape of Personal Digital Archiving Activities and Research

Sarah Kim
University of Texas at Austin

Recordkeeping is not the type of activity that excites most people. However, since the time when records first started to be generated, recordkeeping has become one of the tasks many people do routinely. It is important to note that recordkeeping is more than just putting documents in folders and hoping they will be safe and accessible in the future. In fact, it is a human information behavior that involves complex psychological and social processes.

When people perform recordkeeping in their everyday lives, they often engage in a series of decisions, perhaps without explicit awareness, for example: which documents need be destroyed; which documents need to be kept, why, and for what purposes; for whom the documents are being kept; and where the documents will be stored, in which order or categories, and for how long. Over time, most people will likely revise their previous choices made in the recordkeeping process, corresponding with changes in their lives. Records management norms or rules at work, for instance, may influence people's recordkeeping methods in their private lives. Also, personal preferences play a role in document management at home and work.[1] Thus, recordkeeping actually serves as a practice that is both personalized and socially contextualized.

Recordkeeping has come to mean digital recordkeeping as digital document formats rapidly replace analog ones such as paper. This change, however, is far more than a mere shift in information medium. In digital form, documents become highly flexible in terms of their modifiability and transferability. Using digital tools, documents can be created, altered, remixed, and duplicated much more actively, and the internet makes it easier and faster to retrieve, access, and exchange them. New types of "documents" are emerging in parallel with the evolution of digital technology (e.g., websites, blogs, content on social networking sites, emails, text messages, and tweets). Most documents created and disseminated by individuals using the web are assumed to be accessible to others to some degree. The volume, variety of types/genres, and public visibility of digital documents are only a few of the factors that complicate decision-making processes in recordkeeping. Therefore, it is hardly surprising that scholarly and social interest in personal information management has increased greatly along with the pervasive use of digital tools to create documents.

In recent years, people have begun to pay particular attention to the long-term preservation of personal digital documents, a movement that can be loosely categorized as personal digital archiving. People interested in this topic not only include researchers and practitioners in professional areas (e.g., human–computer interaction [HCI], information science [IS], archives and libraries, digital preservation, media studies, and information technology [IT]) but also individuals who are genuinely concerned about the long-term fate of their digital materials and those who are building their own personal or family digital archives.

Although an understanding of what archiving means varies depending on who is using the term and in what context, people interested in digital archiving would generally share the sense that personal digital documents are more than mere containers of information to be simply created, used, and discarded. Rather, personal digital documents function as evidence of how people live their lives in various kinds of social and private environments (e.g., at home, at work, or on the web). Digital records also serve as evocative objects that help people to recall their memories about past experiences and envision the lives of their ancestors, as well as assisting them to produce their life narratives. They may become objects to which people develop a certain emotional attachment. As a researcher who has investigated this phenomenon for several years, I regard personal digital archiving as part of everyday recordkeeping with the goal of long-term preservation of documents, possibly beyond an owner's lifetime and a lifelong practice of forming a personal documentary heritage collection with objects that are meaningful to the owner, either as evidential resources or as memory objects.

Personal digital archiving is an exciting as well as challenging area to explore, especially from a research point of view. It is relevant to the many individuals who create and collect digital documents, and it is not just about issues of effective management of records. It requires a profound understanding of what the digital documents represent in the context of people's lives.

Personal digital archiving is a relatively young, emerging field, which is already developing around numerous focal points, from utilitarian solutions to conceptual discussions, and from what is personal to what is collective. As a practice dispersed throughout the realm of everyday life, personal digital archiving can be investigated from many different perspectives (e.g., people at different stages of life, types of professions, specific genres of digital materials, legal issues, and cultural differences). In this chapter, I will portray the overall landscape of personal digital archiving activities and research. Rather than seeking to provide a comprehensive overview, my goal is to identify several previous and ongoing research activities related to this topic and to lay out connections between those landmarks based on my own understanding of the phenomenon.

Features of the Landscape: Interest Stimuli

In a person's daily life, the reason for keeping documents is not always clear. Certain documents may be retained due to simple neglect or because an owner forgot they existed. IT researcher Catherine Marshall argues that "the human tendency toward benign neglect" might help the continuing retention of documents.[2] At the same time, there might be "an impulse leading most people to hold onto older records."[3] Whether it is because of benign neglect or human impulse, it is interesting to consider why people tend to keep particular personal documents for a long time. A simple answer is that some documents have an enduring relevance to our life in some way. The enduring value of a document may not be what the document inherently contains but something assigned by its owner at a given moment. People may discover new or different values of documents (e.g., historical or nostalgic value) that have survived when they (accidentally) encounter them many years later.

Value of Personal Documents

Then, we further wonder about what types of values contribute to the enduring value of personal documents. Previous studies that explore functions of personal documents in the context of people's lives offer a broad spectrum of the meanings of personally preserved documents.[4] Although each study was conducted in a different environment, in a workplace or in a private home, for example, it is of particular interest that the following similar themes emerged from the findings of these studies:

1. *Emotional/sentimental value*: Significance of documents based on their emotional bond with a person; for evoking and preserving emotions and memories (e.g., pride, happiness, feeling of accomplishment, and indescribable feeling) relating to the process of creation or acquisition of documents

2. *Historical value*: Usefulness of documents for understanding the past or family history

3. *Identity (formation and expression) value*: Significance of documents in constructing, maintaining, and expressing identity and personality

4. *Personal legacy value*: Significance of documents in exploring professional or career trajectory and/or life achievement and building a personal legacy

5. *Sharing value*: Usefulness of documents for sharing personal life stories, memories, and family histories with others, including future generations

These five values are good starting points for exploring the continuing value of personal documents. It is clear that personally preserved documents play a vital role in assisting people to reflect on their past experiences and to understand who they are and where they come from. These five types of values form the concept of *self-reflective value*, which is the significance or usefulness of documents in constructing self.

The enduring value of personal documents, however, goes far beyond the boundaries of their individual owners' private lives. The public significance of records lies in nurturing our understanding and (re)discovery of the political, economic, and cultural life of a society. Personal documents that have survived as a result of efforts by individuals serve as primary resources for researchers to study our collective past and to conduct historical inquiries. The social and cultural utility of records is the basis of the missions of memory institutions, which collect, preserve, and provide access to personal papers and manuscripts. As Australian archivist Sue McKemmish has asserted, individual archives are transformed from "'evidence of me' into 'evidence of us,' components of our collective memory" when they are gathered into public archives.[5]

In the digital realm, the potential value of personal digital documents for individuals as well as for society is vigorously expanding. Digital technology is contributing to an unprecedented active participation in producing and sharing documents.[6] With the assistance of digital technology, individuals now live in a highly networked environment where they can act as information *prosumers*—producers and consumers at the same time. People are capable of building their own communities without regard to geographical limitations and can educate themselves even as boundaries between professionals and amateurs blur. They can mix what they consider to be their private and public lives, and they have more choices to explore and interact with different groups of people, different cultures, and even different societies, and they can choose to form multiple identities in the digital arena. There are not only more opportunities to record life events but more opportunities to express and actively share one's ideas and life stories with others.[7] People's "creative instincts" seem to be unleashed as they use online digital tools and services.[8] Personal digital documents are by-products of the lively expression of individuals' thoughts, feelings, and opinions about the world around them.

Some would argue that digital content, especially that created and disseminated on the web, is of low quality. Beyond the problem of what "low quality" means, that viewpoint has become outdated. We have not yet seen the scale of what people can do with digital documentation technology or the extent of how the accumulated digital documents can be utilized in the future.[9] The cultural value of the digital documents of ordinary individuals is becoming more apparent, especially with the growing appreciation of "history from the bottom up," or microhistory. An increasing number of scholars and practitioners in cultural heritage institutions consider personal digital documents of ordinary individuals as important bits and bytes that will allow more diverse voices, especially socially marginalized or suppressed voices, to be reflected in the constitution of our collective memory and history.[10]

Preservation Challenges of Personal Digital Documents

The value of personal digital documents, however, is not the only element that ignites interest in personal digital archiving. Managing documents in digital form is different from managing documents in analog form in many ways. For example, it is easy to create backup copies of an entire personal digital collection and store them in multiple locations.

Digital tools can enable users to sort documents in a variety of ways (e.g., by name, type, date, and contents), which can be useful in organizing and retrieving them. Beyond these technical differences, there are more profound changes associated with digital documents: increasing quantity, a greater need for maintenance, and decreasing control over personal digital documents. From a long-term perspective, personal digital archiving practice is likely to be challenged by many new factors.

Quantity: Who Has Time to Manage?

Even without trying to understand that a zettabyte is equal to 1,000 terabytes,[11] we can get a general sense of the number of digital documents that people create and accumulate daily by simply looking at our own experiences in producing digital materials. No matter what kind of enduring value they may or may not have, those digital documents are objects that eventually must be managed. Many people consider the management of digital materials burdensome. They desire "an intelligent automated helper that would magically solve the challenges they face with the management of a personal information collection."[12] Marshall argues that the lack of time and patience to manage large amounts of digital materials as well as difficulties in making value judgments about documents promotes an attitude of benign neglect.[13]

Furthermore, readily available digital storage technology and ever-decreasing costs make it feasible to keep, literally, everything.[14] Observing the technological capability of keeping information as well as recording human activities, Viktor Mayer-Schönberger argues that "in our analog past, the default was to discard rather than preserve; today the default is to retain."[15] This shift represents a dramatic change in our approach to preserving documentary heritage. The space problem that was formerly a major limiting factor for preserving records has been minimized and may soon be eliminated. The focus in appraising records will likely move from reducing the volume to other factors, such as protecting the privacy of people related to the records and respect for the cultural norms of their origin.

Recent research on personal information management reveals that, for people dealing with an overwhelming amount of information, keeping more of everything becomes a convenient choice, which demands less effort than sorting and deleting files.[16] People's tendency to keep everything is understandable since it reduces the chances of regrettable deletions. For society, the abundant accumulation of documents means more resources for research and commercial use. Keeping information, however, is not the end but rather the beginning of the digital recordkeeping process. Once we admit that people are inclined to keep more digital materials, the real question becomes: What will people do with the records, and how will they continue to interact with them in the future?

Maintenance: Keeping Digital Documents Alive

Unlike documents in physical form, digital bits and bytes must reside on a proper device and system in order to be displayed as documents. The necessary reliance of digital documents on a supporting technology makes their long-term preservation difficult, since digital technology changes constantly. Inaccessibility of still relatively young digital objects due to obsolescence of format and equipment has been a problem for many people.[17] In order to keep digital documents accessible through the course of rapid technological change, the timely application of a digital preservation process (e.g., migration and storage media refreshing) is necessary. Digital preservation, however, is a considerable continuing challenge even for information preservation professionals.

Ownership and Control: Who Owns What

Additional problems stem from individuals' lack of control over their documents in a digital environment. Design purposes, policies, and the political and economic intentions of digital tool developers may dictate how people interact with their digital documents.[18] For example, in the case of documents created and stored in the cloud computing environment (i.e., network-based computing), individuals are forced to rely on the technology and options employed by service providers, and there are few ways for end users to make their documents independent from the service providers' systems and to keep them fully under their control. There is a good chance that people's digital contents will disappear due to system failure, cessation of service, or a change in terms and conditions of service. In addition, ownership of content created and stored at service sites is not always made explicit. Even after owners have deleted content from the service site, materials may continue to remain in the service provider's data storage. The indefinite ownership and control over personal digital content created on the web causes many concerns: violation of privacy, infringement of individual intellectual property rights, and a misuse of personal information.

Perspectives on the Landscape: Related Research Trends

The personal and collective value of digital documents and the difficulties associated with long-term retention of personal digital documents represent a challenge that spans technological, social, cultural, cognitive, emotional, and legal considerations. Three research trends are particularly relevant to personal digital archiving phenomena:

- Researchers in IS and HCI, from academia and industry, have led an area called personal information management (PIM).

- Scholars and practitioners in archives and preservation have advocated for the preservation needs of personal digital collections.

- Scholars from media studies and cultural studies have produced literature that links the proliferation of digital media and digital content creation with *digital memory*, a term that also appears increasingly in the literature of HCI and science and technology studies (STS).

As a whole, researchers from diverse backgrounds are uncovering interesting empirical data and engaging in new conceptual discussions, as well as offering visionary suggestions related to personal digital archiving.

Looking for Information Management Solutions for Individuals: PIM Research

Spurred by the problem of information overload—an excessive volume of information and the difficulty of managing it—several research efforts have been aimed at finding alternative or innovative ways for individuals to manage their information more efficiently. These efforts have created the field of PIM. Although the focus of PIM is on information rather than computers, PIM studies actively began when personal computers (PCs) were introduced in the 1980s.[19] Thomas Malone's research about how office workers organize records in their desks and offices is one of the early studies that explored PIM behavior (e.g., filing and piling) and discussed implications for designing computer-based information systems.[20] PIM research has lately expanded into the ubiquitous use of personal digital devices. PIM-related studies are being conducted by commercial companies such as Microsoft as well as by researchers in academia.

Early studies typically focused on the technological aspects of PIM, proposing the development of PIM systems, services, and tools as a major goal, commercially driven in many cases. More recently, however, the psychological and social issues involved in information management activities have been acknowledged. Significantly, Mark Lansdale's pioneering research in 1988 discussed a psychological aspect of PIM in relation to the processes of recall, recognition, and categorization.[21] The necessity of a naturalistic and longitudinal investigation of PIM behavior and PIM tool evaluation has also gained attention.[22] Although the retrieval of personal information (e.g., finding and re-finding) is the most frequently explored topic, various other record-keeping activities are also subjects of PIM studies, including how people collect, organize, classify, and store personal information and how they use information items as reminders. Overall, PIM studies have produced "a significant body of research that suggests definite patterns of behavior in personal creation, management, and use of information."[23]

While many PIM studies target relatively short-term information management (i.e., managing information in current use), the terms *archive(s)*, *archiving*, or *archived* frequently appear in them.[24] In the literature of IT and internet services, however, the word *archive* (without an "s" or as a verb) is often used without a clear distinction between *archive* and the mere backup of data and data warehousing. As leading researchers in the IT industry, Elizabeth Churchill and Jeff Ubois emphasize "good design for archival services" to "guide users between backups, archives, and collections,"[25] which, in fact, requires that service developers comprehend the differences.

Deborah Barreau and Bonnie Nardi recruited managers in a research department at a government agency and Apple employees for their studies and observed their offices or cubicles. Steve Whittaker and Candace Sidner studied researchers, managers, and secretaries in an organization and each person's office space. Boardman and Sasse interviewed "users" and observed their file, email, and bookmark collections on their main work computers. Barreau and Nardi characterize "archived information" as information that "has a shelf life of months or years, but is only indirectly relevant to the user's current work."[26] Barreau adds further detail, saying "[archived information] may be carefully labeled and placed in a folder or subdirectory. As such it becomes part of a person's or an organization's historical record."[27] According to Whittaker and Sidner, "archives are not of immediate relevance to current tasks, but are constructed for reference or anticipated future use."[28] Boardman and Sasse mention that the term *archived* used in Barreau and Nardi's 1995 study is "misleading" since none of their participants archived explicitly. They instead suggest *dormant* as a term for "inactive, but potentially useful information."[29]

The fact that the PIM studies just mentioned were conducted in a work environment[30] may explain the origin of the idea of inactivity. Having a status of "inactive" seems to be the precondition for organizational records categorized as archives in traditional archival thinking as well. For example, in the concept of the lifecycle of records, developed by the U.S. National Archives and Records Administration (NARA), as records age, they become "inactive" and are maintained apart from the site of creation until they are transferred to the archival institution for permanent preservation.[31] Defining archives based on the idea of inactiveness, however, is problematic. An archived document may seem inactive in terms of its original purpose of use; yet it may still be active depending on how it functions in a different context (e.g., the use of records for historical research purposes).[32] Furthermore, associating inactivity with archives has limitations for understanding the characteristics of documents that are generated and maintained outside of organizational or business settings. For example, when and how do digital family photos taken during a family vacation and posted on Flickr become inactive or "unrelated to current activities" even though people may not look at them every day? There is no definite answer for this, since the intention of creating a family picture and the context of its use within a family group are different from these elements of a project report written at work.

Contextualizing Personal Digital Collections in a Social Context: Archival Studies

Archives and cultural institutions have a long tradition of acquiring and preserving various kinds of documentary heritage, including institutional records as well as personal papers. Traditionally, most archival theories and practices have been built around organizational records serving "the needs of ongoing corporate accountability and administrative efficiency."[33] Although the preservation of personal papers has been relatively marginalized within archival discourse, many archival scholars and practitioners have acknowledged the particular value of personal papers, which constitute an important part of our identity and collective memory.[34]

An increasing appreciation of documents generated by individuals is evidenced by the demand within the archival community to extend the traditional boundaries of what archives are, what archives are for, and what archivists do. For example, the concept of *total archives* that emerged in Canada around the 1970s is rooted in the idea that "anything historical was 'archival'—from diaries and letters to government correspondence and corporate files."[35] German archivist Hans Booms, still an influential figure in archival thinking, stressed that "the purpose and goal of the archival formation of the documentary heritage can only be to document the totality of public life as manifested in communities formed by common interests or other ties."[36] Another example of the movement to broaden the vision of archives and the scope of archival holdings is Helen Samuels's idea of "documentation strategy" set forth in 1986 in response to the needs of social historians for personal papers that began in the 1960s.[37] More recently, there are shared doubts about the sufficiency of a Western-oriented archival approach to manage and preserve human heritage, especially from different cultures or places,[38] which requires a shift in archival thinking from top-down to bottom-up, from exclusive to inclusive, and from singular to plural. Injecting postmodern thinking into archival discourse, archival scholars discuss the importance of international, local, indigenous, and ethnic community engagement in the formation of archives, history, and social memories.[39]

As the number of personal records created in digital form increases, some archivists pay particular attention to, and advocate for, the preservation needs for personal digital collections.[40] The uncertainty of the digital information environment seems to threaten the long-term survival of personal digital materials more seriously than the survival of institutional electronic records.[41] The technical longevity of digital records produced in institutions is frequently monitored through a professional records management program backed by institutional IT support, but it is hard to establish any general expectation of the technical stability of private digital records donated by individuals to archives. Individuals have different levels of skills, knowledge, and preferences relating to their digital technology use; traditionally, archives receive personal papers either at the very final stage of an individual's life or following the death of the individual, which can complicate the preservation of personal digital documents.[42] Moreover, private digital records are likely to be highly heterogeneous in terms of their purpose of creation and use, genre, storage media, computing systems, and creating software.[43]

Building a proper archival processing and preservation strategy for private digital collections is a major challenge for digital archivists. The Personal Archives Accessible in Digital Media (PARADIGM) project in the U.K., completed in 2007, is well-known as one of the few examples of personal digital archiving research efforts in the archival profession. Digital archivists and researchers at the University of Oxford Bodleian Library and the University of Manchester sought solutions for preserving digital private papers. Through hands-on work with six living politicians as record creators, the PARADIGM team examined characteristics of the subjects' personal record collections, personal preservation policies, and preservation tools such as digital repository software and metadata extraction tools.[44] Digital Lives Research is another example of a recent project led by researchers in The British Library, in partnership with the School of Library, Archives and Information Studies at University College London and the Centre for Information Technology and Law at the University of Bristol. In recognition of the growing number of personal digital collections as well as their research value, this project focuses on individuals' personal digital archives and their impacts on librarianship and archival practice in research institutions such as The British Library. Through interviews, questionnaires, workshops, focus groups, and literature reviews, the project team members conducted an in-depth investigation into how their research participants (e.g., academics and the "digital public") built their personal digital collections in daily life and addressed related legal and ethical issues.[45]

With the massive influx of electronic records, archivists have recognized the important role of record creators in safeguarding the survival of digital documents in general. To ensure their continued availability, electronic records require timely care, in order to deal with technological obsolescence and incompatibilities. The preservation action should take place when the record creator is still managing or retaining the documents for continuing use. Therefore, the active involvement of record creators in continuing preservation, as well as the proactive engagement of archivists or record managers in a record creator's daily recordkeeping,[46] or "an early intervention approach,"[47] seems necessary. As a result, archives and digital preservation professionals have developed digital records management best practices for record creators.[48]

The fundamental ideas in the research, however, are still mostly centered on how archivists and manuscript curators can capture, manage, and preserve personal digital collections. The act of transferring the custodianship of records to the archival institution seems to remain a key element in archival practices. Furthermore, most memory institutions have focused on acquiring collections from well-known individuals or public figures. This institution-centered view is limited when it comes to promoting a more inclusive collecting and preservation plan for documents from local communities and ordinary individuals.

Several archival scholars have challenged this archival institution-led custodianship. For example, postcustodial theory has been a meta-theme running through postmodern archival discourse.[49] According to American archival educator Patricia Galloway, *postcustodialism* refers to "the practice of an archive's advising and/or supervising records creators in carrying out the preservation of their records themselves."[50] Furthermore, Galloway suggests that digital archiving becomes everyone's concern, "as living on the internet becomes less of a second life and more of a first one for more people, individuals will increasingly take on these issues as their own concerns and perhaps their own responsibility."[51] Australian archival scholar Adrian Cunningham also cautiously points out the mixed reality of digital recordkeeping across public and private realms of life: "The boundaries between work and private life and between work and private information spaces are becoming increasingly blurred. In the future perhaps all recordkeeping, both organizational and personal, will be personal recordkeeping."[52]

Applying postcustodial thinking to the personal digital documents of everyone who wants to hold onto their personal digital materials opens up the possibility of grassroots-level preservation. For example, American archival educator Richard Cox points out that with digital technology, individuals have more ways to administer their own personal documents. He emphasizes the importance of individuals ("citizen archivists") who function as their own archivists in preserving their digital documentary heritage.[53] Cox strongly suggests that a new role for professional archivists and records managers is to nurture and equip citizen archivists in the digital era. Cunningham also notes the idea of "a distributed custody context" or "anti-centralized repository" while stressing that "all archivists should have an interest in helping individuals to become digital auto-archivists."[54] The public outreach and education activity by the U.S. Library of Congress's Preservation Division can be seen as an example of an advocacy effort heading toward grassroots preservation.[55]

Regardless of visionary ideas provided by archival scholars, we need to continue to see how postcustodial theory becomes a practice in archives. Personal digital archives as a research topic for archivists is a complex issue because it challenges what has been done in the archival tradition and offers an uncertain opportunity to expand the scope of archives. A few case studies reporting hands-on experiences with personal digital collections in memory institutions allow us to think about how archives can approach collections from various groups of people without abandoning their own institutional identities and specialties.[56] The continuing accumulation of empirical studies will provide the archival profession with the insight needed to find constructive methods and strategies for empowering individuals as citizen archivists in practice.

Exploring Dimensions of Memory Objects and Practices: Digital Memory Studies

Memory has been a subject of inquiry for a long time in human history. Since the early 1900s, memory studies have greatly expanded, especially following World War II. The rise of attentiveness to "small histories"[57] (e.g., genealogical research and family histories, trauma, emotions, reconciliation, and therapy), along with the development of biotechnology and brain imaging technology, are among the reasons for the proliferation of interest in memory.[58] Studies of memory carried out in specific disciplines, however, never remain in isolation. Rather, as José van Dijck states, "the question of memory ties together the intricacies of the brain with the dynamics of social behavior and the multilayered density of material and social culture."[59] Memory and remembering is also a subject frequently discussed in archival studies and PIM research.[60]

In recent years, the term *digital memory* has increasingly appeared in literature that ranges from media studies to technical fields, such as HCI and STS research. Theories and discussions about digital memory are accompanied by an acknowledgment of the development of digital media and associated technology, and their influence on why and how we remember and forget, including computer memory (e.g., processing memory and storage memory) as a possible extension of, or support for, human memory.

The power of digital or new media in documenting, archiving, and retrieval is linked to maximizing creativity, imagination, and sharing. It frees the process of recording and creating events, making the relationship among memory, media, and technology more intimate. Treating media "as the holistic mix of techniques, technologies and practices through which social and cultural life is mediated," media scholar Andrew Hoskins stresses that "memory is lived through a media ecology wherein abundance, pervasiveness and accessibility of communication networks, nodes, and digital media content, scale pasts anew."[61] Joanne Garde-Hansen offers a similar description of media as the recording of events, as a memory aid, tool, or device, and media as being the key drivers of memory practices (e.g., online memorials and digital storytelling).[62] Van Dijck proposes mediated memory as "the activities and objects we produce and appropriate by means of media technologies, for creating and re-creating a sense of past, present, and future of ourselves in relation to others" with an emphasis on "the mutual shaping of memory and media."[63] Furthermore, the dynamics of digitally mediated memory, its pervasive penetration into everyday life, and especially new media technologies (e.g., online media) seem to facilitate the democratization of memory-making at both the personal and collective levels.[64] In his discussion of a digital biography and "life writing," Paul Longley Arthur points out that technological changes "have made it possible for 'ordinary' lives, that had formerly left no trace, to be recorded and 'saved' for the future."[65]

Concepts and terminologies about memory objects and the practice of memory-making discussed by media scholars seem to serve as an inspiration for digital memory technology studies in HCI and STS.[66] Several researchers from the IS and IT industries explore home and family archives in particular for the purpose of gaining new insights applicable to the development of personal/family digital archives systems.[67] Often, their view of "home archives" centers on the connection between object and personal memory, family history, and emotions. For example, David Kirk and Abigail Sellen explore the material culture of the home and current home archiving practices focusing on *sentimental artifacts*. In their research, sentimental artifacts are defined as two- and three-dimensional physical objects and digital materials that people keep and display in their home environments and "feel in some way attached to."[68] The issue of preserving digital documents beyond a lifetime is another newly emerging topic that, from an HCI perspective, comes under the category of digital memory-related research. Researchers active in this area start with the question of how digital technology can help with bereavement by treating personal digital documents as memorial and mourning objects. For example, Michael Massimi and Andrea Charise introduce a concept called *thanatosensitivity* as "a novel, humanistically-grounded approach to HCI research and design that recognizes and actively engages with the facts of mortality, dying, and death in the creation of interactive systems."[69] Many of these HCI studies focus on storytelling and sharing memories through the design of virtual memorial systems, digital heirlooms, and family digital archives.[70] Rapidly emerging online commercial services offer assistance to individuals and families for planning how to bequeath personal documentary assets, sending posthumous emails and messages, and building memorial sites where people can share photos of, or stories about, a deceased person.[71]

Inspired by the technological promise of capturing and keeping everything as an opportunity to actualize the vision of Vannevar Bush's memex, "an enlarged intimate supplement to his [one's] memory,"[72] HCI researchers are attempting to design devices and applications to automatically capture, store, and provide access to an entire lifetime of activities in digital form, the so-called lifelog. The potential benefits of lifelog data are certainly appealing. Lifelog data can assist in remembering, replaying, and sharing past events as well as improving personal time management, security, and health,[73] and can also be used for many other purposes, such as information behavior research and micro-advertising. Microsoft's MyLifeBits is a pioneering project that stemmed from Gordon Bell's project of digitizing every document (and some three dimensional objects) that he owns, an undertaking that has evolved into lifelogging technology research.[74] While still rooted in an "engineering-like epistemological and methodological stance,"[75] a similar project, Memories for Life (M4L), set up by U.K. computing and engineering communities, seeks participation from researchers in a relatively wide range of fields, including cultural heritage preservation, knowledge management, neuroscience, and psychology as well as computer science.[76] Along with its innovativeness, however, lifelogging technology research raises many serious questions. For example, what will having lifetime data about oneself actually mean to a person? How will individuals live with massive amounts of lifetime data about themselves? While there is no single answer, it is obvious that usable lifelog technologies for individuals need to be built upon a thorough understanding of the complexity of how human memories and minds work,[77] including the psychological and social functions of forgetting as well as remembering along with the relationship between active forgetting and intentional deletion of the recorded past.[78]

Emerging Landscape: Cross-Field and Undisciplined Exploration

How researchers from different backgrounds share similar yet diverse views about the phenomenon of personal digital archiving is fascinating to observe. PIM studies respond to the growing concern about the practicality of information management methods. Related studies of digital memory in HCI are driven by the view of the influence of digital technology on the creation of and interaction with digital memory objects. Overall, both areas are based on a utilitarian motivation that is geared toward developing digital archiving tools that can help people to manage digital objects and thereby manage their life activities. In these studies, people who are creators, primary users, and preservers of their own personal digital information are basically "customers" or "users" of potential digital archiving tools and services.

Archival studies are concerned with a historically oriented demand for safeguarding our collective documentary heritage. The significant amount of literature generated by archival scholars and practitioners provides a foundation for in-depth discussions about how the personal digital archives of individuals are situated in an overall societal and cultural context. Archival literature and practices often presuppose the archivist as an intermediary and the archival institution as a permanent repository. Therefore, the creator of records and the user of the records (e.g., potential researchers or visitors to memory institutions) are not usually the same person, while the record manager and the preserver of records (e.g., archivists and manuscript curators) usually serve as intermediaries. Discussions on digital memory in cultural and media studies bring perspectives from the humanities, communication, and sociology into personal digital archiving research and stimulate us to think of the layers of memory (e.g., from autobiographical to collective and from private to public) embedded in and captured through digital media.

In fact, the shared phenomena of inquiry and the substantially distinct positions taken by researchers across various fields point to a desperate need for cross-disciplinary research.[79] Application of PIM studies to day-to-day task performance will support the exploration of "the business of creating our records as documents, capturing them as records, and keeping and discarding them over time" that resembles the activities of professional archivists.[80] HCI researchers' interests, directed more toward digital materials as memory objects, will be useful in investigating people's self-reflective and emotional associations with their digital possessions. A refined definition of the meaning of archives and a focus on the preservation needs of personal digital documents supplied by archives professionals will assist us in understanding and differentiating "archival" documents from other documents based on their values and meanings to the owner as well as to others, including the larger society. For example, bringing in their archival perspective, Peter Williams, Jeremy John, and Ian Rowland address the necessity of *archivally oriented PIM* studies and PIM technology design. They urge the incorporation of objectives of the professional archivists into PIM research, which will make information "interpretable and maximally useful for future as well as current generations."[81]

The demand for an archivally oriented PIM is timely, since PIM researchers seem to be less active in investigating knowledge and practices from the archival profession. When Marshall[82] claims that "personal archiving revolves around the same basic technological issues as other types of digital archiving" in memory institutions,[83] her view of the universe of the archival profession is rather passive[84]—the technological aspect of the problem is the bare minimum of what is shared or should be shared among researchers from these various fields. The overlapping concerns need to be expanded into a series of questions about the delicate relationship between people and their digital documents, and the meaning of *archiving* as a practice at both the individual and collective levels: Why have people as individuals, communities, and societies tried to keep and organize documents? What kinds of functions and values do personal documents have in different settings, from one's private life to relatively public environments such as the web or a memory institution's reading room? How do people perceive and experience digital archiving that is personal as well as social?

Collaboration among experts with different backgrounds is already taking place. The Personal Digital Archiving conferences, first hosted in 2010 at the Internet Archive in San Francisco, are an example of an effort to build bridges. Participants in the conferences include IT entrepreneurs, researchers in IT companies, working archivists and preservation professionals, scholars in academia, and individuals genuinely interested in the topic.[85] While conversations among these participants may or may not be compelling to one another yet, it is certain that this kind of interdisciplinary conference provides a forum for people concerned with personal digital archiving to exchange their findings and ideas. In addition, it should be noted that individuals who are interested in constructing digital archives for themselves, their families, and their communities are the essential driving force of personal digital archiving activities and research. The keynote address by Mike Ashenfelder of the Library of Congress at the 2012 Personal Digital Archiving Conference was preceded by Stan James's presentation about his ongoing personal family photos and memorabilia scanning project that he and his father have been working on for the past several years.[86] Although not everyone wants to actively build their own or family digital archives, our private desires and actions, as represented by James's case, inspire us to contemplate what additional factors need to be explored in terms of personal digital archiving research and development.

Bedrock: Documenting and Understanding Human Experience

PIM researchers Jones and Teevan describe digital technology as a double-edged sword that both accelerates the phenomena of information overload and offers opportunities for creativity.[87] If we view the negative connotation of information overload in a positive way, it can be interpreted as producing and accumulating more information to utilize—so-called Big Data. When this view of information overload is combined with technological creativity, it appears that we have multitudes of interesting opportunities as well as the capability to document and preserve human experiences at an unprecedented scale and level of detail.

Personal digital archives as collections constructed by people throughout their lives offer a potentially huge body of material, which is especially useful for enriching our understanding of ourselves and our collective histories, as well as the nature of society and culture for present and future. Personal digital archiving is a practice that focuses on assigning and extracting meanings from a massive amount of material. From this perspective and with cautious optimism, we can regard personal digital archiving activities and research as a particularly interesting way to explore the possibility of capturing—and better comprehending—the human experience.

Endnotes

1. Patricia Galloway, "Big Buckets or Big Ideas? Classification vs. Innovation on the Enterprise 2.0 Desktop" (paper prepared for the ARMA International Educational Foundation, Pittsburgh, PA, 2008). www.armaedfoundation.org/pdfs/BBpaper30.pdf.

2. Catherine C. Marshall, "Challenges and Opportunities for Personal Digital Archiving," in *I, Digital: Personal Collections in the Digital Era*, ed. Christopher A. Lee (Chicago: Society of American Archivists, 2011), 113–114.

3. Richard J. Cox, "Human Impulses and Personal Archives," *Records & Information Management Report* 22, no. 3 (2006): 4.

4. For examples, see Steve Whittaker and Julia Hirschberg, "The Character, Value, and Management of Personal Paper Archives," *ACM Transactions on Computer-Human Interaction* 8, no. 2 (2001): 150–170; Joseph Kaye, Janet Vertesi, Shari

Avery, Allan Dafoe, Shay David, Lisa Onaga, Ivan Rosero, and Trevor Pinch, "To Have and to Hold: Exploring the Personal Archive," in *Proceedings of the SIGCHI Conference on Human Factors in Computing Systems* (New York: ACM, 2006), 275–284; David S. Kirk and Abigail Sellen, *On Human Remains: Excavating the Home Archive* (Microsoft, 2008), research.microsoft.com/apps/pubs/default. aspx?id=70595; Peter Williams, Katrina Dean, Ian Rowland, and Jeremy L. John, "Digital Lives: Report of Interviews with the Creators of Personal Digital Collections," *Ariadne55* (2008), www.ariadne.ac.uk/issue55/williams-et-al; Daniela Petrelli and Steve Whittaker, "Family Memories in the Home: Contrasting Physical and Digital Mementos," *Personal and Ubiquitous Computing* 14, no. 2 (2010): 153–169.

5. Sue McKemmish, "Evidence of Me … ," *Archives and Manuscripts* 24 (1996): 38.

6. For examples, see Neil Beagrie, "Plenty of Room at the Bottom? Personal Digital Libraries and Collections," *D-Lib Magazine* 11 (2005), www.dlib.org/dlib/june 05/beagrie/06beagrie.html; Joanne Garde-Hansen, Andrew Hoskins, and Anna Reading, "Introduction," in *Save As … Digital Memories*, ed. Joanne Garde-Hansen, Andrew Hoskins, and Anna Reading (New York: Palgrave Macmillan, 2009), 1–26.

7. Paul Longley Arthur, "Saving Lives: Digital Biography and Life Writing," in *Save As … Digital Memories*, ed. Joanne Garde-Hansen, Andrew Hoskins, and Anna Reading (New York: Palgrave Macmillan, 2009), 44–59.

8. Peter Williams, Jeremy L. John, and Ian Rowland, "The Personal Curation of Digital Objects: A Lifecycle Approach," *Aslib Proceedings* 6, no. 4 (2009): 348.

9. Some companies (e.g., Recorded Future) are developing services that identify predictive signals from public data, such as newsfeeds, Twitter, and blogs, by using information extraction algorithms and visualization software. See Dian Temple-Raston, "Predicting the Future: Fantasy or A Good Algorithm?" *National Public Radio*, October 8, 2012, www.npr.org/2012/10/08/162397787/predicting-the-future-fantasy-or-a-good-algorithm?sc=tw.

10. For examples, see Beagrie, "Plenty of Room at the Bottom?"; Richard J. Cox, *Personal Archives and a New Archival Calling: Readings, Reflections and Ruminations* (Duluth: Litwin Books, 2008); Andrew Flinn, "Other Ways of Thinking, Other Ways of Being. Documenting the Margins and the Transitory: What to Preserve, How to Collect," in *What Are Archives?: Cultural and Theoretical Perspectives: A Reader*, ed. Louise Craven (Burlington, VT: Ashgate Publishing, 2008), 109–128; Caroline Williams, "Personal Papers: Perceptions and Practices," in *What Are Archives?: Cultural and Theoretical Perspectives: A Reader*, ed. Louise Craven (Burlington, VT: Ashgate Publishing, 2008), 53–67.

11. In an attempt to measure the amount of information produced, Gantz and Reinsel estimate that the digital universe will surpass 1.8 zettabytes in 2011. See John Gantz and David Reinsel, *Extracting Value from Chaos State of the Universe*

(report prepared for IDC and EMC Corporation, 2011, www.emc.com/collateral/analyst-reports/idc-extracting-value-from-chaos-ar.pdf).

12. Harry Bruce, Abraham Wenning, Elisabeth Jones, Julia Vinson, and William Jones, "Seeking an Ideal Solution to the Management of Personal Information Collections," *Information Research* 16, no. 1 (2011): 1.

13. Catherine C. Marshall, "How People Manage Information over a Lifetime," in *Personal Information Management*, ed. William Jones and Jaime Teevan (Seattle: University of Washington Press: 2007), 57–75; Catherine C. Marshall, "Rethinking Personal Digital Archiving," *D-Lib Magazine* 14, no. 3/4 (2008), www.dlib.org/dlib/march08/marshall/03marshall-pt1.html.

14. Jim Gemmell, Gordon Bell, and Roger Lueder, "MyLifeBits: a Personal Database for Everything," *Communications of the ACM* 49, no. 1 (2006): 88–95; Mary Czerwinski, Douglas W. Gage, Jim Gemmell, Catherine C. Marshall, Manuel A. Péres-Quiñonesis, Meredith M. Skeels, and Tiziana Catarci, "Digital Memories in an Era of Ubiquitous Computing and Abundant Storage," *Communications of the ACM* 49, no. 1 (2006): 44–50.

15. Viktor Mayer-Schönberger, *Useful Void: The Art of Forgetting in the Age of Ubiquitous Computing*, paper prepared for Harvard John F. Kennedy School of Government Faculty Research Working Paper Series, Cambridge, MA, 2007, research.hks.harvard.edu/publications/getFile.aspx?Id=25. Mayer-Schönberger's viewpoint corresponds with what Mark Weiser, former head of the Computer Science Laboratory at the Xerox Palo Alto Research Center, said in his 1991 article about ubiquitous computing: "A terabyte of space makes deleting old files virtually unnecessary." See Mark Weiser, "The Computer for the 21st Century," *Scientific American* 265, no. 3 (1999): 110.

16. Peter Williams, Katrina Dean, Ian Rowland, and Jeremy L. John, "Digital Lives: Report of Interviews with the Creators of Personal Digital Collections," *Ariadne55* (2008).

17. Personal Archives Accessible in Digital Media (PARADIGM) Project, *Workbook on Digital Private Papers*, (2007), www.paradigm.ac.uk/workbook/index.html.

18. Joanne Garde-Hansen, "My Memories?: Personal Digital Archive Fever and Facebook," in *Save As … Digital Memories*, ed. Joanne Garde-Hansen, Andrew Hoskins, and Anna Reading (New York: Palgrave Macmillan, 2009), 135–150; Nancy Van House and Elizabeth F. Churchill, "Technologies of Memory: Key Issues and Critical Perspectives," *Memory Studies* 1, no. 3 (2008): 295–310.

19. William Jones and Jaime Teevan, "Introduction," in *Personal Information Management*, ed. William Jones and Jaime Teevan (Seattle: University of Washington Press, 2007), 18.

20. Thomas W. Malone, "How Do People Organize Their Desks?: Implications for the Design of Office Information Systems," *ACM Transactions on Information Systems* 1, no. 1 (1983): 99–112.

21. Mark Lansdale, "The Psychology of Personal Information Management," *Applied Ergonomics* 19, no. 1 (1988): 55–66.

22. For examples, see Diane Kelly, "Evaluating Personal Information Management Behaviors and Tools," *Communications of the ACM* 49, no.1 (2006): 84–86; Deborah K. Barreau, "The Persistence of Behavior and Form in the Organization of Personal Information," *Journal of the American Society For Information Science and Technology* 59, no. 2 (2008): 307–317; Charles M. Naumer and Karen E. Fisher, "Naturalistic Approaches for Understanding PIM," in *Personal Information Management*, ed. William Jones and Jaime Teevan (Seattle: University of Washington Press, 2007), 76–88.

23. Christopher A. Lee and Robert Capra, "And Now the Twain Shall Meet: Exploring the Connections between PIM and Archives," in *I, Digital: Personal Collections in the Digital Era*, ed. Christopher A. Lee (Chicago: Society of American Archivists, 2011), 13.

24. For examples, see Catherine C. Marshall, Sara Bly, and Françoise Brun-Cottan, "The Long Term Fate of Our Personal Digital Belongings: Toward a Service Model for Personal Archives," in *Proceedings of Archiving 2006* (Springfield, VA: Society for Imaging Science and Technology, 2006), 25–30; Catherine C. Marshall, Frank McCown, and Michael L. Nelson, "Evaluating Personal Archiving Strategies for Internet-Based Information," In *Proceedings of Archiving 2007* (Springfield, VA: Society for Imaging Science and Technology, 2007), 151–156; Marshall, "How People Manage Information over a Lifetime," 57–75; Marshall, "Rethinking Personal Digital Archiving." Additionally, Lifestreams is an example of the early PIM-related projects that aimed to develop a virtual storage model for personal electronic data including "old information." Lifestreams uses time-based ordering (i.e., past, present, and future streams) as its key mechanism to archive/store and organize documents created and received. See Eric Freeman and David Gelernter, "Lifestreams: a Storage Model for Personal Data," *SIGMOD Record* 25, no. 1 (1996): 80–86.

25. Elizabeth Churchill and Jeff Ubois, "Designing for Digital Archives," *Interactions* 15, no. 2 (2008): 11.

26. Deborah K. Barreau and Bonnie A. Nardi, "Finding and Reminding: File Organization from the Desktop," *SIGCHI Bulletin* 27, no. 3 (1995): 42.

27. Barreau, "The Persistence of Behavior and Form in the Organization of Personal Information," 308.

28. Steve Whittaker and Candace Sidner, "Email Overload: Exploring Personal Information Management of Email," in *Proceedings of the SIGCHI Conference on Human Factors in Computing Systems* (New York: ACM, 1996), 276.

29. Richard Boardman and Angela M. Sasse, "'Stuff Goes into the Computer and Doesn't Come Out': A Cross-tool Study of Personal Information Management," in *CHI'04: Proceedings of the SIGCHI Conference on Human Factors in Computing Systems* (Vienna, Austria: ACM Press, 2004), 583–590.

30. For example, Barreau and Nardi recruited managers in a research department at a government agency and Apple employees for their studies and observed their offices or cubicles. Whittaker and Sidner studied researchers, managers, and secretaries in an organization and each person's office space. Boardman and Sasse interviewed "users" and observed their file, email, and bookmark collections on their main work computers.

31. Anne Gilliland-Swetland, *Enduring Paradigm, New Opportunities: The Value of the Archival Perspective in the Digital Environment* (Washington: Council on Library and Information Resources, 2000), 14.

32. For example, the Australian model of a records continuum offers a contrasting view of the linear time- and stage-based lifecycle of records. Archival scholars of the records continuum model emphasize records as something "always in a process of becoming." This model is founded on the ideas of the continuity of the evidential qualities of records, transactionality documented in records of any kinds, and the identity of a record creator as long as records exist. Under this model, recordkeeping is a process of contextualization of records. The records continuum theorists stress that recordkeeping professionals (archivists and records managers) need to establish integrating and dynamic understandings of records throughout different time and space—from creation to accumulation, management, and use, while opposing the idea of making a "distracting" division between records managers and archivists. See Sue McKemmish, "Evidence of Me … in a Digital World," in *I, Digital: Personal Collections in the Digital Era*, ed. Christopher A. Lee (Chicago: Society of American Archivists, 2011), 122, 118.

33. Adrian Cunningham, "Beyond the Pale?" *Archives and Manuscripts* 24 (1996): 22.

34. For examples, see Robert A. J. McDonald, "Acquiring and Preserving Private Records—A Debate," *Archivaria* 38 (1994): 155–157; Cunningham, "Beyond the Pale?"; Catherine Hobbs, "The Character of Personal Archives: Reflections on the Value of Records of Individuals," *Archivaria* 52, no. 2 (2001): 126–135; Riva A. Pollard, "The Appraisal of Personal Papers: A Critical Literature Review," *Archivaria* 52 (2001): 136–150; Judith Etherton, "The Role of Archives in the Perception of Self," *Journal of the Society of Archivists* 27 (2006): 227–246; Cox, *Personal Archives and a New Archival Calling*; Williams, "Personal Papers: Perceptions and Practices."

35. Laura Millar, "Discharging Our Debt: The Evolution of the Total Archives Concept in English Canada," *Archivaria* 46 (1998): 110.

36. Hans Booms, "Society and the Formation of a Documentary Heritage: Issues in the Appraisal of Archival Sources," *Archivaria* 24 (1987), (original 1972: translation by Hermina Joldersma and Richard Klumpenhouwer): 106.

37. Helen W. Samuels, "Who Controls the Past," *The American Archivist* 49, no 2. (1986): 109–124. Cook says that Samuels urges a connection of "official government and other institutional records with personal manuscripts and visual media, as well as published information and even oral history." See Terry Cook, "What Is Past Is Prologue: A History of Archival Ideas since 1898, and the Future Paradigm Shift," *Archivaria* 43 (1997): 32.

38. Richard J. Cox, "Conclusion: The Archivist and Community," in *Community Archives, the Shaping of Memory*, ed. Jeannette Bastian and Ben Alexander (London: Facet Publishing, 2009), 251–264.

39. For example, McKemmish, Gilliland-Swetland, and Eric Ketelaar argue for broadening notions of records and archives from textual material to "orality, literature, art, artifacts, the built environment, landscape, dance, ceremonies and rituals as archival forms." See Sue McKemmish, Anne Gilliland-Swetland, and Eric Ketelaar, "'Communities of Memory': Pluralising Archival Research and Education Agendas," *Archives and Manuscripts* 33 (2005): 152. Exploring the history of the survival of orally transmitted culture, Galloway suggests the idea of "archivist-as-apprentice," who undertakes to play the role of a tradition-bearer by apprenticing, learning, and performing the intangible cultural heritage. See Patricia Galloway, "Oral Tradition in Living Cultures: The Role of Archives in the Preservation of Memory," in *Community Archives, the Shaping of Memory*, ed. Jeannette Bastian and Ben Alexander (London: Facet Publishing, 2009), 81. Flinn and his colleagues shed light on the emergence of independent, nonprofessionalized community archives—versus mainstream archives—in connection with social movements, which inherently involves issues of identity, power, and struggle. See Andrew Flinn, Mary Stevens, and Elizabeth Shepherd, "Whose Memories, Whose Archives? Independent Community Archives, Autonomy and the Mainstream," *Archival Science* 9, no. 1–2 (2009): 71–86; Andrew Flinn and Mary Stevens, "'It Is Noh Mistri, Wi Mekin Histry.' Telling Our Own Story: Independent and Community Archives in the UK, Challenging and Subverting the Mainstream," in *Community Archives, the Shaping of Memory*, ed. by Jeannette Bastian and Ben Alexander (London: Facet Publishing, 2009), 3–27; Andrew Flinn, "Archival Activism: Independent and Community-Led Archives, Radical Public History and the Heritage Professions," *InterActions: UCLA Journal of Education and Information Studies* 7, no. 2 (2011): 1–20.

40. For examples, see Tom Hyry and Rachel Onuf, "The Personality of Electronic Records: The Impact of New Information Technology on Personal Papers," *Archival Issues* 22, no. 1 (1997): 37–44; Beagrie, "Plenty of Room at the Bottom?"; Susan Thomas, *Paradigm: A Practical Approach to the Preservation of Personal Digital Archives* (report prepared for the Joint Information Systems

Committee (JISC), Bristol and London, UK, 2007, www.paradigm.ac.uk/project docs/jiscreports/ParadigmFinalReportv1.pdf.

41. For example, see Lucie Paquet, "Appraisal, Acquisition, and Control of Personal Electronic Records: From Myth to Reality," *Archives and Manuscripts* 28 (2000): 71–91.

42. For example, password-protected digital files and personal computers donated after a record creator passes away make it difficult to process them for archival preservation. See Sarah Kim, Lorraine Dong, and Megan Durden, "Batch Archival Processing: Preserving Arnold Wesker's Digital Manuscripts," *Archival Issues* 30, no 2. (2006): 94.

43. Williams, John, and Rowland, "The Personal Curation of Digital Objects: A Lifecycle Approach," *Aslib Proceedings* 6, no. 4 (2009): 340–363.

44. For examples, see Susan Thomas, "Using the Papers of Contemporary British Politicians as a Testbed for the Preservation of Digital Personal Archives," *Journal of the Society of Archivists* 27, no. 1 (2006): 29–56; Susan Thomas, *Paradigm: A Practical Approach to the Preservation of Personal Digital Archives*; PARADIGM Project website, www.paradigm.ac.uk.

45. See Jeremy Leighton John, Ian Rowland, Peter Williams, and Katrina Dean, *Digital Lives: Personal Digital Archives for the 21st Century. An Initial Synthesis. Essays in Criticism* (report prepared for the Digital Lives Research Project, The British Library, London, 2010, britishlibrary.typepad.co.uk/files/digital-lives-synthesis 02-1.pdf, 14.

46. Adrian Cunningham, "Waiting for the Ghost Train: Strategies for Managing Electronic Personal Records Before It Is Too Late," *Archival Issues: Journal of the Midwest Archives Conference* 24, no. 1 (1999): 55–64.

47. Rachel Onuf and Thomas Hyry, "Take It Personally: The Implications of Personal Records in Electronic Form," in *I, Digital: Personal Collections in the Digital Era*, ed. Christopher A. Lee (Chicago: Society of American Archivists, 2011), 252.

48. For example, one of the outcomes of the PARADIGM project is the *Guidelines for Creators of Personal Archives*, which covers how people can manage and maintain their personal digital materials for the purpose of long-term preservation. See PARADIGM, "Workbook on Digital Private Papers: Guidelines for Creators of Personal Archives," in *Workbook on Digital Private Papers* (2007), www.paradigm. ac.uk/workbook/appendices/guidelines.html. Another project, International Research on Permanent Authentic Records in Electronic Systems (InterPARES), has also distributed *Creator Guidelines Booklet - Making and Maintaining Digital Materials: Guidelines for Individuals*. See International Research on Permanent Authentic Records in Electronic Systems (InterPARES), *Creator Guidelines Booklet—Making and Maintaining Digital Materials: Guidelines for Individuals*, www.interpares.org/display_file.cfm?doc=ip2(pub)creator_guidelines_booklet.pdf.

49. The *postcustodial* idea was first introduced into the archival discourse by Gerald Ham, in his article "Archival Strategies for the Postcustodial Era," *American Archivist* 44, no. 3 (1981): 207–16. In general, the postcustodial theory in archives has been elaborated as a new paradigm for electronic records. For example, see David Bearman and Margaret Hedstrom, "Reinventing Archives for Electronic Records: Alternative Service Delivery Options," *Archives and Museum Informatics Technical Report* 18 (1993): 82–96; Terry Cook, "Electronic Records, Paper Minds: The Revolution in Information Management and Archives in the Post-Custodial and Post-Modernist Era," *Archives and Manuscripts* 22 (1994): 300–329.

50. Patricia Galloway, "Oral Tradition in Living Cultures: The Role of Archives in the Preservation of Memory," 78.

51. Patricia Galloway, "Digital Archiving," in *Encyclopedia of Library and Information Sciences*, third edition (London: Taylor & Francis, 2010), 1526.

52. Adrian Cunningham, "Ghosts in the Machine: Towards a Principles-Based Approach to Making and Keeping Digital Personal Records," in *I, Digital: Personal Collections in the Digital Era*, ed. Christopher A. Lee (Chicago: Society of American Archivists, 2011), 81.

53. Cox, *Personal Archives and a New Archival Calling*, vii.

54. Cunningham, "Ghosts in the Machine," 82.

55. The U.S. Library of Congress's Personal Archiving: Preserving Your Digital Memories website, www.digitalpreservation.gov/personalarchiving, provides promotional video clips, tips, and other resources on how ordinary individuals can preserve their own digital materials in their everyday lives. See also Chapter 3, "The Library of Congress and Personal Digital Archiving" by Mike Ashenfelder.

56. For examples, see Leslie Johnston, "Making It Usable: Developing Personal Collection Tools for Digital Collections," in *I, Digital: Personal Collections in the Digital Era*, ed. Christopher A. Lee (Chicago: Society of American Archivists, 2011), 257–279; Susan Thomas, "Curating the I, Digital: Experiences at the Bodleian Library." In *I, Digital: Personal Collections in the Digital Era*, ed. Christopher A. Lee (Chicago: Society of American Archivists, 2011), 280–305.

57. José van Dijck, *Mediated Memories in the Digital Age* (Palo Alto, CA: Stanford University Press, 2007), 10.

58. Referring to French historian Pierre Nora's reasons for increasing attention to memory, Garde-Hansen provides a brief explanation of the explosion of memory-related studies after the Second World War. See Joanne Garde-Hansen, *Media and Memory* (Edinburgh: Edinburgh University Press, 2011), 13–14.

59. van Dijck, *Mediated Memories in the Digital Age*, xiii.

60. For example, archival scholars have produced a large amount of literature exploring the relationships between institutional archives and the construction

of collective memory and identities. The archival literature on memory is too substantial to refer in detail here. For examples, see Joan Schwartz, and Terry Cook, "Archives, Records, and Power: The Making of Modern Memory," *Archival Science* 2, no. 1 (March 2002): 1–19; Laura Millar, "Touchstones: Considering the Relationship Between Memory and Archives," *Archivaria* 61 (2006): 105–126. PIM researchers have investigated the role of memory in retrieval of information objects. For examples, see Lansdale, "The Psychology of Personal Information Management," 55–66; Liadh Kelly, Yi Chen, Marguerite Fuller, and Gareth J. F. Jones, "A Study of Remembered Context for Information Access from Personal Digital Archives," in *Proceedings of the Second International Symposium on Information Interaction in Context'08* (New York: ACM Press, 2008), 44–50.

61. Andrew Hoskins, "Media, Memory, Metaphor: Remembering and the Connective Turn," *Parallax* 17, no. 4 (2011): 20, 29.

62. Garde-Hansen, *Media and Memory*, 52–53.

63. van Dijck, *Mediated Memories in the Digital Age*, 21.

64. For example, see Garde-Hansen, *Media and Memory*, 71–87.

65. Arthur, "Saving Lives: Digital Biography and Life Writing," 44.

66. For example, see Nancy Van House and Elizabeth F. Churchill, "Technologies of Memory: Key Issues and Critical Perspectives," *Memory Studies* 1, no. 3 (2008): 295–310.

67. For examples, see David S. Kirk and Abigail Sellen, *On Human Remains: Excavating the Home Archive* (Microsoft, 2008); Daniela Petrelli, *Personal and Shared Memories in the Home* (2007), citeseerx.ist.psu.edu/viewdoc/summary? doi=10.1.1.103.9803; Petrelli and Whittaker, "Family Memories in the Home"; David S. Kirk, Shahram Izadi, Abigail Sellen, Stuart Taylor, Richard Banks, and Otmar Hilliges, "Opening up the Family Archive," in *Proceedings of the 2010 ACM Conference on Computer Supported Cooperative Work* (Savannah, Georgia: ACM, 2010), 261–270.

68. Kirk and Sellen, *On Human Remains*, 1. See also Chapter 11, "Our Technology Heritage," by Richard Banks.

69. Michael Massimi and Andrea Charise, "Dying, Death, and Mortality: Towards Thanatosensitivity in HCI," in *Proceedings of the 27th of the International Conference Extended Abstracts on Human Factors in Computing Systems* (New York: ACM, 2009), 2464.

70. For examples, see David S. Kirk and Richard Banks, "On the Design of Technology Heirlooms," in *International Workshop on Social Interaction and Mundane Technologies* (Cambridge, U.K., 2008); William Odom, Richard Harper, Abigail Sellen, David Kirk, and Richard Banks, "Passing On & Putting To Rest: Understanding Bereavement in the Context of Interactive Technologies," in *Proceedings of ACM Conference on Human Factors in Computing Systems* (New

York: ACM, 2010), 1831–1840; Michael Massimi and William Odom, "HCI at the End of Life: Understanding Death, Dying, and the Digital," in *Proceedings of the 28th International Conference on Human Factors in Computing Systems* (New York: ACM, 2010), 4477–4480; Siân Lindley, "Passing on Memories in Later Life," in *CHI 2011 Workshop* (Vancouver, Canada, 2011); Michael Massimi and Ronald M Baecker, "Dealing with Death in Design: Developing Systems for the Bereaved," in *Proceedings of ACM Conference on Human Factors in Computing Systems* (New York: ACM, 2011), 1001–1010.

71. Evan Carroll and John Romano provide a list of the commercial digital services related to death in their website, "Digital Beyond," www.thedigitalbeyond.com/online-services-list. See also Chapter 4, "Software and Services for Personal Archiving," by Donald T. Hawkins.

72. Vannevar Bush, "As We May Think," *Atlantic Monthly* 176 (1945): sec. 6.

73. For example, see Czerwinski et al., "Digital Memories in an Era of Ubiquitous Computing and Abundant Storage"; Gordon Bell and Jim Gemmell, "A Digital Life," *Scientific American* 296, no. 3 (2007): 58–65; Abigail Sellen and Steve Whittaker, "Beyond Total Capture: A Constructive Critique of Lifelogging," *Communications of the ACM* 53, no. 5 (2010): 70–77.

74. See Gordon Bell and Jim Gemmell, *Total Recall: How the E-Memory Revolution Will Change Everything* (New York: Dutton, 2009); Gordon Bell and Jim Gemmell's Total Recall blog, totalrecallbook.com/blog.

75. Nancy Van House and Elizabeth F. Churchill, "Technologies of Memory: Key Issues and Critical Perspectives," 299.

76. Kieron O'Hara et al., "Memories for Life: A Review of the Science and Technology," *Journal of the Royal Society Interface* 3, no. 8 (June 2006): 351–365.

77. For example, van Dijck, *Mediated Memories in the Digital Age*; Sellen and Whittaker, "Beyond Total Capture: a Constructive Critique of Lifelogging," 70–77; Daniela Petrelli, Elise van den Hoven, and Steve Whittaker, "Making History: Intentional Capture of Future Memories," in *Proceedings of the 27th International Conference on Human Factors in Computing Systems* (New York: ACM, 2009), 1723–1732.

78. For example, see Viktor Mayer-Schönberger, *Delete: The Virtue of Forgetting in the Digital Age* (Princeton, NJ: Princeton University Press, 2009).

79. For example, Lee and Capra discuss how concepts, principles, and practices developed in Archives and Records Management and PIM can be relevant to each other. See Lee and Capra, "And Now the Twain Shall Meet: Exploring the Connections between PIM and Archives," 29–77.

80. McKemmish, "Evidence of Me … ," 29.

81. Williams, John, and Rowland, "The Personal Curation of Digital Objects," 343.

82. See Chapter 6, "Social Media, Personal Data, and the Fate of Our Digital Legacy," by Catherine C. Marshall as an example of her recent research.

83. Marshall, "How People Manage Information over a Lifetime," 61.

84. For example, see Amber L. Cushing, "Highlighting the Archives Perspective in the Personal Digital Archiving Discussion," *Library Hi Tech* 28, no. 2 (2010): 301–312.

85. For example, in 2012, participants presented a variety of topics such as ongoing software development projects, case studies, and work experiences in memory institutions, and results of scholarly research.

86. See Stan James's family photo scanning project websites, scanwithstan.com and archive.scanwithstan.com.

87. Jones and Teevan, "Introduction," 3–20.

CHAPTER 10

Active Personal Archiving and the Internet Archive

Aaron Ximm
Internet Archive

Author's note: This chapter extends and unifies comments on Internet Archive efforts in archiving generally and in active personal archiving presented by Brewster Kahle and Aaron Ximm at Personal Digital Archiving 2012, a 2-day conference organized and hosted by the Internet Archive on February 23–24, 2012, in San Francisco.

Active personal archiving is a research area at the Internet Archive, a nonprofit internet library and repository of digital cultural materials. In this chapter, after introducing the Archive and reviewing some of its better-known projects to illustrate the nature and scope of our familiarity with issues of data acquisition and retention, I review in some detail the Archive's mechanisms for ingesting, preserving, and sharing data arising from both analog and digital domains. Particularly close attention is given here to its existing work with personal archives, which leverage our core capacity as an archive of public collections and works.

Next, I discuss our interest in how existing capabilities might evolve to accommodate *active personal digital archiving*, which would evolve existing capabilities in both active and personal archiving.

At Internet Archive, we define *active archiving*, in this context, to mean archives or components of archives that autonomously collect themselves, on behalf of their owners. We define *personal archiving* to mean on behalf of, and (at least for some period) exclusively for, the use of an individual person or institution. Such archiving is in contrast with, but not necessarily at odds with, the Internet Archive's mission to make holdings as accessible as possible to contemporary and future users.

I conclude the chapter by considering the unique capabilities of institutions such as the Internet Archive to develop (and preserve) such collections and the unique role that institutions such as ours might play by virtue of their particularly altruistic set of stakeholders.

The Internet Archive: An Overview

The Internet Archive is a San Francisco-based 501(c)(3) nonprofit organization (Figure 10.1 shows its headquarters building). It was founded in 1996 as an internet library, with a mission to enable and provide "universal access to all knowledge" and offer permanent access for researchers, historians, scholars, people with disabilities, and the general public to historical collections that exist in digital format. In executing that mission, the Archive has evolved into a very high use, very large capacity, publicly accessible repository of digital cultural materials.

The Archive's website (www.archive.org) consistently ranks among the 250 most popular websites worldwide, in terms of both unique visitors and total traffic. Its servers average well over 2 million unique visitors each day, with average bandwidth in and out of data centers averaging at least 10 gigabits per second. At the time of this writing, the Archive maintains a collection of over 10 petabytes (10 million GB) of material in its collections, and its holdings are growing at a rate of approximately 1 petabyte a year. Usage and total storage requirements are both increasing faster than linearly.

While the majority of the Archive's collections are drawn from public materials that are published across many media, the Archive

Figure 10.1   Internet Archive headquarters in San Francisco

includes many collections and works constituting personal archives. We shall review our evolved experience with personal archiving to date.

The Archive's Heterogeneous Collections

Personal or public, the Archive's collections are heterogeneous in the sense that they include both digitally collected and digitized materials. Each category includes distinct subtypes as well, according to medium and provenance. Ingesting and providing access to each class of material has required development of different capabilities:

- *Digital materials* in the Archive include digitally created media objects (e.g., sound, film, video, and images), current and historic software and firmware, electronic documents of all kinds (e.g., ebooks, schematics, patents, census data, and personal documents), and, famously, web-crawl data on a vast scale.

- *Digitized materials* in the Archive include scanned physical books and microfilm, digitized analog media (e.g., film and video transfers, recordings of historic radio broadcasts, and vinyl records), and scanned or otherwise digitized curated personal documents from individual and institutional collections and contributing archives.

In its collections, both personal and public archives may comprise both digital and digitized materials, though often specific collections are limited to one subtype.

Active personal archiving, which I will discuss in the following section, represents a novel collection type distinct from or evolving out of the collections and related service types that exist today. Conventional personal archives, however, are readily ingested and shared, using practices developed and refined through working with public materials. Current Archive holdings contain both individual and institutional personal archives at all scales.

Given the relatively recent advent of digital materials generally, the majority of personal archive collections consist of *digitized* materials. We anticipate that as we partner with or obtain archives from contemporary and future sources, more and more material will come to the Archive already in digital form.

Core Capacities for Personal Archiving Derive From Existing Projects

The Archive's ability to collect, maintain, and disseminate both conventional and active personal archives is rooted in capabilities that the organization has developed in pursuit of myriad large-scale, long-term, public data collection and preservation projects. Most of the Archive's best-known projects have arisen as a result of ambitious (some might say, audacious) aims, such as "archiving the public web" or "preserving a digital copy of every book published in English."

As might be expected, moving toward goals on this scale has led to a habit of deconstructing problems into specific technical challenges generally formulated internally as, "how do we deal with X," where X can be as broad as a media type (e.g., public television, BitTorrent) or as specific as a narrow subtype (e.g., "how do we adapt our existing scanning infrastructure to ingest mounted newspaper clippings, oversized laboratory journals, etc. at scale?").

To provide a sense of the scope of the Archive's efforts and provide a context for discussion of the specifics to follow about how data enters, resides within, and is shared by the Archive, I examine several such projects and consider how they have been used in the service of collecting personal archives.

Web Archiving

The Archive is perhaps best-known for snapshots of the World Wide Web captured over time by web crawling shared through the Wayback Machine (www.archive.org, Figure 10.2). The Machine uniquely affords users the opportunity to browse the web backward through time, providing a reasonably representative, if admittedly incomplete, view of an otherwise vanished digital heritage. Individual documents that have been altered; sites that have been taken offline or lost through domain ownership changes, neglect, and lack of interest, retirement,

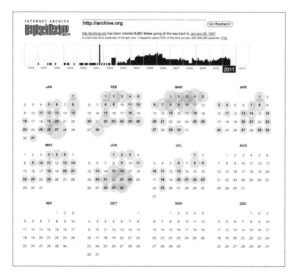

Figure 10.2   The Wayback Machine interface, showing captures of archive.org

and so on, of their originators; and in a growing number of cases, entire online communities' histories and documents are all preserved with static, canonical URLs. This web collection comprises more than two petabytes of data consisting over 150 billion webpages; it is growing by up to 50 terabytes (50,000GB) a week and billions of pages every year as a result of accelerating and perpetual crawl cycles.

The significance of the web archiving service to both current and future users is worth explicitly noting. Through the Machine, the fabric of the highly ephemeral World Wide Web itself has in a real sense been made into a medium of both reference and record, albeit with some key limitations (primarily because individual domain owners may request exclusion of their domains from our archives).

In the context of personal archiving, many contemporary lives are largely determined in relationship to online materials. Preserving those materials in the general web archive is thus an unprecedented exercise in maintaining the context in which private lives were lived. Entire subsets of crawl data (i.e., all of the data collected during particular crawl cycles) are now being made available for research purposes to the public.

As an aside, the question of how and whether the Archive can continue to play the same role in preserving a collective digital heritage as more and more online content moves behind paywalls, credential walls, and the like, and as more and more of it is composed programmatically and targeted personally, is an interesting one. The answer is certainly not yet known.

Television News

In 2012, the Archive launched the Television News Search and Borrow Service (archive.org/details/tv; Figure 10.3), through which approximately 350,000 television news programs captured from dozens of channels from 2001 to the present are now full-text searchable through closed caption transcripts and electronic program guide (EPG) metadata.

As the Wayback Machine did for the web, the Search and Borrow Service aims to accelerate the transition of news television into a citable

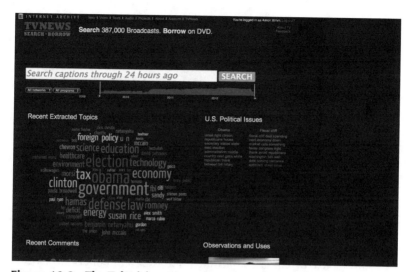

Figure 10.3   The Television News Search and Borrow Service

medium of record and research. It builds on the model of Vanderbilt University's Television News Archive (tvnews.vanderbilt.edu), extending beyond that service's search capabilities by enabling on-demand online access to very brief, but in-context, streaming excerpts from available programs. As with the Vanderbilt service, digital copies of full programs (and when possible, closed caption transcripts) are available to be borrowed on DVD under interlibrary loan terms, for a small fee.

The scale of digital media processing and serving required to enable the service is significant. That it is within the reach of a relatively small, if highly accomplished, technical staff should serve as inspiration for other institutions with similar missions or mandates to empower an informed citizenry.

As discussed in the following section, personal archives including or entirely consisting of moving images are well-represented in the Archive generally. The capacity to transclude (or link) material preserved from broadcast television in a manner analogous to that possible with webpages, however, represents a nascent but provocative new capability, especially should such inclusion ever become possible via active personal archiving techniques, which even in our prototyping have only extended to conventional digital presence.

Book Scanning and Lending

The Archive is increasingly known for its efforts to amass and make as widely accessible as possible an online lending library of an almost unprecedented scale, primarily through the collection, scanning, and preservation of physical books but also (as we can) through the acquisition of ebooks and other already digitized texts. As of 2013, the Archive has collected more than 2 million books (primarily in English, but in dozens of languages), comprising more than 150 million pages. Five hundred thousand of these, after scanning by the Archive, have been preserved in climate-controlled shipping containers in a dedicated facility, the "Physical Archive" (Figure 10.4), which is growing toward a current target of 1 million volumes in that facility.

These physical books provide the root copies necessary to enable one-at-a-time loans of digital copies and provide for restoration of the collection in the event of some catastrophic loss of digital data.

Scanning occurs in 20 scanning centers located in five countries, staffed by over 100 employees, partners, and volunteers. More than

Figure 10.4   Climate-controlled shipping containers at the Physical Archive

1,000 new books are added to the Archive's collections each day. Book collections include public domain works, orphaned works (those under copyright of some kind in at least some jurisdictions but which are no longer published or available within them), and contemporary or recent works for which rights are maintained by various parties. A primary mission of the Archive, and a primary driver of our book scanning efforts, is to provide access to all of our print materials to the print-disabled, a community championed under U.S. law in this regard.

A related secondary mission is to support online book lending. The Archive is recognized by the State of California as a library, and by virtue of that status, it provides residents of California (and citizens in other participating partnered jurisdictions, which now include many states) with access to the over 200,000 ebooks in our loanable collection. Works not already checked out may be borrowed from our collections for 2 weeks using the loan-management capabilities of Adobe Digital Editions. (Public domain works are available to the general public without restriction.)

The Archive's capability for ingesting print materials has readily (and regularly) facilitated our ability to absorb and preserve personal and institutional archives. Most such materials are personal documents, not printed publications, but the infrastructure and processing efficiency in place is a direct outgrowth of our focus on book scanning.

Community Collections

The Archive hosts user-uploaded collections and contributions on a large scale. User-uploaded collections include texts, images, video, audio, software, and more. One of the most well-known collections is the Live Music Archive (LMA, archive.org/details/etree), consisting of over 100,000 concert recordings contributed by authorized tapers and, in some cases, the musicians themselves. (Among the thousands of other artists, the LMA includes at least one recording of every known public Grateful Dead performance.)

While much highly curated user-uploaded content represents personal or institutional interests in preserving published materials of various kinds (for example, minutes or video from community meetings, online and conventional radio programs or podcasts, out-of-print technical manuals, and many other types), individuals also regularly contribute *ad hoc* personal archives. At present, without a mechanism for identifying such materials explicitly, Archive use for this purpose is fragmented and incoherent. As much as active personal archiving constitutes a research interest at the Archive, the related question of providing for personal archiving generally incorporates the question of how better to support users in managing disparate contributions that cross media boundaries and may require or deserve restricted access of some kind (at least originally).

The Data Lifecycle at the Internet Archive

The Archive's experience with intake and preservation of personal archives builds on the procedures and technology acquired to serve all our collections, for which, the story of the Archive is one of *bits in, bits out,* and *bits preserved.* The policies and capabilities for personal archives diverge from those of our public holdings in the bits in (acquisition) and bits out (dissemination) stages. Generally speaking, all data within our collections, personal and private, is maintained and protected using the same strategies.

Bits In

Bits in at the Archive means the mechanisms through which data enters our collections from both online and offline sources. The specifics for any given item in our holdings naturally depend on the form of the data at the time of its ingestion. Pre-20th century materials consist of pre-digital physical artifacts with demonstrated physical longevity, well-understood types of (often gradual) degradation, and few rights issues. While our collections include significant holdings of such material (particularly, scanned media), this domain is also well-addressed by countless other institutions, and its preservation is not a core focus of the Archive.

Twentieth-century materials, however, present several challenges, often simultaneously, for us as well as other archivists. They may exist only in dead, dying, or unstable digital media formats, and, from a rights perspective, they may be orphaned works. These qualities make their capture, preservation, and dissemination considerably more involved, resource-intensive, and, in many cases, constrained. Much of the Archive's effort today therefore focuses on collecting and preserving them, despite their unique challenges to archivists in terms of capture, presentation, and use/accessibility. Of specific interest in this context is that while contemporary archives may incorporate contemporary materials, most personal archives entering our collections consist primarily of 20th-century materials (both digital and digitized) and, to a small but increasing extent, personal web presence (e.g., blogs, personal websites and projects, and other online assets).

Contemporary (i.e., 21st century) materials, by comparison, largely consist of already-digital assets, for which rights issues are at least clearly defined or the subject of explicit scrutiny by the broader community. For these materials, preservation is less immediately urgent, provided for at least to some degree by its originators, or, often, taken on by conceptually allied organizations such as the Archive Team members, who specialize in rapid comprehensive distributed archiving of online communities and resources at risk of "going dark."

Conventional Digital Content

Existing digital files of all types may be contributed to the Archive through several straightforward means. At the Archive, we often characterize data of this type as coming from, or representative of, the "hard drive era."

Content on hard drives and other contemporary digital media may be received and ingested directly (for example, television news arrives from partners on high-capacity hard drives), but the vast majority of content comes into the Archive from the internet via well-established high-bandwidth interfaces. Principal among these, which also include a Flash (soon, HTML5) file uploader, and (antiquated) FTP, is an Amazon S3-like interface. This interface is our recommended mechanism for any ongoing or large-scale contribution.

The Archive's S3 (Simple Storage Service) implementation is closely modeled on, and indeed intended to be "bug compatible" with, the S3 API developed by Amazon. Like Amazon's cloud-storage service, the Archive's S3-like server interface provides a straightforward mechanism for contributing arbitrary numbers of files (or arbitrarily large size ones) using simply constructed HTTP PUT requests.

The system provides for data integrity with a clear permissions system that controls who can read what after upload and collections management settings that control who can write what and where. The Internet Archive S3-like (IAS3) interface is easy to script for and works with a variety of third-party tools (created for use with Amazon S3 and/or other compatible APIs) on many platforms. IAS3 has therefore become the standard mechanism through which the Archive ingests most external content. The interface currently takes in approximately 10 terabytes of user-uploaded content a day; it can ingest up to 10 files per second.

Archiving the Public World Wide Web

As many aspects of contemporary life are increasingly documented and lived online, preserving online presence is a core component of many contemporary personal archives. We consider archiving the public web a core mission (as reflected in our name). The Archive's well-known history and expertise in this area provide a proven mechanism for capturing this online presence, although personalization and customization of both the capture and subsequent presentation of online materials (e.g., through scoping of crawls and limitations in browsing and access) is an open-ended and growing challenge.

Generally, website archives are collected primarily through a distributed web-crawling infrastructure based on the Heritrix web crawler (webarchive.jira.com/wiki/display/Heritrix/Heritrix) and served through the Archive's Wayback Machine (github.com/internet archive/wayback). These tools come from open source projects originated at the Archive.

Crawls retrieve public web assets through HTTP (and to a minimal degree, FTP) and archive them in open Web Archive formats such as Web Archive (WARC). Web data is collected through crawls of various kinds. Most data in our collections is public, not private; it comes from broad shallow crawls of as many domains as possible and from perpetually crawling the web over several-month cycles, or narrowly focused crawls of specific domains meeting specific criteria (e.g., news sites and popular websites). A large amount of crawling, however, is undertaken in the service of amassing personal or institutional archives (e.g., contract crawls undertaken for, or with, partner organizations on all scales). Crawl rates vary but can exceed 50 terabytes a week.

Web archive contributions originating outside the Archive are also increasing. The Archive has always received data contributions from Alexa Internet, and we are currently beginning to accept data from outside archivists who have engaged in systematic preservation of online communities and services that "go dark" for various reasons. As long as crawl data is appropriately packaged in the WARC format, it can be ingested and presented through the Wayback Machine interface.

A promising area of potential contribution to the Archive web collections is the capacity currently being developed to allow direct, instantaneous archiving (into the Archive) of materials published online using popular tools such as WordPress, through tight integration with our public APIs. Such collections would serve as an interesting hybrid of personal and public archive, preserved at personal request but (most likely) entering the pool of publicly accessible web archives. Similarly, the Archive is interested in expanding the extent to which it serves as a mirror for resources such as Wikimedia, Project Gutenberg, and similar open or public community resources to leverage our bandwidth and storage capacities in support of them, and to provide a permanent archive of those resources.

Scanning Physical Materials

Book and microfilm scanning is the primary example of the conversion of analog and physical cultural objects into digital assets, such as can be preserved and disseminated by the Archive. Internally, we consider data of this type broadly as coming from the "analog era."

The majority of the printed matter that enters the Archive collections is scanned at our own and partner scan centers, using the Scribe book scanner digitization stations (Figure 10.5) that were developed for Archive use.

The Scribe uses open-source software and consumer components including high-end digital cameras (currently the Canon EOS 5D Mark II DSLR) and LED digital lighting arrays, which provide constant illumination with a known color temperature and intensity to capture printed materials through a known and consistent high-quality mechanism. Experienced operators can scan over 800 pages of books an hour (with a goal of accelerating to 1,000 pages an hour consistently);

Figure 10.5   Scribe book scanner at the Internet Archive scanning center (Courtesy of Jason Scott)

speeds for other printed material such as newspaper clippings are considerably slower.

Once available as raw images, scanned data is processed in a variety of ways to rapidly produce ebook assets that can be read online, downloaded, or borrowed, as appropriate. Optical character recognition (OCR) is used to process texts in roman characters, enabling full-text search. When working with conventionally published materials (e.g., books, magazines, and journals), a significant portion of the Archive's efforts to enhance scan-center throughput is focused on rapidly identifying whether or not a given text is already present, or in process, within our extensive holdings.

Personal archival materials such as newspaper clippings, notebooks, artworks, and so on are also subject to scanning using specialized Scribes and as-needed per-project techniques. Figure 10.6 shows an example of one such collection.

Given current efficiencies and requirements, we estimate that non-book printed personal archives can be ingested by the Archive at an average cost of approximately $500 for one conventional box or tub of

Figure 10.6   Scanned print materials in the personal archive of Dr. Timothy Leary on the Internet Archive

materials. We predict that the price for ingesting such materials would drop considerably on a significantly increased scale.

Scanning of non-print-based analog materials also takes place at various scales. For example, scanning stations with similar capabilities for digitizing microfilm are also used in scan centers. Audio CDs, laserdiscs, and vinyl LPs are also ingestible through conventional digitization; and in the past year, the Archive has added the capabilities to rapidly scan 8 and 16 mm film at very high quality and ingest analog videotapes in various formats in parallel.

Rick Prelinger of the Prelinger Archives (archive.org/details/prelinger), whose popular collections are hosted on the Archive, estimates that while commercial video and film scanning has typically cost $200–300 an hour, current efforts at the Archive to develop capacity may make $20 an hour a reasonable target cost for ingestion. Under his direction, a pool of volunteers are currently being trained in film archiving practices to allow full-time scanning of VHS and film collections into the Archive. Much of the material in the Prelinger collections comes from personal home movies.

The Archive is interested in, but has not yet begun, efforts to scan three-dimensional artifacts.

Bits Preserved

The Archive considers future users as well as current ones as part of the communities it is mandated to serve in its mission to provide universal access to all knowledge. It is assumed that part of the organization's charge is to preserve its holdings in perpetuity, through the "Long Now"—the 10,000-year timeline for our civilization proposed by the Long Now Foundation (www.longnow.org)—as a metric for true sustainability.

Planning for the worst, if hoping for the best, with this mandate in mind has driven many architectural and policy decisions at the Archive, such as the on-disk representation of holdings and how to enable the distributed preservation of our collections. The overarching goal is that items in our collections are individually recoverable (e.g., from single hard drives), even should the rest of the collection be lost. Toward these ends, we eschew RAID and databases, and embrace simple file hierarchies, open and human-readable metadata formats, and co-locate primary (original) content, adherent metadata, and derived secondary formats in the same logical location. This is true for personal archives as well as for our public holdings.

Most data at the Archive is redundantly stored in at least two physical locations, supported by internal tools that maintain synchronization between copies and perform data integrity checks. Although we use off-the-shelf components and have pioneered techniques and designs for achieving high data density, high reliability, low power consumption and waste heat generation, and a long working life using consumer-grade server and network components, a primary expense for the Archive is the simple physical infrastructure required to maintain "hot" data for the long term. Physical components of our rack systems are regularly replaced, with many drive replacements required every week given the extent of our holdings.

As a result of the infrastructural overhead required to make holdings available on demand 24/7, we estimate that our current cost to preserve 1 terabyte of data in perpetuity to be approximately $2,000, which is on the order of 40 times the street price for a single 1 terabyte drive. While significant, this cost is considerably below commercial alternatives. The preservation of extensive personal archives at this price point, however, often is supported by institutions or partnerships.

Bits Out

Access Concerns

The Archive's mission to provide universal access to all knowledge necessarily entails that any shareable item in our collection is shared. How and when to restrict access to personal archives presents an interesting, and admittedly still unanswered, policy and philosophical question for the Archive. Generally speaking, we accept contributed materials provided that the contributor avers that the materials are in the public domain or under a Creative Commons license, or, when appropriate, the contributor releases the materials into the public domain or assigns such a license.

Some collections allow for nuanced or mediated access, however. One example is web-crawl data contributed by, or collected on behalf of, partner organizations that request various embargoes before their data is available to the general public. A different kind of nuanced access is that some recordings within the LMA are made available as streaming media only and not for download. Finally, some collections may be accessible only to users with specific privileges by virtue of ownership of those collections or (much more commonly) by virtue of being a member of a specific class of users. The chief examples of this type of restricted access are scanned books and related materials made available in the DAISY format (www.daisy.org) to the print-disabled community.

Access Challenges for Various Collections

As just described, the Archive's heterogeneous collections comprise a wide variety of digitized and digital materials. Some of these materials (e.g., those that originated in the digital domain as well-encapsulated documents in living formats, such as images, common audio and video formats, and many common text formats) may be accessed directly via browsing. Others, however, present disparate access challenges:

- Uncompressed or antiquated media objects may require conversion into derivative formats to enhance access. For example, FLAC (Free Lossless Audio Codec) audio recordings are automatically made available not only in the original FLAC format but in MP3 and Ogg audio formats as well.

- Web-crawl data stored in archival formats such as ARC and WARC may to some extent technically be human-readable, but in practice, website captures are meaningful in human terms primarily when rendered through the Wayback Machine using a variety of heuristics. Ever-increasing usage of sophisticated JavaScript and other scripting and dynamic web components relying on server-side data present a significant challenge for making web captures meaningfully available via the Wayback Machine.

- Scanned physical materials, such as books, require "players" of some kind to be cognizant of their internal structures. Our scanned books for example provide a very good user experience through our own online book reader but may not provide the best possible experience or even be viewable at all on hardware ebook readers such as the Amazon Kindle or Barnes & Noble NOOK, which may require proprietary hypertext formats, DRM and/or distribution via closed private ecosystems, or support only for text-based formats.

One concern that may become ever more pressing for the Archive is to what extent it is possible and advisable to provide playback and browsing mechanisms to provide access to digital material with a high degree of internal structure and/or complexity.

One example is the challenge posed by sophisticated websites with well-developed ontologies and specific (but evolving) user interface philosophies such as Facebook, whose current Timeline is essentially impossible to reproduce without re-coding its own interface. Such problems arise even with much simpler forums, which are only mean-ingfully browsable by an interface that understands the intrinsic nature of thread-based discussions. Another example is media with specific idiosyncratic formats, such as DVD video, in which the on-disk file structure must be understood to render on-screen menus, switch between various audio and subtitle tracks, and so on.

Innovative work has enabled interesting advances in this area; for example, the Archive's capability to render CD-ROM ISO file and Zip file contents directly browsable (and canonically linkable); and the JavaScript MESS project, an effort to port the MAME and MESS emu-lators to JavaScript and thereby allow any contemporary webbrowser to fully emulate a large number of classic computing environments.

Active Personal Archiving

Having described the Archive's mission and, at a high level, some of its capabilities and challenges in fulfilling that mission with respect to personal archives of a conventional sort, I now describe active personal archiving—an area of ongoing research.

Active Personal Archiving Defined

Active personal archiving is simply the automated collection by an archive of its own contents on behalf of a specific individual human or institution by simple software agents. This agency is understood for the purposes of our current research to be specifically constrained to the capture and preservation of the digital self.

Capturing the digital self is understood to require, at a minimum, the retrieval of personal documents and traces from explicitly engaged online services, such as email, social media, media sharing, and file sharing services; preservation of known and discovered web materials, such as blogs or personal websites; and preservation of other forms of digital presence, such as discovery and archiving of a secondary, semi-anonymous, or anonymous (but indicated) online presence in specific forums. Popularly, this presence is often described as (and hence conceived of) as existing "in the cloud," but at the Archive, we try instead to internally describe this data as hosted by "commercial services"—institutions that may be as ephemeral as clouds and whose intentions may be as hard to define, contain, or accurately describe as one.

Although many materials in the Archive have traditionally been ingested as a result of specific one-time curatorial decisions or specific types of heuristic discovery (e.g., link discovery during web crawls and attendant scoping rules), active personal digital archiving obviously requires a wide portfolio of strategies undertaken in parallel on a recurring basis. Some of the specific mechanisms in that portfolio, such as those based on web crawling, are existing and well-understood capabilities at the Archive; others, however, are more experimental or nascent.

At its boundaries, active personal archiving touches on notions of agents using heuristics to identify unknown digital traces through inspection of regular search results, use of social profiling tools such as Klout (www.klout.com), clipping services, and perhaps carefully scoped web crawls.

As traditional media such as television become increasingly subject to digital inspection and capture via closed caption data, they too may be subject to capture and encapsulation in a personal archiving context. The Television News Research and Borrow Service described earlier already permits post-facto research if topics cluster in a nuanced way. It is easy to imagine monitoring content as it is added for inclusion, or rather transclusion, in specific personal archives.

Today, however, most retrieval is performed in a mechanistic fashion under predetermined constraints, using explicitly provided credentials for third-party services with well-defined APIs. Providing for flexible and nimble tools to engage those services and use those APIs is still the subject of research. We anticipate that the various cloud-based service providers will continue to rapidly evolve their own APIs, access models and requirements, application and end-user agreements pertaining to data retrieval, subsequent preservation and presentation, and so on.

Additionally, the set of services, which at any given moment seem to collectively define most aspects of online presence, will of course continue to itself mutate. The path to coherent digital personhood is littered with a thousand profiles (on AOL, Tribe, Friendster, Myspace, Google+, MobileMe, etc.). All of these mechanisms constitute the "bits in" side to the personal aspect of active personal archiving. Collection of personalized data is essentially uncharted territory for the Archive; our purview and specialty in retrieval of online (as opposed to offline) assets has almost entirely been in wholesale data ingestion via web crawling at scale. Even in the web-crawling domain, focused and targeted crawls are currently scoped in terms of domain, not in terms of subject areas of interest.

The bits out side presents at least as many challenges, particularly when it comes to the access model applied. The personal is also usually often (at least, from the general public's perspective, in terms of access) private. Generally speaking, when we collect a given medium (e.g., the web, books, and television broadcasts), we do so using the "front door"—we do not crawl behind paywalls, archive subscription services, and so on. Furthermore, most of our existing collection efforts take place (when the distinction is relevant) anonymously. If possible, we do not maintain an identity, preferring to capture archetypal, generic, or default (rather than targeted, tailored, and personalized) versions of content. Yet an individual's digital presence is inherently almost entirely personal. Developing our capacity in this area would require not only new tools but likely refinements or enhancements to existing ones, such as the Heritrix web crawler. If and when the broadcast media we archive also become individually tailored, the same issues will apply.

Retrieval, playback, or re-animation of even well-gathered content will also be increasingly difficult. As described, current mechanisms for retrieving such data are, alas, not sufficient to provide for an entirely reliable or useful living copy of it. For example, a retrieved copy of one's own Facebook stream does not provide more than a transcript. It does not replicate the venue or even capture all the nuances of the relationships implied by various data structures.

In sum, then, we have an unsolved bits-out problem with regard to active personal archiving. This is true not just for us, but for anyone who wishes to provide nuanced or deep access to materials liberated from various highly evolved closed sources. And yet, it is still much better to have a static liberated copy than nothing in the locker, especially in an era in which online communities can "go dark" with little (or in some cases no) warning, and years of collective and personal history vanish without recourse. Nevertheless, hard questions will remain around access to personal archiving, who is permitted to access materials, and when.

The Case for Active Personal Archiving

To an ever-increasing extent, personal identity is effectively interchangeable with a digital (mostly online) presence. Yet, a digital presence is increasingly stored in that curiously nebulous thing: the cloud.

On the surface, the cloud is convenient shorthand for a myriad of web service providers. But under scrutiny, it is a collection of sometimes mercurial—if not mendacious—and truly fallible institutions, many for-profit and many whose motivations are at best obscure and at worst genuinely a cause for reasonable concern.

We does not need to engage in paranoia or be a Luddite to recognize that our online presence is distributed among players whose commitment (and ability) to preserve their fraction of our digital selves is undemonstrated or demonstrably absent. We believe therefore that until online identity is maintained in better trust and in the hands of institutions with more angelic motivations with an ability and commitment to long-term preservation, a mechanism is needed to ensure that personal data and traces are preserved, independent of the fates or decisions of specific institutions.

It is worth noting that it is not simply "gray-hat" institutions that pose a challenge to maintenance or preservation of a coherent or comprehensive online presence and history. Our own institutional genesis at the Archive, after all, was the experience of the World Wide Web as an ephemeral resource and the recognition of a need to preserve what we could while we could (hence our name).

The mechanism needed to preserve our personal data, under our own care, and in perpetuity, so long as we see fit seems to be active personal archiving: the intentional, continual, wholesale extraction of an up-to-date archive of personal data (that is, a record of one's digital shadow) from the services on which the originals (temporarily) reside.

The Unique Role of Institutions Such as the Internet Archive

Active personal archiving, under other names and to varying degrees, has of course already been undertaken by a variety of interested players. Tools are available to liberate one's data from various hosting services, and many of these services now provide reasonable mechanisms for exporting personal data. But even with those tools, we would argue that the Archive serves as a superior model for an active personal archiving service, for both technical and philosophical reasons. It is to make this case that I have spent considerable space here reviewing some of our projects, statistics, and accomplishments to date.

Technically and specifically speaking, the Archive has already developed the specific capabilities required to capture data from some sources, in some cases, uniquely. In some areas, such as web crawling and book scanning, it has pioneered or has emerged as a consistent thought leader. Moreover, the Archive is now almost synonymous with large-scale, scalable, high-bandwidth, high-usage services. Indeed, efforts are focused now on unifying the computational and storage infrastructure of the Archive for all of our services and projects, with the explicit intention of allowing rapid minting of new virtual servers on newly deployed "cookie-cutter" physical racks, so as to provide additional capability for any of our service offerings on demand.

Although we have defined active personal archiving in terms of capturing digital presence, it is worth noting that the Archive is uniquely capable, through its facilities for digitization of physical materials and ingesting arbitrary pre-existing digital assets, of capturing and preserving a distinctly more three dimensional (if still ultimately virtual) version of the digital self. Less unique, perhaps, but a prerequisite for any such service, is the Archive's proven strategy for indefinite data retention.

It is not technical prowess *per se* that is the most important argument for participation of the Archive or a comparable institution in some version of active personal archiving; instead, it is the fact that the Archive is a nonprofit institution with a commitment to a fundamentally different set of stakeholders than most other organizations. The overtly communitarian and humanitarian mission of the Archive and its extensive track record in defending online civil liberty ensure that there is no possibility that data in the collections will be subject to misuse.

More subtly, nonprofit organizations are uniquely suited to planning and managing for the long-term. As mentioned, at the Archive, the mandate to provide for universal access is understood to require a commitment to, and service to, not just our own generation of users but those to come, as close to the ideal of "in perpetuity" as possible.

Indeed, to these ends, the Archive is actively investigating strategies for distributed redundant preservation of our collections.

These observations are made not to argue that the Archive should, or shall, pursue an active personal archiving capability. Rather, they are made to argue that whichever institution does (inevitably, we hope) offer such a service, it should be similarly constituted and serve a similar constituency. Thus, it should be a high-tech nonprofit organization motivated by service to its current users and those to come.

Active Personal Archiving and the Internet Archive Itself

Given that the Archive has the capacity to provide for active personal archiving and is in a unique position as a high-tech nonprofit to do so with appropriate motivation, should it? A fully functional proof-of-concept infrastructure for active personal archiving was constructed and deployed by the Archive early in 2012. It collected and kept current private personal content from Facebook, Twitter, and Flickr, using their various APIs, and it also crawled personal websites of interest via targeted web crawling.

There is undeniably a near-term tension between the role the Archive could play by evolving this infrastructure into a full-fledged active personal archiving service, and the traditional interpretation of our mandate to provide for universal access to our collections, but we have never offered personalized storage lockers. Considering the issue closely, one analysis of that tension could be construed in terms of the conceptual axes implicit in the taxonomy of collections within the Archive, *stasis* and *access*. Briefly, an item's position along the *axis of stasis* defines the degree to which the item is static, or, alternately, mutable. Differences along this axis imply a difference in the techniques or technologies necessary to ingest materials. That is, it is a *bits in* distinction.

An item's position along the *axis of access* defines the degree to which the item is accessible, or, alternately, restricted. Differences along this axis are, explicitly, *bits out* distinctions.

Traditionally, the Archive has primarily collected generally accessible materials that are both static (e.g., most user-contributed materials and digitized artifacts such as books) and mutable (e.g., websites collected by crawling). Items in the first category are for the most part ingested once. Those in the second category are in many cases, by definition, only current if they are regularly revisited.

In contrast to these archived websites, we contend that, historically speaking, personal archives have resided primarily in the opposite quadrant, as private or perpetually access-restricted collections of mostly static (e.g., posthumous) materials. Active personal archiving occupies the remaining quadrant: access-restricted materials that are highly mutable. We find it interesting that this is not actually unprecedented or unfamiliar conceptual territory for the Archive.

Our service offerings include both contracted web crawls of various sizes (including the very, very large) and user-managed web crawling via the Archive-It subscription service. In both of these offerings, mutable materials, in this case web data, are commonly collected on a recurring basis and made available (initially) only to the contracting partner. Such services provide a model whereby data might be embargoed in exchange for a subscription to offset operational costs.

As described, we currently estimate the cost to archive 1 terabyte of data in perpetuity at about $2,000. This may be prohibitively expensive for most individuals or institutions, but there may be ways to offset this cost or underwrite it, which are not yet defined. Alternatively, one might construe such an offering as isomorphic to existing access-restricted collections, such as the restriction of some textual material to the print-disabled community. In the case of personal archives, the community with access might simply be narrowed further, to a single user.

Conclusion

On the one hand, I hope I have made a case for the need for active personal archiving, as an antidote to, or at least a hedge against, the untenable reliance on for-profit institutions and ephemeral web presence; and on the other, I hope I have made a case for the need for such a service to be predicated on a comprehensive set of capabilities, and commitments, such as are demonstrated by the Internet Archive. For now, active personal archiving remains a research area at the Archive, not a service offering. It is not clear that it is within our mission to provide this service ourselves. It certainly should be, or should become, someone's mission. Too much is at stake, both individually and collectively.

Our original motivation to attempt to preserve what we could of the web was predicated on, and fired by, the observation that our culture, and by extension our cultural identity, was being defined on a fabric that was not (then) being preserved. Our current observation is that our online identities, which is increasingly to say, our identities, and by extension our collective culture, are again being written on a fabric that is not being preserved.

We have a well-defined problem and an obvious solution. All that remains is the implementation.

CHAPTER 11

Our Technology Heritage

Richard Banks
Microsoft Research, Cambridge, U.K.

When my grandfather passed away in 2005, he left behind a lot of physical things, in addition to his home, but no digital artifacts. It was not that he was averse to technology. He was born in the early 20th century and had had a career as a pilot in the Royal Air Force and subsequently as a test pilot, which exposed him to what would have been the state of the art in aerodynamics and engineering. He was not averse to tinkering with technology at home, either. I remember making an old radio receiver with him in his shed, twisting wire around a solid carbon rod, and assembling a few other components, including a small earpiece, to listen in to radio broadcasts. So although he had embraced the technology of his day, by the time he was elderly, he was not willing to be swept away by the tide of "digitalness" on which we have been cast adrift over the last 2 decades.

My father did have more of a digital life, which seems natural since he came from the generation that followed my grandfather's, and from which personal computing emerged. He had had a career as an aviation engineer, again exposed to bleeding-edge technology, and had tinkered with electronic components as they had started to be miniaturized and as high-end stereo systems became popular in the 1970s. I remember seeing boxes full of capacitors and resistors at home

215

when I was little. When he passed away in 2010, he had started to live some aspects of the digital life we take for granted today. He had a cellphone and a digital camera, and he left a laptop and a PC behind in his quiet little cottage in Yorkshire. His PC was a classic no-name beige brick, beaten up and surrounded by his trademark cigarette ash, and as such had very little sentimental value to me.

I am interested in considering the gradual shift of our lives from physical to digital and the increasing role of technology as part of legacy. My life now is consumed by digital experiences. I spend a good deal of my day online. So, considering this trajectory—from my grandfather's digital-free existence through to my father's mild use of the internet and through to a life like mine—it seems worthwhile. In addition, I am interested in understanding what role technology can play as a tool for reflecting on the past. How might I use technology, for example, to represent, and perhaps get a better sense of, my grandfather's life?

Visiting Digital Places

When I inherited my father's PC, I was less interested in the external, physical object than the content of its hard drive. I assumed it would contain personal information that I should sort through, much as I had sorted through his paperwork as executor of his estate. In addition to pragmatic data, it might also contain sentimental content, photos he had taken, for example, that I might like to keep.

I removed the hard drive from its cradle (Figure 11.1) and discarded the battered old beige box it had been in. I had imagined I could just plug the drive into my PC at home and view it as if it was an addition to my existing system; that way I could look through it for things that might seem important. After a discussion with a colleague at work, though, we came up with a different way for me to see the drive's content. He offered to create a virtual PC from it, so that rather than just seeing the files and folders that it contained, I could launch the whole operating system. My colleague borrowed the drive and a few days later gave me back a single, large digital file, which I copied to the desktop of my own laptop. When I double-clicked on it, the welcome screen of my father's version of the Windows operating system appeared. This was identical in every way to the one he had run on his own physical computer. I was looking at his desktop and icons just as he would have seen them (Figures 11.2 and 11.3). Suddenly, the contents of this lit-tle digital world were available to me, accessible through an icon sitting on my own machine.

Although I was running the most recent version of the Windows operating system, my father had not upgraded his machine for quite a while, if at all. He was still running Microsoft Windows Millennium Edition, released in 2000. In this sense, to me, the outside of his PC— the old and battered beige box—resembled the inside: a low-resolution desktop of primitive icons and beveled panes.

I had expected to simply start looking through the folders of items on my father's PC, trying to pick out items that I might care about or needed to deal with as part of his estate. Instead, though, I was struck by the sense that I was an interloper, that what I had entered was actu-ally quite a personal world. This was not a world for the uninvited and

Figure 11.1   My father's hard drive

Figure 11.2   The welcome screen for the virtual PC of my father's version of Windows

Figure 11.3   The desktop of my father's PC

unexpected guest. He had not anticipated that a visitor like me would ever appear in it and had not put any effort into arranging and organizing the content of his PC in a way that might make sense to a visitor. It was cluttered and felt disorganized to me.

Although we keep certain areas of our homes private, friends and family who come to see us have access to many of the more public spaces. We have an awareness of this that can influence the choices we make about what they should or should not see. That's not to say our homes are pristine or that we might not sometimes be embarrassed by visible clutter (despite its being a normal part of the loose organization of most homes) when we have visitors. This space of my father's that I was visiting, a digital environment in which he had spent time, did not operate under the same rules. He would have never expected visitors to drop by, so he never prepared for them.

The limited amount of physical space we have in our homes also encourages us to make decisions about what we keep and do not keep (Kirk and Sellen 2010). We have to choose between the things we throw away and the things we cannot bring ourselves to part with, because we only have so many places to put things on display or space to store them out of sight. The capacity of a modern hard drive, by contrast, as a digital container for our digital things, far outstrips our ability to fill it. We do not feel the same pressure to organize our digital lives as we might with our physical environment because we do not run out of space as often. And if we do, we simply buy more.

What I was looking at then, in the virtual version of my father's PC, was the content of his digital life "in the raw." In its cluttered state, it seemed unlikely that I would be able to make any sense of what mattered to him and what did not, or what he might have wanted to preserve or would have discarded if he had known that I would one day visit. It was not the clutter that bothered me so much, though. His digital desktop felt as badly organized as most of the rest of his physical environment. It was more the sense that I might simply stumble across some piece of content that, had it been physical, he may have been careful to discard. Since deleting things in the digital realm takes effort and is not actively encouraged, I was worried that I might come across content that was unexpected, embarrassing, or even shocking, and that I was never intended to see. I feared that seeing these items might undermine the way in which I chose to remember him and change my relationship with him even after his passing.

So I have left well enough alone. The icon for his virtual PC still sits on my desktop, and I have only gone as far as seeing his own desktop. I have avoided delving deeper out of respect for him and fear of what I might find.

Physical vs. Digital

The lesson for me from my father's virtual PC is that digital artifacts and digital spaces do not operate under the same rules as physical things and places. While physical things require effort and need caretaking, we create many digital artifacts with little effort, as a by-product of what we do day-to-day, with no pressure to filter or organize. This contrast between our behavior toward, and our treatment of, physical and digital things redefines our relationship to them. Things we once thought of as solid and tangible become virtual and disembodied instead.

We are in the middle of this process of digitization, as our documents, letters, CDs and DVDs shift from atoms to bits. These virtual versions of things we could formerly hold and touch are not simply proxies for their physical equivalent, though. They come with new properties and enable new activities. They also have an impact on the way in which we formulate and craft our personal legacies, since we have to think in new ways about how they will be inherited and what they will say about us.

Issues of legacy and memory continue to matter to people. We can see this both in an anticipatory way—in the effort that people are putting into recording and marking their life through tweets, status updates, and check-ins—as well as through the sense of anxiety that comes through in the potential loss of digital data and the growth in services such as LegacyLocker.com, which allow people to set up systems for archiving and bequeathing digital things.

While the properties and affordances of these digital things are quite different to physical items, our motivations for caring about them are not. The arrangement of objects in the home, for example, can be seen as a form of personal expression in which the things we put on display both set us apart from others and show us what we have in common. We display photos of our children, for example, that both say "our kids are great and unique" and "I am part of a family, just like you." Our artifacts have always played a role in meeting the seemingly contradictory human need to show others how we are different from them while at the same time showing how we are the same (Csikszentmihalyi and Rochberg-Halton 1981). The digital things we share with others are no different. We want them to meet this need, too. We make choices about what we share, and through those choices, we express our individuality while also connecting ourselves more closely with others with whom we share something in common. While the material of our artifacts is changing, from atoms to bits, human values like these, which drive our care for them, are not.

So people still care about their legacy, but their new objects of legacy do not have the same properties as the old ones, as they are now digital and not physical. While our needs and values may be the same, new attributes for these digital objects may mean that they are expressed in different ways (Odom, Banks, and Kirk 2010). Following are a few examples of how digital and physical things differ.

Physical Things

Each physical item we own comes to be unique. While we can often tell apart objects that are handmade or that have been somehow crafted into being from the outset, a sense of uniqueness emerges even for the most mass-produced objects.

We might purchase a mobile phone, which rolled off the assembly line with millions of other seemingly identical copies. As we start to use it, it becomes even more "ours." The surface of objects like these can start to change, or be changed, as we use them in ways that are additive or reductive. As they *age*, they start to develop a natural patina that shows signs of use. This change in the surface of the object may come about simply through the way we interact with it, as material is removed. A bright, polished spot might appear on an item showing where we have handled it the most, or more significant dings and scrapes might start to show up as it is knocked and dropped.

We might start personalizing the object, too, if we feel a particular affinity toward it, *adding* new layers to its skin that associate the item more closely to us. We might put our name on an object using permanent ink, afix stickers to it showing our support for a favorite band, or envelop the item in a new, carefully selected protective cover. These additive and reductive changes in the skin of an object tell their own story of personal use.

Physical things *take up space*, of course, and, as we described earlier, that fact can encourage us to make decisions about where each belongs, even if that means they no longer belong with us and have to be discarded. The use of space can reflect something about an object's meaning in our lives. Arranging items in a public space in our home, putting things on display, raises some items above others.

Physical things *play on our senses*, too, in ways that the digital cannot. Although there has been a recent growth in technological interfaces that rely on touch and gesture, such as those found on digital tablets and phones or devices like Microsoft's Kinect (Figure 11.4) that allow for whole-body interaction with games, these still pale in comparison to the range of senses that physical objects can address. We can see and feel the minute details in the rough surface of an old book; we can smell its aged pages and listen to the comfortable sounds it makes when we snap it shut; and we can taste the air that surrounds it.

Digital Things

Digital things are full of contrasts to the physical. Many digital attributes can feel cheap in comparison, but they are powerful when taken outside the context of physical things. Digital things can be infinitely

Figure 11.4   Microsoft's Kinect

duplicated, for example. Each copy is, to all intents and purposes, identical to the original. The capacity to instantly duplicate a digital photo seems to cheapen it somehow. Physical photos often seem more meaningful or precious. Yet, I can take a digital photo, make a copy of it, and put it somewhere safe, knowing that it will be preserved in the event of some accident or catastrophe, knowing that the digital copy will be indistinguishable from the original, and knowing that it will be basically the same. Suddenly, loss becomes less of an issue, and permanent preservation seems possible.

Duplication is an amazing attribute when it comes to legacy. Rather than making agonizing choices about which family member should get a particular object as part of a bequest, for example, duplication makes it possible to *share* a copy with every family member, which they can keep as their own. There's no antagonism over ownership or decision about where an object should physically "live." It can live in many places, each of which is equivalent.

Digital things can have *properties* that allow them to carry some of their story with them. When digital photos are taken, for example, they can have data stored in them that gives context to the shot. A typical digital camera stores information about the time the shutter was opened in the picture itself. Some cameras, which are GPS enabled, can even find out the coordinates of where the shot was taken and embed that in the photo. When the photo is shared with others, those details go with it. While an issue with organizing old physical photos is in figuring out when and where they were taken, digital photos have some of the details we need and can therefore self-organize chronologically, helping reveal a progression of moments or events to us automatically.

These embedded properties allow a digital item to be *connected* with other items. A digital song, for example, has the details of the recording artist and the album on which it was featured embedded in it. It is therefore related with other songs automatically. It becomes part of an album, or part of the discography of an artist, almost by default.

The idea of the interconnectedness of digital things is extended when I put them online. There, new properties and relationships are added, binding an item with others. When I post a photo to Facebook, for example, it can be connected with others automatically through time because of the date tag embedded in the file. Manual connections can be created, too. I can tag a photo with a friend's name if he or she is featured in it, and suddenly it becomes part of their profile, too. Each of these connections adds a new level of detail to the image and binds it with specific people, places, and events.

So digital items have the potential to deeply enrich our relationship with the past because these interconnections are a very powerful way of understanding the context and stories of the person with whom they are associated. While physical things can end up orphaned in terms of their meaning, the details of them lost as friends and family pass away, digital things can carry archaeological detail with them that has the potential to tell others about their history and ours.

While this list of properties for physical and digital objects is in no way exhaustive, hopefully you have some sense that both have value (for a longer discussion, see Banks 2011). In the next section, I will describe a number of working prototypes that we have made in our research lab in Cambridge, U.K., that were created to explore the relationship between some of the physical and digital attributes described (Odom et al. 2012).

Exploring Legacy Through Designed Objects

This section describes four different devices—Shoebox, Timecard, Digital Slide Viewer, and Backup Box—that have both a physical and digital component. They are designed with the home in mind, as objects that might bridge personal and digital spaces. Our hope in designing them is that people will put them on display and that value would be seen in both their physical form and digital content.

Shoebox

I described earlier how we make decisions about whether to hide physical objects away or put them on display in our homes. Often, things are put on display as a reminder to us of some event in our life or to act as a point of interest for visitors. Digital content, by contrast, cannot be made available to us in our homes in quite the same way. The technology makes it hard to expose digital things in our environment. While printed images, for example, can easily be framed and hung, casually propped up on the mantelpiece, or displayed in the kitchen on a family fridge using magnets, digital images lack these simple properties. Instead, they tend to stay hidden away on PCs and laptops. Even when they are shared online, the primary point of access for them is through a web browser. They become public online but not public at home.

Shoebox (Figure 11.5) was created to explore whether this lack of presence of digital objects in the home is necessary. It is designed to act much like the hard drive on a laptop, onto which we might download our digital photos by default, except it is a drive that has a screen built

Figure 11.5   Shoebox

into it and is housed in an attractive wooden box. It is designed to be put on display—perhaps placed on a bookshelf—so that when photos are downloaded to it they are visible immediately. The owner of Shoebox can then leave the photos displaying in a slide show or can lift the lid and use a linear touch surface to navigate forward and backward through its contents.

Unlike a digital photo frame, Shoebox is intended as a default location for the photos, accessible much like networked storage. It has a memory card slot in it that allows content from a camera to be downloaded quickly and made available to other devices in the home through the network. These show up immediately on the screen, too. It is both storage and display. Digital photo frames, by comparison, do not act as default storage in the home. They are rarely on the network, and the memory cards onto which their photos are typically placed are awkward to manage since they require a PC to transfer the content from the camera.

This simple act of including a screen in a unit with the hard drive and creating Shoebox to be put on display in the home by default, suddenly elevates the content on it because it starts to have a visible presence in the home without requiring the awkward storage management of a digital photo frame. An object like Shoebox gives the digital photos a sense of physical place that is often lacking when they are buried on a PC. I suddenly have a strong sense of where they are. If my house caught fire and I needed to rescue my photos, I would know where to go for them.

Shoebox has a simple label holder built into the front of it that invites you to think about the thematic content of the Shoebox as a whole. You might have a Shoebox that contains all of your wedding photos for example, with the word "Wedding" written on a slip of paper and tucked into the label holder. Another Shoebox might be about a specific person or place. The label holder is a simple addition that invites a sensitive consideration of content.

I like to think that my father could have had a Shoebox containing the digital photos he had taken. This would have kept them isolated from the rest of the items on his PC. I would have been able to take it from my father's home and put it on display in my own, as both a physical and digital reminder of him, as a form of technology heirloom. Like any heirloom, it would have taken on new meaning with me. While it was at his home, it would have been there to remind him of the things he had seen and done. Once it had moved to my home, after he had passed away, it would have become an object that enabled me to remember, reflect on, and honor his life.

Shoebox, then, focuses simply on the act of making digital photos, and therefore an individual or family's activity and history, accessible in the home. However, the experience of Shoebox is "all or nothing": Photos downloaded to the device are shown in the slide show by default, and while it allows an image to be viewed in the home very easily, there is little actual functionality built in to allow the device's owner to omit images he does not want to have appear, for example, or to use the device to tell a story the way he might with a photo album. That is something the next device is designed to do.

Timecard

Photo albums are inherently objects of legacy. They act as a crafted record that helps preserve the memory of people, places, and events through time. Without the creative act of making a photo album, we might inherit boxes full of loose images, disconnected from context, with no real detail to tell us what they represent. Actually, we often inherit those, too, but we value the photo album for its structure and narrative. When someone takes the effort to create a photo album, they add a layer of detail and connect potentially disparate content, which is invaluable in the long term in providing historical record. Photo albums may potentially be read in the future by known or unknown family members, or maybe even by strangers acting as archaeologists of personal histories, and the detail they contain helps to humanize the subjects. Scrapbooks and baby books can serve a similar purpose.

A by-product of photo album creation is a deeper insight into the album's subject because of the time we spend thinking about its content. A photo album might tell the story of a person, a place, or perhaps an event such as a wedding, and the time during the creation of the album allows for reflection as our hands are busy. While we are making decisions such as what photos to include, how to lay out the pages, how to annotate the content, and so on, we learn new things about our subject.

Timecard was created to enable something similar to photo albums in the digital realm, to allow a family to craft digital content in a way that allows for storytelling and to create an opportunity for reflection on that content during and through the act of creation.

The Timecard device itself (Figure 11.6) is designed, like Shoebox, to be put on display in the home. Also like Shoebox, the device can display content (typically photos) randomly as part of a slideshow. Unlike Shoebox, though, each displayed image on Timecard has been chosen and arranged as part of a broader chronology. When a photo appears

Figure 11.6   Timecard

on the device, it can be touched using the touchscreen, and the display will shift to show a timeline, moving to the point in time where the touched photo occurs.

I have created a timeline on my Timecard that is all about the life of my grandfather, for example. It shows his early career as a pilot in the Royal Air Force in the U.K. and subsequently as a test pilot. It also shows content about him from the time period after I was born, when I knew him personally. My Timecard has my grandfather as its subject, and when I have visitors to my home and they see a photo of him on the device, I can just press on it, view the timeline, and use its structure to tell them more about his life.

The act of creating this timeline about my grandfather gave me time to think about his life. I had to find out what material I had about him, such as photos at different points in his life, scans of objects that he had owned, and figure out what point in time they belonged to on the device. Thinking about his chronology made me aware of the different places he had lived and the arc of his life in a way I had not thought about before. I am conscious now, for example, that he seemed to leave very little record of his life between the time he stopped flying and became a grounded air-traffic controller, and his retirement. He seemed to have decided not to keep much material about his life during this period, and I wonder if he found the time boring in comparison to the excitement of flying.

These interpretations of his motives are very much my own, though. My mother—my grandfather's daughter—would have a very different version of the narrative of his life. Her life obviously overlapped far more with my grandfather's life than mine did, and so her interpretation would be driven much more by her memories of events in which she was a participant, as well as the complexities of a father–daughter relationship. Timecard acts as a device to perhaps draw out some of these contrasting or complementary stories about a person and perhaps to even present them as parallel, overlapping narratives.

One feature we enabled with the Timecard device was the ability to add reference material. Using Wikipedia, the author of the timeline can search for contextual material (details about world events, for example) to add as a complement to the more personal content. On my grandfather's timeline, I added references to events he may have been involved in, such as the Battle of Britain (a famous skirmish involving the Royal Air Force), so I had a sense of broader occurrences that may have affected his life directly. I also added some entries that were more generic in nature, but which helped me get a sense of a period of time. For example, I added an entry showing when the first television broadcast occurred in the U.K. In addition to events, I also added details of places he lived at different periods in his life, aircraft he may have flown, and so on. This contextual material acts to flesh out the more personal entries, adding more content on which to reflect. In the case of my grandfather, it aided me in thinking about where he may have been and what he may have been doing at different points in his life.

Timecard is a device, then, that can be dedicated to a specific person and that can be crafted over time to show more and more detail of that person's life. It is like a photo album that keeps accruing new stories and new value as the repository for a history related to family. As the value of the content increases, so does that of the device it is on. It becomes a technology heirloom of sorts—an object a family will care about looking after because of the stories it contains.

Digital Slide Viewer

The data for Timecard is deliberately stored on the device so that it persists even if the online service and tools that allowed for its creation disappear. We are in an age now, though, in which we are pouring many of the facts and stories of our lives—the things I could have imagined belonging on Timecard—into online services such as the social networking site Facebook and the photo-sharing site Flickr. These are now the places in which we record what we have been doing, where we have been, who we have spent time with, and so on.

What happens to data on these services when they become part of an inheritance? Taking on another person's online services and profiles once they pass away is an onerous task. Services need maintaining, both financially and socially. For many people, an inherited service is likely to be a burden. Why would they want to become the administrator of another person's online life, when they are often already so invested in looking after their own?

That is not to say that the online remains of a deceased relative do not have value. Of course they do. The question is where that value lies and for whom. There is value in the persistence of an online profile as a nexus for bereavement, for example. The Facebook profiles of people who have passed away often become the center of memorialization for that person, with people adding comments and media that reflect on their lives. Yet even a memorialized profile is likely eventually to succumb to time.

With the Digital Slide Viewer (Figure 11.7), we have explored the idea that for many families what they care about is the persistence and comfort of content, particularly once the process of immediate bereavement has come to an end. As with Timecard, they want to keep

Figure 11.7   Digital Slide Viewer

the details and stories of a life alive and store that data somewhere where they become the caretaker, rather than the service.

The Digital Slide Viewer concept imagines that a family member who recently passed away was an avid user of Flickr, the photo-sharing website. During this person's life, he invested time editing and uploading his favorite photos to the site and organizing them into sets of related items. He tagged these images with keywords that helped to describe their content and then shared the photos with others.

We imagine that the inheritors of the Flickr user's estate would want their relative's account to persist so that family and friends around the world could continue to see its content. In addition, they might be both concerned about the account's ongoing maintenance—that they might somehow fail to take care of it adequately—and wish that the content was available in a form that, like a photo album, was more conducive to face-to-face reminiscence.

With the (still conceptual) Digital Slide Viewer system, loved ones can pay a service to repackage the content of the Flickr account, archiving it in a hybrid digital–physical form that can then be put on display in the family's home, alongside other mementos of the deceased person. Like Shoebox, this physical form reassures the family that valuable sentimental content is safe and secure, while at the same time acting as a reminder of their loved one.

The Digital Slide Viewer is stored in an oak presentation case, which the family could put on display in their home, on a bookshelf, or in another visible space. Inside the box is an old analog photo slide viewer, which has been repurposed for the digital age. It has had a small digital display installed into it, as well as a memory card onto which the content of the Flickr account is archived. Next to the slide viewer in the case are a large number of white "slides," which can be placed into the viewer in order to access different sets of photos. Each slide corresponds to a different organizational collection created on the site by the deceased.

The slide viewer form encourages family members to look into the device and interact with it. Once they have accessed a set of photos by inserting one of the slides, they can tilt the viewer to the left and right to proceed to the next or previous images. They can then pass the device around to friends and family in the same physical location as they find images that they want to share and talk about.

The Digital Slide Viewer is a fully working prototype, but it is entirely conceptual, designed to elicit questions about the relationship between digital content and physical needs. One question we are interested in, for example, is the value of metadata accrued by the digital photos while they were stored on Flickr. Flickr is a social service, and each photo picks up new properties as other people interact with it. Flickr keeps track of the number of views of each image by people other than the owner, for example, as well as the number of times other people have marked it as a favorite of theirs. Photos that are shared through the service can be commented on, for example, or added to galleries of photos assembled by other members of Flickr.

What value does this new layer of social properties offer to friends and family? Should those new properties also be downloaded into the Digital Slide Viewer along with the photos? It might be interesting, for example, if the family wants to know which of their relative's photos were viewed or marked as favorites most on Flickr. This would indicate how the images were valued by the community that their relative was a part of. Since the photo archive could number in the thousands, these properties might also aid the family by drawing their attention to items with more activity around them than others.

These properties on Flickr, as with many online services, are not isolated but are interlinked. A comment left on a photo, for example, has an author, and that author's name is visible next to the comment itself. This name is a live property, linked to a real person. Clicking on it takes you to that person's profile. That person has photos of their own, which are also commented on.

These properties are deeply interconnected and part of a seemingly endless web of related data with only a few degrees of separation between one person and another, or one photo and another. How much of this web would we want to archive on a device like the Digital Slide Viewer? If simple properties like views and favorites add some insight into our relative's photos, what other aspects of this web might, too? If we can imagine downloading one or two properties on to the Digital Slide Viewer, might it not also be valuable to download the properties connected to those properties such as the names of the viewers? At what point might we have to draw a line before the whole interconnected mess of properties that make up a service like Flickr find themselves on our device?

Backup Box

Shoebox, Digital Slide Viewer, and even Timecard, to some extent, focus on visual material. When we think of the materials of legacy, we often are drawn to photos, which were taken with the goal of capturing moments and preserving for memory, and are often evocative and visceral. Since the motive for the creation of images is often for them to act as triggers of the past, they have an implicit long-term value.

But much of the digital content that we create as an output from our lives is not visual but textual. We write documents and emails, and, more recently, create status updates on Facebook and tweets on Twitter. Does this content offer value to us in the long term, as a resource for reflecting and reminiscing? Might it potentially form an important part of our digital legacy, too, just like photos?

Online content shared with others through social networking sites can tell us much about what a person has done, where they have been, who they have spent their time with, and so on. For an individual who is an active participant in online communities, that picture can be quite full and can form a detailed, data-driven narrative of a life lived. In many ways, the creation of this content is not unlike the act of diary writing, except that diaries are purposefully crafted and kept private. These online diary entries, by contrast, are a by-product of socialization, and are provocatively public.

In the world of online communities, it is not just the personally authored word that has value in telling our tale. We produce data, too, either consciously (as we register our GPS coordinates through "check-in" services such as Foursquare) or not (as Amazon finds patterns in our purchases, for example). This personal data provides an alternative layer of information about our life, one based on what we do, whom we see, and where we spend our time. This material may provide some context to our more personal, crafted output. This notion of personal data strongly distinguishes old forms of diary-keeping from new.

Diaries really stand out as objects of legacy since they provide a first-hand account of the life of the deceased. Even as they are being authored, there can be a sense of their value to a future reader. Social networking content often has this personal orientation, and we might expect, therefore, that our attitudes toward online content would be similar to that of a diary—that we would understand the content's value in the long term as a record of our own lives. Oddly, though, the sense we get talking to people about their online output is quite different. They see it as quite mundane and valueless in the long term. It may offer some brief value in the short term, during those few minutes when a friend or stranger responds to it with a comment or the press of the Like button on Facebook. This value is perceived as fleeting, though. The content is written very much in the moment, is about now, and so considering it in the long term may seem odd.

This short-term emphasis on the content we produce online seems to understate its potential value as a resource for reminiscing in the long term. As part of our research work into the area of legacy, we talked to a woman who had inherited 40 years of diaries from her mother and grandmother. These were full of detail, but it was often the most mundane entry, such as "cleaned the kitchen today," which provided the most insight into the everyday, domestic lives of the authors. After 30 or 40 years, the mundane can become special.

As people age, they tend to look for ways to peer into their past and draw on objects like photos that can aid their recall, as they start to reflect on their lived lives. Our online output seems to offer amazing potential, in this regard, for sparking our memories. The body of data about us could be valuable for our own reflection and potentially for that of our offspring. The danger is that today we take the attitude that this content is disposable, so we do not worry about its preservation. If it does survive, it will be through happy accident, through the accidental preservation of the service on which it was authored, for example, rather than through our own effort.

Backup Box (Figure 11.8) is designed to explore a few of these issues. Like the other artifacts, it is a working system, but one that was created to explore conceptual ideas. In this case, Backup Box focuses on the issue just described: mundane digital content.

Backup Box is a wooden container with a closed lid, containing both a hard drive and a display. It is connected to the internet and designed to do nothing but back up your tweets day after day. (Although we focused exclusively on Twitter with this device, it might also be used for archiving other short-form social media content, such as status updates on Facebook.) We imagine that it would just sit in some corner of its owner's house performing this task. It might do this for days, then years, and then decades. Its owner may never attend to it, forgetting about it, until one day he starts to feel the urge to revisit aspects of his past, at which point he lifts the lid on the Backup Box. Underneath, the touch-sensitive display shows a timeline of all the tweets that have been collected.

Figure 11.8   Backup Box

The owner of the Backup Box can scroll back in time to view old Twitter content. At first, the more recent entries are likely to seem mundane, since they are the freshest in memory. As the owner reaches further back, though, he starts to see tweets about events, people, and places he had forgotten. At some point, the content has shifted from being valueless to valuable.

When the Backup Box's owner eventually passes away, the device would become an object of legacy and might be passed on to family or friends who personally knew the deceased. The content of the box would provide another source of material, along with other inherited objects that might mix with the owner's own personal reminiscences, providing additional context and perhaps unexpected insight. They might be drawn to particular tweets that record events at which they were also present or that describe people they also knew.

As the box is passed on further through the generations, the device would inevitably become the property of family members who never knew the original owner. Now the content of the box is archaeological, devoid of direct personal memory. What now might the new recipients of the box find interesting in its content? They would probably be drawn less to personal entries that describe people or events that they do not know, and more to those tweets that give them some sense of the period in which they were posted. The further we look back, the stranger things appear, so details that seem mundane—what we were wearing, the technology we were using, the amount that something cost—jump out at us because they emphasize how times have changed. (For more on memory and technology heirlooms, see "Things We've Learnt About ... Memory.")

Conclusion

Shoebox, Timecard, Digital Slide Viewer, and Backup Box each highlight the potential value, as well as some potential pitfalls, in the role of contemporary technology in personal legacy. There are some specific, pragmatic issues that fall out of the creation of this set of "technology heirlooms," for example. All four devices have digital displays in them. Most digital displays are fragile things that would barely last 5 or 10 years, let alone the decades that we might hope for. The same is true for most of the components we have used to prototype these devices, which are similarly delicate. These conceptual devices raise other questions worth discussing further, though, beyond their physical fragility.

Designing More Nuanced Physical and Digital Experiences

As the objects that surround us in our homes become digitized—our books, music, and photos, for example—they disappear from our immediate surroundings, reappearing online or in devices like cellphones and tablets. Items that were previously visible to all are moving into technological formats optimized for the individual. Home continues to be important to us, but it is being stripped of an important physical layer that reminds us of our connection to others and to our past, that tells visitors something about our interests and personality, and that simply acts to create a domestic aesthetic.

There is something uncomfortable about the way that digital things fit in our lives, even when we do try and make them a part of our home. We experience digital photos, for example, primarily through screens, and things with screens tend to be self-consciously technological, which seems to be at odds with the choices, driven by aesthetics and comfort, that we make concerning many of the non-digital things in our lives.

I have a diverse set of printed photos and pictures on display at my home. Some are shots of my family, and some are paintings my wife and I have bought together. I have some watercolors by my mother-in-law and a print of the Yorkshire countryside I inherited from my father. Each plays a dual role, as an aesthetic object and as an object connected with memory. The paintings serve to bring beauty into my home. The print from my father is a beautiful image, too, but it also acts as a reminder of him. Through it, I fulfill my duty (willingly) of remembering his place in my life and honoring his memory.

For each of these images, I have carefully selected a frame to match and picked a spot on a wall in my home where it hangs. Like a digital display, the photo frame is an aid to the presentation of content. The frame, however, fulfills this role in a way that that puts me in control and puts the emphasis on my environment. I had a huge choice of frames for these images, and when I selected each, I was allowed to focus on how it matched the picture as well as on how it matched my home.

Digital picture frames, by contrast, have very little diversity in terms of material and aesthetic choice. They tend to be made from plastic or metal and be a little brash in design. They seem to seek to draw attention to themselves as objects in their own right. The manufacturer invariably insists that its logo be clearly visible on the front, for example. This seems to be a strange choice. Imagine buying an analog picture frame for a printed photo that had the frame manufacturer's logo as a prominent element on the front. It would seem incongruous, yet that seems to be a default for these devices because of their digital nature. These devices do not seem to offer sympathy or subtlety either to their content or to the environment in which they will sit.

There seems to be a disconnection, then, between digital content and the way it is presented in our home. The digital picture frame seems ambivalent about its role as a device that puts the emphasis on its content. This kind of design seems to do that content a disservice, though, particularly if it is highly personal. If we want to put that content on display as a reminder of someone, as a way of honoring them, we want attention drawn to that content and not to its presentation medium.

Getting Things on Display

This disconnection between the ways we are able to present physical things and digital things matters in the context of legacy because of the way we use our homes as a display space for material related to the people, events, and places that form part of our history and that of our family. Digital content also needs room in this space now, to do the same. It is a vehicle for carrying memories, just as the physical objects it replaces were before it. It is not enough to simply *have* the digital content stored away somewhere on a PC or online. That is a little like putting all of the objects in our home out of sight in our basement. Some of it needs to be made visible to aid us in remembering things that matter.

I am not arguing that all digital material, inherited or not, must have a physical instantiation. The technological component of our lives has grown too large and too complex for that to be likely or even possible. What I am arguing is that "placeness" still matters, just as the "placelessness" of our lives online does. We need to be able to make nuanced choices about how our digital content is arranged and that should include making it accessible to us in our physical environments as well as our digital.

The four technology heirloom devices I have described attempt to do this in a diverse set of ways. They attempt to intertwine hardware and software together in a way that is sympathetic, with an emphasis on bridging the gap between our digital and domestic lives. Shoebox is a device for simplifying the act of displaying digital content in our home. Timecard offers a tangible experience for interacting with images and exploring the stories associated with a person's life. Digital Slide Viewer allows families to archive the content of an online photo service so they can view and share it in their homes. Backup Box gives the content of a service a physical instantiation, the comfort of knowing that that content is secure and available for us when we decide to use it for reflecting on our past.

The Permanence of Services

We should not underestimate the comfort of physical things in terms of the reassurance they give. People care about inherited material, be it digital or physical, and when they accept it, they take on the responsibility for its safekeeping. Being able literally to point to that material in a way that is not abstract, as it often is with content stored online, can provide a sense of security around it. Knowing that a deceased relative's digital photos are in a Shoebox-like device on display in the home is reassuring in a way that is different to entrusting them to Flickr. It places the responsibility for preservation with the individual. It puts people in control. They might not want this sense of control for more trivial content that they care less about, but they may for content that is highly precious to them.

This issue of control is one of many tensions that are highlighted by our increasing reliance on online services for the safekeeping of our digital things. These services are not yet tested through time. Many of the services we used a decade ago (a very short time when it comes to issues of legacy) are obsolete or have changed their nature. Only a few years ago, for example, millions of people spent large amounts of their time carefully creating and crafting a personal domain on Myspace, an early social network. That content has been left behind or lost now that the service has diminished in popularity and people have moved on to new sites like Facebook.

While the services themselves have not been tested through time, neither have we. We do not yet understand the value or potential of the things we are creating and sharing through them in terms of legacy. We regard this content as novel and spontaneous, but not yet a concrete part of the record of our lives. We can see that we are in the middle of this transition from physical to digital, but we cannot yet see which of these are the things that will constitute our legacy. There is a danger that we will lose this content, and in the long term, regret its loss once it has gone.

References and Recommended Reading

Banks, Richard. 2001. *The Future of Looking Back*. Cambridge, U.K.: Microsoft Press.

Csikszentmihalyi, Mihaly, and Eugene Rochberg-Halton. 1981. *The Meaning of Things: Domestic Symbols and the Self*. Cambridge, MA: Cambridge University Press.

Kirk, David, and Abigail Sellen. 2010. "On Human Remains: Value and Practice in the Home Archiving of Cherished Objects." ACM *Transactions on Computer-Human Interaction* 17, no. 3, Article 10, 43 pages. D01:10.1145/1806923. 1806924.

Odom, William, Richard Banks, and Dave Kirk. 2010. "Reciprocity, Deep Storage, and Letting Go: Opportunities for Designing Interactions With Inherited Digital Materials." *Interactions* 17, no. 5, p. 31–34. D01:10.1145/1836216.1836224.

Odom, William, Richard Banks, Richard Harper, David Kirk, Siân Lindley, and Abigail Sellen. 2012. "Technology Heirlooms? Considerations for Passing Down and Inheriting Digital Materials." In *Proceedings of the 2012 SIGCHI conference on Human Factors in computing systems (CHI 2012)*, ACM, Austin, TX, May 5–10, 2012, p. 337–346 D01:10.1145/2207676.2207723.

"Things We've Learnt About ... Memory." Microsoft Research, 2012. research.microsoft.com/projects/thingswevelearnt.

CHAPTER 12

New Horizons in Personal Archiving: 1 Second Everyday, myKive, and MUSE

Donald T. Hawkins
Christopher J. Prom, University of Illinois
Peter Chan, Stanford University

Editor's note: There is a great deal of research going on in research laboratories as well as in entrepreneurs' proverbial "garages," and we never know when a significant new product will emerge. In the course of my study of software products and services for personal archiving (see Chapter 4 in this volume), I became aware of three promising research projects that appear well on their way to becoming new products: 1 Second Everyday, MUSE, and myKive. I am pleased that Christopher Prom, principal investigator of myKive, and Peter Chan, digital archivist at Standford University who has played a leading role in introducing MUSE to the archives community, have contributed substantive overviews of their work in this chapter.

1 Second Everyday
Donald T. Hawkins

When he turned 30 years old, Cesar Kuriyama began using his smartphone to record 1 second of video from his activities every day. After a year, he had 6 minutes of video stored in his phone and discovered something:

> This particular project has had such a profoundly positive impact on my life that I think everyone could benefit immensely from doing it too. ... Recording one second every day suddenly allowed me to easily reflect back on my life—to look back at my day-to-day decisions. I started re-evaluating how I approached each day. ... Recording a moment daily started encouraging me to wake up and seize each day. ... This project continues to provide me with priceless data on how I'm living my life, and it can do that for you, too.

Kuriyama was interviewed on CNN and was also invited to make a presentation at the prestigious TED conference (talk at www.ted.com/talks/cesar_kuriyama_one_second_every_day.html) in 2012. He then applied for funding using Kickstarter (www.kickstarter.com) and received enough funding to begin development on an iPhone app to automate the process. One of the functionalities of the app will be to create a personal archive in the cloud. 1 Second Everyday (www.1second everyday.com) is now available in the iTunes App Store.

***

myKive: Facilitating the Aggregation of Dispersed Archives

Christopher J. Prom

The myKive project (www.mykive.org) proceeds from a simple working assumption: One of the biggest challenges facing archivists in the digital era is the fact that the evidence of an individual's activities is scattered across many computers and servers. This problem is not wholly new. Even when dealing with the hard copy papers of an individual who lived before the invention of the personal computer, the archivist sometimes needed to track down documentation from multiple rooms, buildings, cities, states, or even countries. However, the widespread use of networked computers (and, in particular, cloud services) has exponentially increased what might be termed the documentation dispersion rate.

To address this challenge, the myKive project is testing the feasibility of developing a free and open source software application that can be used to copy, preserve, and manage personal social media records, email, and desktop files that are stored in disparate virtual locations. The project seeks to weave existing and/or newly developed open source tools into an integrated package of services that can be installed on a web server and administered via a web dashboard.

The myKive service will allow people to push or pull records and information from email accounts, blogs, Facebook pages, Twitter feeds, local computers, or other sources that are connected to the internet or a local network and save them to a redundant, cloud-based server in a standardized, preservation-read format. Regular integrity checks will be run against duplicate copies and the checksums will be generated at the time of packaging. Content will be stored with sufficient technical and structural metadata to permit its long-term preservation. Technically, the service will be based on very common web standards or technologies (Ruby on Rails, PHP, AJAX, REST, and JSON). In providing these functions, the myKive project does not seek to replace a person's existing applications or to affect their daily behavior but simply to provide a method by which they can aggregate and make useful content that is currently scattered to the virtual winds.

As part of the myKive pilot project, the University of Illinois will wrap four pieces of software into a web-based dashboard application. Initially, the dashboard will provide access to tools to perform these four functions:

- Social media archiving
- Email archiving

- Desktop archiving

- Visualization and mining

By focusing on three critical formats (social media, email, and desktop files), the project targets the format types that are most widely used by people in their personal and work lives. Providing visualization tools will render the records useful immediately. We suggest that preservation is provided as a critical but secondary benefit to the end user. While users of the system will surely benefit from its preservation aspects, the project is based on the presupposition that the service is much more likely to be used if it provides its users with an immediately tangible benefit, rather than a distant, disembodied one.

During the pilot stage, we developed the provisional technical model (Figure 12.1). We anticipate that the application will use and extend existing open source software, wrapped within middleware to be developed by the University of Illinois Library. The middleware will link the individual system components into an overall archiving application, managed from a web-based dashboard. The service core will consist of an application programming interface (API), linking these components from a dashboard to a backend preservation service.

Within this overall framework, the application will consist of the following elements: myKive API, myKive Social, myKive Email, myKive Desktop, and Dashboard with Visualization Tools.

The myKive API will be comprised of user and account management, system security, and preservation packaging. The system will use a model/view/controller (MVC) framework to segregate application control and data views from the object and data model, which stores and manipulates information in user accounts. As of June 2013, the basic modeling work for user registration and authentication has been completed.

For myKive Social, when we developed the provisional project architecture, we suggested that the ThinkUp application (www.thinkup.com) be used as the basis for social media harvesting, with appropriate extensions and links to our application core.

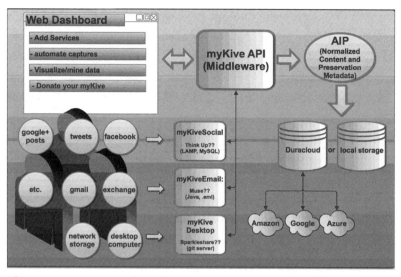

Figure 12.1   Proposed myKive architecture (as of September 2012)

ThinkUp, which is described as a "social media insights platform," provides people with a way to harvest and aggregate tweets, Facebook content, and Google+ postings, then visualize and understand the ways in which social media are being produced, consumed, and repurposed. During fall 2012, we installed the tool and conducted preliminary testing. While the tool works well for its stated purpose, several technical factors (including the lack of a theming system and API) impeded its effective integration into external services. In addition, it is not a preservation tool, and some of the most important elements of a user's social media account (e.g., photographs) are not captured by the system. As of June 2013, we started exploring whether changes in the beta version will alleviate some of these technical hurdles. We hope to integrate preservation services directly into the application by code contributions to the overall project, but based on early results, it appears more likely that we will need to develop a separate project fork or stand-alone API to accomplish the overall project goals.

For myKive Email, the open-source MUSE software described later in this chapter is suggested as a candidate technology for incorporation into myKive, since it uses an open storage format that facilitates data reuse and transformation, including visualizing, graphing, searching, and browsing. Currently, MUSE operates as an extension to popular web browsers, such as Chrome, Firefox, and Safari, and it installs a Java applet on the user's computer. A copy of the email is then downloaded, and MUSE provides visualization tools to make the email searchable and more useful. We propose to utilize the MUSE core to build a server-based version of the software.

For myKive Desktop, we propose using secure socket layer technologies and standard encryption techniques to capture and store desktop files from a local computer on a synchronized and replicated server. The SparkleShare application (www.sparkleshare.org) is suggested as a candidate technology. SparkleShare is an open source alternative to file sharing and backup applications like Dropbox and Carbonite, using Git as its backend architecture.[1A] Our hypothesis is that it will be possible to establish the server on which myKive is installed as a Git repository, then integrate the SparkleShare synchronization tools into our myKive application core/dashboard. We hope to add automated desktop file backup, synchronization, and even version control into the system. In theory, users will be able to choose whether to keep a complete record of the desktop over time or only the latest version of the files.

Finally, with the Dashboard with Visualization Tools element, users will be provided a dashboard application to manage the system components described here. Once they complete the initial setup, they will need to perform little or no maintenance other than keeping passwords current. However, we believe that by providing visualization and data mining tools, such as those integrated into MUSE and ThinkUp, we will provide users with a reason to remain interested in and use the application. Over time, we propose to integrate other data mining and visualization tools into the service. This work is anticipated to take place after the pilot service has been developed.

One element of the service not shown in the figure is the core API. This API will include a plug-in architecture, allowing people from the computer science, archives, library, and digital curation communities to preserve information from other social media services, thereby extending the application and allowing for its evolution over time. Using those extensions and plug-ins, people will be able harvest records from other services into their myKive. For example, the following record types might included in an individual's myKive, once appropriate extensions are developed:

- Blogs, using backup tools such as ArchivePress and Simple Backup

- Photographs, using capture tools such as parallel-Flickr

- Webpages, using harvesting tools such as Wget, WARC, and NutchWAX

- Personal reference and citation libraries, using tools such as Zotero's application programming interface

At this time, myKive is a pilot service in very early stage feasibility testing, with funding from the University of Illinois Library Innovation Fund. As we develop the technical model, we will seek to engage external partners for pilot testing. If the pilot is successful, we hope that the project will garner widespread interest and may serve as the basis for a collaborative international project. Depending on the results of the pilot project, we anticipate seeking external funding to develop the service into a production application. Current information on the project is available at www.mykive.org.

Endnote

1A. See en.wikipedia.org/wiki/Git_%28software%29. Git is an open source revision control system, typically used for source code management in open source projects. However, it can be used as part of any distributed file-sharing project.

***

MUSE: An Experiment in Appraising, Accessioning, Processing, Discovering, and Delivering Emails in Special Collections

Peter Chan

David S. Ferriero, archivist of the United States, reports that emails have been collected from every U.S. administration since the 1980s and that the archives in the George W. Bush Presidential Library include about 240 million email messages.[1B] Similarly, many large archival repositories, including Columbia University, The New York Public Library, Smithsonian Institution Archives, Stanford University, and Oxford University, are collecting emails but currently lack the tools necessary to adequately provide access to them.[2B] Six key functions that a tool for managing emails in special collections must address are:

- Appraisal (collection development/review)
- Accessioning (transferring emails to a repository)
- Processing (arrangement and description)
- Discovery (online via the web)
- Delivery (access in reading room)
- Preservation

In 2011, I came across MUSE (Memories USing Email, mobiso-cial.stanford.edu/muse), a research system designed at Stanford University (primarily by Sudheendra Hangal, a PhD candidate in the Computer Science Department) specifically to explore and interact with the contents of email archives. MUSE uses data mining and text-analysis techniques to analyze an email archive and generate visualizations of it as well as cues to messages likely to be of interest. The cues serve as entry points into a browsing interface that supports faceted navigation and rapid skimming of messages. MUSE was originally designed for individuals working with their own email archives and therefore does not explicitly support the six functional activities related to managing email within archival repositories mentioned above. However, it has a number of features that can be further developed and adapted to support these functions. This chapter describes the six functional activities and shows how MUSE supports them.

Appraisal

MUSE enables repositories and researchers to perform collection development and review related to email collections. It provides a chronological summary overview of an archive by identifying statistically the most significant terms in the archive by month.[3B] Terms, including people, places, and organizations, are extracted from message contents by using the Named Entity Recognition (NER; nlp.stanford.edu/software/CRF-NER.shtml) package from the Stanford Natural Language Processing toolkit. In order for the terms to appear in the monthly summaries (Figure 12.2), they must be "statistically significant terms." Terms are scored taking time into account. For example, if a person develops a new hobby such as music, MUSE will score terms related to music highly during the initial months but lower their score as they become relatively common.

MUSE also provides a thumbnail of every image attachment for people to scan. Since image attachments are an important part of an email archive, the thumbnails can provide a quick view of all images for appraisal (Figure 12.3).

Accessioning

MUSE also facilitates accessioning, or the process of transferring email to a repository. It can read files stored on computer hard drives in the open "mbox" format (an open, text-base format for email) and can see all folders via IMAP (internet message access protocol). Gmail or Yahoo! accounts can be accessed by logging in with the email address and password. MUSE can then download and store the emails on a local drive, from which they can be exported in mbox format and transferred to an institution's computer server.

Processing

Arrangement and description can also be accomplished in MUSE. It performs a number of data cleaning tasks such as removing duplicate

June 2001	July 2001	August 2001
377 MESSAGES	544 MESSAGES	577 MESSAGES
Robert Creeley	Maine	Buffalo
Waldoboro	SLS Russia	Allen
Robert	Robert	Robert
Maine	NYC	Kenneth
NYC	Russia	Olson
Helen	Hannah	Adrienne
Buffalo	Michael	Waldoboro
Carmen	France	Maine
Michele	American	Amherst Street
Miranda	Olson	David Cast
Avis Roberts	Skowhegan	Danny
Dad	Charles Olson	Jack
Ireland House	Bob	Bob
Bob	Robert Creeley	NYC

Figure 12.2   Significant terms by month

Figure 12.3   Thumbnail view of images in emails (intentionally blurred to protect privacy)

messages and resolving situations where a person has multiple email addresses. To reconcile this, MUSE merges identities that have the same RFC-822 name (the name that appears in parentheses alongside the email address) and treats them as the same person. MUSE also applies some intelligent guesses. For example, the name *Barack Obama* will be treated the same as *Obama, Barack*, and an email address such as *john.doe@example.com* will automatically infer the name *John Doe*, even if the email address does not have a name associated with it. In most places in the MUSE interface, the user can hover over a name or email address to see a list of all email addresses and names associated with that person. In addition, MUSE can automatically identify important groups of people in an email archive based on co-recipiency patterns, allowing researchers to explore all messages involving a particular group of people (Figure 12.4).

MUSE incorporates sentiment analysis techniques to identify subjective categories such as love, anger, and so on, since these messages are likely to be of special interest (Figure 12.5). The sentiment lexicon can be edited according to the needs of a repository or researcher. For example, a repository may add terms to the lexicon in order to aid in searching for private/sensitive material in the collection.

Discovery

Special considerations must be made when making personal email freely available over the web. Aside from emails collected under the Freedom of Information Act, institutions cannot publicly expose the contents of emails on the web due to privacy and copyright issues.

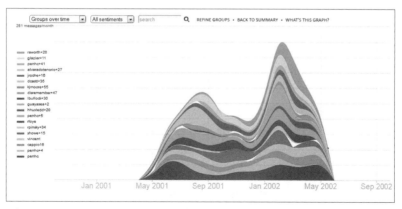

Figure 12.4   Groups over time

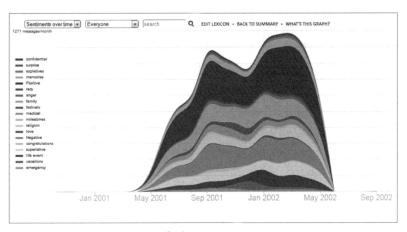

Figure 12.5   Sentiment analysis

Thus, we needed to strike a balance between these limitations and the goal of providing as much information as possible to researchers. Since MUSE already performs NER to extract terms from the message contents, we worked with a consultant to create an index of just the extracted entities and the names of correspondents, which will be accessible to the public to allow for discovery of the contents of the emails. A researcher in New York can therefore review the named entities in an email archive housed at Stanford University and get some sense of the contents of the archive. Based on this knowledge, she can determine whether the time and expense for a trip to view the email in the Special Collections Reading Room at Stanford is warranted.

In addition, MUSE has a browsing lens feature that acts like an extended browser that carries an entire personal archive in its memory. While browsing the web with this extension installed (in Firefox or Chrome), the lens extracts entities (people, location, events, etc.) on the page and looks up these in the email archives, highlighting the matching ones.

During a recent internal grant-funded project, we added a "bulk" search function into the discovery mode (via the web) to allow researchers to paste a piece of text to this bulk search box. For example, if a researcher knows the names of 40 people who are associated with the Black Mountain Poets, she can paste all 40 names in the bulk search box. MUSE performs an entity extraction on the text pasted in the bulk search entities box and then compares the extracted entities with an index of entities generated from the whole email archives. Matching entities are highlighted in the results presented to the users. Clicking on a highlighted name in the MUSE interface will show the researcher the number of email messages in the archive associated with that name (Figure 12.6).

Delivery

The MUSE delivery environment at a repository provides access to the full text of the emails within a collection. The facets panel can be used to turn on or off Sentiment, Group, People, Folder, and Direction filters for the messages within the view. One can also activate or deactivate a facet by clicking on it. The number in parentheses indicates the

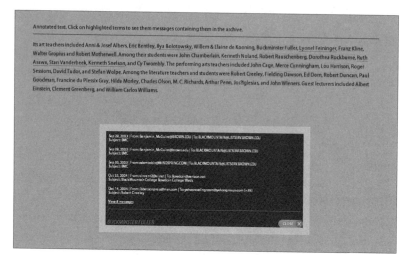

Figure 12.6   Result of bulk search after clicking on Buckminster Fuller

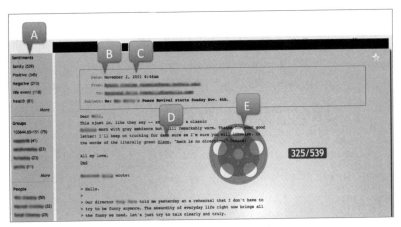

Figure 12.7   The messages view in MUSE, with 539 messages loaded. (A) Facet panel for Sentiments, Groups, and People. (B) Link to all messages for month and (C) for a year. (D) Hyperlink inserted into message contents. (E) Jog dial for rapid skimming. Some details are blurred to protect privacy.

number of messages in the current view that reflect the corresponding facet (Figure 12.7). A full-text search function is also included.

Preservation

MUSE exports emails in mbox. These exported files can then be ingested to an institution's digital repository for long-term preservation.

More technical information about MUSE can be found at mobisocial. stanford.edu/papers/uist11m.pdf. Readers are encouraged to download and use the current prototype of MUSE, which can be found at mobisocial.stanford.edu/muse.

Acknowledgments

Peter Chan wishes to thank Laura Williams, project archivist at Stanford University Libraries, and Sudheendra Hangal, for editing and commenting on this work.

Endnotes

1B. David S. Ferriero, "Prepared Remarks of Archivist of the United States David S. Ferriero," Closing Plenary at Wikimania 2012, Lisner Auditorium, George Washington University, Washington, DC, www.archives.gov/about/speeches/2012/7-14-2012.html.

2B. Stanford University submitted an application for the Innovation in Archives and Documentary Editing 2013 grant (working with Columbia University, New York Public Library, Smithsonian Institution Archives, and Oxford University) to produce an open-source tool that will consist of four modules, each supporting a different functional activity: processing (arrangement and description), appraisal (collection development/review), discovery (online via the web), and delivery (access in reading room).

3B. Sudheendra Hangal, Monica S. Lam, and Jeffrey Heer, "MUSE: Reviving Memories Using Email Archives, UIST–2011," In *Proceedings of the 24th Symposium on User Interface Software and Technology*, ACM, 2011.

CHAPTER 13

The Future of Personal Digital Archiving: Defining the Research Agendas

Clifford Lynch
Coalition for Networked Information

In this concluding chapter, I will first try to frame and situate the various developments that are now being considered (appropriately or otherwise) under the catchphrase *personal digital archiving* and explore some of the many places where these developments interconnect with other (often not academic) fields of endeavor. In part, my approach will be through the autobiographical lens of my own encounters and engagement with various streams and tributaries of research over the last 15 years that have converged into what is now personal digital archiving. These include efforts to digitally capture life as it is lived (e.g., Gordon Bell's "Total Recall" work, ARPA's LifeLogs, and Microsoft's SenseCam).

This work was strongly influenced by information retrieval research in many ways, but it reached into very interesting potential applications, such as helping people with deteriorating memories. The major U.K. study on digital lives, led by Jeremy Leighton John, started from consideration of how to acquire and manage new special collections that included extensive digital materials. It grew to a broader inquiry into the nature of these new digital materials and their implications, not only to cultural memory organizations but to a wide range of scholars and to the general public, culminating in the milestone Digital Libraries Conference hosted by The British Library in 2009. There are still many broken links under www.bl.uk/digital-lives, but most of this material is available through the U.K. Web Archive (www.webarchive.org.uk/ukwa/target/9175069/source/subject), interestingly enough. The final report of The British Library's Digital Lives Research Project (britishlibrary.typepad.co.uk/files/digital-lives-synthesis 02-1.pdf) includes some information on the conference and is a major resource.

Over the past decade, personal information management has emerged as a new subfield of information retrieval research. A team at the Maryland Institute for Technology in the Humanities (MITH) at the University of Maryland, College Park, has taken the lead in exploring applications of digital forensics tools (primarily developed to support the intelligence and law enforcement communities) to capture and understand personal digital archives. Since 2010, the Personal Digital Archiving conferences organized by Jeff Ubois and hosted by the Internet Archive have served as primary focal points for people interested in personal digital archiving (the 2013 meeting moved to the University of Maryland, College Park). These conferences have provided a broad and generous stage for a very wide array of work in digital archiving, personal and otherwise, as well as developments in related fields such as genealogy, analysis of social media platforms, media studies, and public history. They brought together researchers, engineers, activists, entrepreneurs, archivists, librarians, and collectors among others.

But looking over this vast body of work with the benefit of hindsight, much of it feels like *context* to the study of personal digital archiving, or *external viewings* of personal digital archiving from well-established vantage points situated in other disciplinary traditions, rather than a direct engagement with the core issues themselves. Personal digital archiving as a field of study still awaits clear definition and delineation, and my hope in writing this chapter is that, as someone not intellectually committed to any specific one of the many adjacent disciplines, I can help to advance this definitional process.

The remainder of the chapter sketches what I believe are the central research agendas for personal digital archiving today, as these are shared among researchers, archivists, librarians, and curators. I focus on issues that seem to me to be specific to personal digital archiving and do not often consider the many broader fundamental problems in digital preservation (such as ensuring that a Microsoft Word or Excel document created in 2008 is still meaningfully readable in 2058). Progress in basic digital preservation will be important to personal digital archiving and will, to some extent, probably shape developments, but the personal digital archiving area introduces new issues—many not primarily technical in nature—that go far beyond digital preservation.

While this concluding essay has not been explicitly coordinated with the other chapters in the volume in hand beyond a sharing of chapter authors and titles, it is my hope that it will help the reader to synthesize many of the perspectives presented in the earlier chapters, some of which look at personal digital archiving explicitly from the perspective of well-established older adjacent fields, such as the development and management of special collections in libraries.

Scoping the Personal Digital Archiving Challenges

For the last 3 decades, I have been trying to understand the ways in which information technology and ubiquitous computer communications networks are reshaping the scholarly and cultural record of our civilization. I have also been concerned with the effects of these technologies on individuals and how they live their lives: how they communicate and share, remember, and learn. And, of course, the migrations and connections between the private sphere and the public (or collective) record are central.

I should also note at the outset that, even within the overall "Western" tradition, there are great variations in both legal and social traditions and understandings from nation to nation. Thus, personal digital archiving can be explored within a national context or from a comparative international perspective. The international perspective has an increasingly pragmatic element, as networks cross national boundaries and legal and regulatory frameworks very casually. Issues beyond the Western traditions are almost completely unfamiliar to me, and I will not pretend to offer an understanding of how these considerations might broaden the research agendas in question here.

Digital Records of Individuals

It is clear that for many people, much of their communication is now recorded in email, text messages, and social media systems such as Twitter, Facebook, Tumblr, Flickr, and the like, and even in phone logs and occasional records from cellphones or multiplatform systems such as Skype. Communication and sharing have become constant and casual, and much more day-to-day experience is documented through these tools. With digital cameras, and particularly with the merger of cellphones and cameras, this collection of records takes on a much more visual dimension, incorporating enormous numbers of still and moving images. Documents of all types, including to-do lists, may well persist in digital form. Bills, invoices, account statements, and other records of commercial transactions have moved into email or various online systems.

Interesting contested areas exist: Search logs, records of purchases, and other kinds of interaction history may be held by the individuals who initiated the transactions or by the businesses that will provide them back to the individual under various terms. Related (particularly in important public policy ways) but slightly out of scope here is the vast and ever-growing set of records *about* specific individuals and their activities held by retail businesses, credit bureaus, insurers, the medical system, background check services, various levels of government, and others. In many cases, it is very difficult for the individuals in question even to obtain copies of these records, let alone address issues about their accuracy or dissemination.

Additional forms of personal records are currently moving into the digital realm, notably medical and genomic information. With the rise of the new generation of instructional technology (massive open online courses, or MOOCs), advanced learning management systems and course delivery platforms, and similar developments, individuals will create learning records as detailed, and perhaps even more revealing, than medical records today, and some individuals will doubtless at least try to have shared custody of these records with the learning platforms.

A small but growing number of individuals has embraced various technology trends and has deliberately tried to intensify the amount of data collected; we find movements such as *sousvellience* (a term popularized by Steve Mann, a play on *surveillance* that speaks to individuals surveilling themselves and events around them from the bottom up), life logging, quantified individuals (popularized by Larry Smarr, among others), and some of the personal genotyping (and soon, sequencing) sharing communities organized by companies such as 23andMe.com, as well as those keeping records from time and task management systems.

The actual custody and storage of all of this information is very messy, and it is getting more complex as time goes on. A decade ago, most of it was on local storage media, though even at that time there was an important class of information that was housed by service providers. A service provider in some sense shares ownership or use of the data, and it may or may not let the individual even download copies in useful forms. Today, we find more information scattered about the network, in some cases in remote storage offered as a service, but in many other cases, it is actually embedded in some network-based system—at stores, banks, hospitals, social media platforms—that attends to its housing, structuring, and sharing. Very few of these network systems make any meaningful commitment to stewardship or preservation, though all too often users assume that such commitments exist, in spirit if not in an explicit contract. And, of course, some information lingers in discontinued or abandoned services or vanishes (consider the fates of some of the early social media platforms, such as GeoCities, as case studies).

More and more of the cultural products that individuals acquire, enjoy, collect, share, and keep—books, music, videos, games—are moving to electronic form. In digital form, they are often jumbled together with materials that individuals have themselves created, along with records of their acquisition and use (purchase histories on Amazon, playlists and play frequencies for music, etc.). It is interesting to think about how scholars have exploited the (fairly rare) records of book acquisition and the building of personal collections by important historical figures, or occasionally have been able to systematically study the annotations that those historical figures may have added to the works that they owned, and then compare these scholarly practices to analogous research that will be enabled by today's records of digital lives.

Individual back-up practices and even commitments to maintaining meaningful backup vary tremendously, and until the last few years, effective ongoing back-up strategies were substantial technical challenges for casual computer users. Factoring in the complexities of information stored in a wide range of independent systems and services, the interactions between computer security threats and information persistence, and the long-time horizons involved in the records of a lifetime, it is inevitable that for many people at least some material will be lost over the years.

Clearly, there is a vast research area in understanding the nature of these personal records and how they are changing year to year; understanding how people think about these collections of records, what importance they assign to them, and how these views change over time; and understanding the issues involving records about individuals that are held in remote systems, sometimes with limited access. It is important to study not only what people are doing with personal records they create today, but also what has happened to the personal records that they created a decade or 2 ago. There is an enormous variation in individual behaviors in all of these areas, and it is valuable to try to correlate various kinds of behavior with demographics, to try to understand how behaviors develop, how they are learned, and how and why they change.

Many useful pathways already exist that can advance this research agenda. A variety of humanistic and social science techniques can be applied to understand individuals' behavior in depth or to survey large groups of individuals. But there are also methods involving the use of personal computers, social media and ecommerce platforms, and various software packages that can potentially provide a complementary set of insights; unfortunately, the vast of majority of this information, assuming that it is even collected and stored, is viewed as highly proprietary. Opening up some of these system-side data sources to individual researchers could offer a very high payoff.

An additional research agenda deals with pragmatic advice and best practices that can be offered to the broad public for dealing with life in the digital world, for ensuring the long-term survival and usability of the electronic records that they create, and the cultural materials that they acquire. This area also connects with guidance about how to maintain privacy where desired, and how to secure identity and property in the digital environment. Libraries, in particular, are increasingly being called upon to provide advice in this area. Technology developers can also benefit from this agenda. It is interesting, for example, to see the very welcome vendor investments in developing easy-to-use consumer-oriented integrated backup, recovery, and migration software after long decades of neglecting these problems (consider, for example, Apple's Time Machine, Migration Assistant, and the automatic recovery features incorporated in its recent operating system releases).

How the Private Is Managed Over Time

The issues raised by the death of an individual and what happens to his or her possessions cast a spotlight on the nature and scope of those possessions. Fifty years ago, when someone died, it fell to the executor or an heir to sort through the deceased's personal papers. Typically, they were stored at home, with perhaps a few critical documents held by a family attorney or in a bank safe-deposit box. On very rare occasions, if the deceased had been perhaps a writer or a composer, copyrights would be recognized as an integral and specific part of the estate, and there might be something like a "literary executor" put in place specifically to deal with copyrights and the fate of unpublished materials.

Today, for the vast majority of the general public, simply determining the scope of an estate that includes digital materials (private, shared, and acquired) scattered across a wide range of services and storage is a formidable task. Resolving issues around ownership, inheritance, and meaningful transfer of access, possession, or control (the clumsiness of the language here itself suggests the complexity of the problem) is a tangle of legal, contractual, and technical challenges, further complicated by a lack of overall social consensus in many areas. Tragically, many of the cases that have highlighted the shortcomings of the current level of understanding and practice have involved young people who were enthusiastic users of social media platforms and who died suddenly, often in military service, leaving grieving parents, spouses, or friends to try to salvage their memories.

At the time of an individual's death, his or her digital life is always a mixture of the deliberate (intentionally saved and retained) and the accidental (once saved and never subsequently weeded or just there by happenstance and never cleaned up). This mix will vary. Determining the intent of the collector/creator may be difficult or impossible in many cases, which will greatly complicate the interpretation of these materials. Further, identifying things that were being kept for personal sentimental value is very hard, and the longer-term significance and importance of such materials may be very difficult to evaluate. Understanding the current situation and helping to structure better practices and solutions through legal and public policy means with respect to digital possessions of all kinds (including perhaps new best practices in estate planning) is an important part of the research agenda. But the overall research agenda is actually much broader and deeper and extends to the public understanding of what constitutes a "digital estate," what expectations surround the disposal of that estate, and the extent to which this is in conflict with current legal understandings or commercial practices. For example, to what extent can a collection of digital music or ebooks be inherited in the way that physical books and sound recordings have been, and how is this transfer actually accomplished?

The Ambiguity of Shared Materials and Spaces, New and Old

Individuals have always been contributors to, and custodians of, collections of shared but generally not public materials, which are typically viewed as belonging to a family (photo albums, narratives, letters, documents, or diaries of deceased or elderly family members). Sometimes, usually less formally, similar materials are encountered that are shared by a group of friends of long standing. And, of course, these groups, family or friends, have always been subject to fracture through feuds, divorces, and so on—disputes that can create controversy and hard feelings about who has access or who can have copies of the material in question. One advantage of digital materials is that shared materials can be easily and cheaply duplicated, so everyone can have his or her own copy, in contrast to the treasured family photo album (the negatives being long lost) or the collection of handwritten letters, which were typically held "in trust" by one individual. But new questions arise with respect to digital materials: How are family records managed when third-party social media or media sharing platforms are in play, and who should be responsible?

The boundaries of family are being stressed by many developments. More frequent divorces, remarriages, and longer lives create more complex extended families. The ability of the internet to reconnect people has made family relationships even more complex in recent years. What do we make of an (alleged) distant cousin who contacts you on a genealogy site offering to trade information about a common great-great-great-grandmother you have both been researching? (In effect, this is an offer to merge personal or family databases in a very controlled way; commercial genealogy sites today host much more than genealogy, using such records as an armature for all kinds of documentary material about individuals and families.)

The internet can reverse diasporas originating from a village in the Balkans or Somalia; the individuals involved are linked by a complex web of relationships based on kinship and family, friendship, and shared heritage. It can reassemble most of the members of an elementary school class, or a group of high school students who graduated together, 50 years later. What, if anything, is the common digital archive of such a group, and how is it assembled and managed?

On current social media platforms, it is quite common for *ad hoc*, dynamic groups (not just of close friends or family but sometimes of rather casual acquaintances) to collectively create a corpus of interlinked material. The nature of social media platforms is to facilitate the movement of material, often by sharing (copying), from one circle of people to another. When is it appropriate to share in this way? When can someone demand that material be taken down, and is that request likely to be effective? What are the tacit social understandings about archiving and reuse? The law is not enough (and is not particularly clear on these points). How do third-party platforms alter the picture, where terms of use (contracts) may also come into play, and where the platform operator itself may claim some rights of ownership and control?

Sometimes the common interests that bind are those of love, friendship, or even just collective endurance and participation in disasters or other great events. Other times, however, these common interests are defined by shared intellectual interests, common political or social beliefs, artistic collaborations or similar ideas, and perhaps shared experiences. Any of these can form the basis for the creation of shared but private digital collections. The period of creation or aggregation can be relatively brief (a common disaster or an infatuation), enthusiastic, passionate, and trusting, but the unraveling and bickering about the ongoing fate of this shared collection can span lifetimes.

Imagine a continuum that begins with very small groups, families, and intimate friends and extends through to formal *organizations*, which define and structure information-sharing interactions and preservation, establishing frameworks surrounding shared materials through organization policies, terms of employment or participation, records management, government, legal or financial regulations, and related strictures. Among families and friends and formal organizations, there is a fascinating ambiguous territory that has been incredibly fertile in the past, offering a home for intellectual movements, creative collaborations, artistic collectives, protests, and political movements. Think of the range of activist movements in the 19th and 20th centuries: the Bloomsbury circle, the Beats, the Surrealists, and the Futurists. But the nature and variety of this territory, along with family archives, was historically quite circumscribed and simple. In the digital era, in the time of social media platforms, it has become much more complex and variable. We need to develop a much better understanding of the content and social structures that shape this space in the digital world, and the connections between the personal and the collective in this area, as well as the space of families, intimates, and friends.

Individuals typically cannot be understood in isolation, only in the context of their times and their relationships, families, friends, lovers, colleagues, and so on. So it is with the personal digital archives that individuals create. These archives overlap with those of their families, friends, and others with whom they may share common cause. The evidence so far suggests that these interpenetrations and overlaps are so intimate and so complex that personal digital archives cannot be considered in isolation. Indeed, to understand the nature of personal digital archives, we must also understand these small-scale, intimate, collective digital archives and how they relate to the personal, which is an essential part of the personal digital archiving agenda.

How, When, and Why the Private Becomes Public

How the private becomes public is probably the least understood, almost certainly the least studied, and yet perhaps the most important area within the overall personal digital archiving research agenda. It is central to understanding both the cultural record in general and personal digital archiving specifically, because it focuses on the connections between one and the other.

There is no mandate or requirement that personal digital archives or digital lives ever become public. The heirs of some public figures (and sometimes the public figures themselves) despise and distrust biographers; characterizations like "jackals" are common. Throughout history, it has been common for people to ask that various parts of their letters, personal papers, manuscripts, and the like be burned or otherwise destroyed; sometimes they have seen to this personally, and other times they have relied on executors or heirs. In the latter case, sometimes their wishes are honored, and sometimes they are not. The choices that have been made over the centuries have had a profound effect on the materials that have reached us as part of the cultural record. The ethical dilemmas, the alternatives, and the consequences in this area have been well-studied, at least anecdotally, and, in some cases, comparatively.

Today, we operate in a legal framework that distinguishes between ownership of a specific physical copy of a work and the rights to the *content* of the work under copyright. After enough time has passed, copyright ceases to protect materials, even unpublished works, and they fall into the public domain (though given the legislative propensity to extend copyright terms, this may take a *very* long time). After that, materials are kept private only by possession and access control. I doubt that very much genuinely private digital material will ultimately find its way into the collections of cultural memory organizations by accident, in the way that centuries-old manuscripts, diaries, and similar materials survived simply by chance until copyright expired and their contents came to belong to the culture as a whole (though the *artifacts* themselves may well be owned by specific memory organizations). The situation where digital artifacts pass to memory organizations even though their contents remain under copyright, and use of these contents is highly constrained, is going to be unusual in the world of personal digital archives, I think. Perhaps someday, we will see antiquarians making treasure hunts through 2-century-old memory sticks, but that seems unlikely. In the digital world, I believe that most personal digital archives will become public only through deliberate action, not by chance and the passage of time.

Ownership of an artifact typically persists as long as the artifact survives, but there are some interesting counterexamples, and specialized transition paths exist for objects that can be characterized as "national patrimony" to reach the cultural memory sector. These are rare and particularly foreign to American law (though we do recognize international treaty obligations in this area, and we also have legislation such as the Native American Graves Protection and Repatriation Act). But this, too, is an area that demands fresh examination in the digital world, particularly when it is possible to create very sophisticated digital representations of objects. How do we decide who gets the object and who gets a (perfect) copy of the digital representation? We also need to consider under what circumstances material in a personal digital collection or archive might be considered national patrimony.

So, if the vast majority of the movement of personal digital archives and collections from the private to the public sphere is going to occur through deliberate action, how does this happen? Clearly, the process is connected to the questions about inheritance and estate discussed earlier. A personal digital archive might be contributed or sold to a library or archive (indeed, today important collections of personal papers are commanding seven-figure prices). To be most effective, this transfer probably should take place with the active collaboration of the individual in question, while she or he is still alive, rather than posthumously, in collaboration with the individual's estate. The recent acquisition of the Salman Rushdie archives (with the ongoing engagement of Rushdie himself) by Emory University is an excellent case study. Note that the marketplace for the acquisition of personal archives is very different now than it was in the pre-digital world, where individual items might be sold and resold; here the stock in trade is rights to a *collection*, most commonly gathered with some help from the creator, help that will become ever more necessary as large segments of a "digital life" leave an individual's personal devices for locations on the web, in social media systems, in the cloud, and so on.

In the future, the acquisition of personal digital collections is going to be more and more about relationships and intent, and about an acknowledgment (grudging or otherwise) of the interests of the scholarly and biographical world. Consider, as an illuminating thought experiment, the market for acquiring Thomas Pynchon's (as far as I know imaginary) personal digital archive (or pick your own favorite important literary author). Would it make a difference in the archive's value if it were known that he wrote (and edited for publication) all of his books since 1995 in Microsoft Word with change tracking enabled and had saved the draft versions? We can only imagine the range of unintended consequences in a race to identify and recruit authors and other potentially important figures early in their professional lives to be part of the acquisitions program of particular special collections in libraries and archives, and the kinds of constraints to which they might be asked to agree.

Some of the personal digital archiving research agenda is framed by memory organizations that are trying to manage the transition from private personal digital archives to a curated, relatively public environment hosted by the library, archive, or museum. The issues include negotiation of suitable contracts or deeds of gift, privacy, embargoes, and redaction; the appropriate application (if any) of forensic technologies; and, of course (more and more), how to handle material that is spread across various servers on various networks rather than housed on local storage media that can simply be copied. I think that the research agenda should legitimately include guidance for prospective donors to the cultural record on what they need to consider in making choices and negotiating such donations. The research agendas here can also take a wider view, considering not only best practices in acquiring personal archives, but also best practices for curating and providing access to these collections, and examining the ways that scholars can make best use of them. We see questions about:

- When and how digital lives should be linked to one another—typically spanning different cultural memory organizations—and when they should stand alone; to what extent should these links be created computationally and to what extent should they be created by human intellectual analysis; when is the creation of such linkages the appropriate work of curators, and when of scholars. Note that the options here are much more extensive, and it is much easier to make progress than has historically been the case with physical collections of personal papers, which are often extensively fragmented and scattered across memory organizations.

- The appropriate use of sense-making and information-retrieval tools and technologies, including forensic tools originating in the law enforcement and intelligence communities and those developed to support legal discovery in large-scale electronic records collections, both by curators and by scholars, to gain an understanding of what is in a given personal digital archive and to locate specific materials of interest.

Beyond the portion of a digital life that is basically "owned" by the individual (including the parts that interconnect with shared social spaces), there are other segments of personal digital archives, lives, and collections that also need to be examined. One such part is the collection of cultural materials that an individual has amassed during his or her lifetime—ebooks, sound recordings, downloaded webpages, video games, and so much more. Some of this is licensed in consumer markets in very structured ways, and they may or may not be able to be moved into a collection that is public in some sense. Sometimes inventory records are as important as the materials themselves, particularly if the underlying ebooks, videos, or other materials are still widely available; annotations and marginalia are another very important resource.

But digital collections can be much more complex. Consider music: We might find a personal collection that includes commercial music from multiple sources such as Amazon or the Apple iTunes store, live materials acquired from various online sources, audio tracks taken from YouTube, and ripped CDs (that may or may not have been entirely legal in the first place). It is a safe bet that the provenance information will not always be quite as thorough as a lawyer might like, although the metadata may be extensive and add very considerable value. This kind of collection is a challenge at two levels for the cultural memory organization: first, in capturing the inventory, evolution, and use of a digital collection by its owner; and second, and equally important, in ensuring the survival and availability of perhaps ephemeral, "gray," or similar material that the owner chose to collect, curate, and preserve, and which might otherwise not find its way into the long-term cultural record. We may need new legal provisions allowing cultural memory organizations that undertake stewardship of these collections to seek safe harbor from liability for copyright infringement, at the very least, if we are to be able accurately to preserve what is in these personal digital archives.

Equally problematic, but for very different reasons, are the massive amounts of information *about* a given individual that are held by corporations, government, the medical establishment, and similar sectors. In some cases, a living individual has some right at least to obtain copies of these records (though often in unhelpful printed forms rather than as digital files); the passage of these rights through inheritance is complex, messy, and limited. Some bits—airline frequent-flyer records, credit card histories, perhaps even credit bureau records—will likely vanish within a few years after the individual's death (or when the holding corporation becomes cognizant of the death, which can take more years) because they have vanishingly small commercial value. (This area has yet to be fully exploited; imagine a potential marketplace in credit card records, itineraries, or interactions with Amazon, for dead public figures. Many of these records are relatively small; it may cost more to delete them promptly than to treat them with benign neglect.) Records of interaction with commerce or social media sites may persist longer. We do not yet know how rapidly the contributions from old interaction records decay in value as recommender systems use these interaction databases to make suggestions (and the answer is likely to be highly proprietary, and perhaps vary wildly from one applications domain to the next).

In social media spaces, often the contributions of the dead are heavily linked to the ongoing, active contributions of the living, and there seems to be no pressure by the platform operators to remove material; indeed, some social sites appear willing to host memorial pages indefinitely and presumably view them as assets.

Medical records are likely to be an emerging battleground in the coming years. Historically, in the United States, access to these has been controlled by a byzantine mix of federal and state legislation that seems to serve everyone poorly, but until today, the interested parties have been limited: a few biographers; family members, mainly concerned with understanding hereditary conditions; and people pursuing lawsuits, usually around alleged errors in end-of-life care. In the near future, medical records will commonly include genotyping or gene sequencing data, detailed machine-readable medical history records, perhaps prescription or insurance claim information, tests, and imaging. Whether the individual is dead or alive, this is prime material for data mining on a large scale. Some countries, such as the U.K., are setting policy about access to these medical records as a matter of national public health strategy, international competitiveness as a partner with multinational pharmaceutical firms, and medical entitlement cost-control strategies. There is a great deal of money at stake. It is not clear to what extent, if any, a person's heirs have control over the disposition of his or her medical records; while patients are alive, they usually have some right to view or perhaps obtain copies of these records, but typically they do not "own" them, and the healthcare or insurance providers that do claim ownership may be free to destroy them under some circumstances. We could imagine a very desirable—though perhaps currently impossible—future option where an individual could choose to place his or her medical records (before or after death) in a genuinely public research commons, perhaps somewhat like signing up to become an organ donor.

Dossiers held by various government agencies on deceased individuals will be another point of contention, especially as these dossiers apply to more and more people and expand seemingly without limit. There is some precedent in the treatment of military records, FBI files, and similar material. We can see a mix of public policy considerations and pragmatic issues shaping the research on how this part of an individual's "digital life" might move from the private to the public sphere.

Personal digital archives are, in a very real sense, an optional, even accidental, part of our collective cultural record. I know of very little systematic research (as opposed to endless anecdotal case studies) on how personal document collections have been acquired and integrated into the cultural record historically. There is a pressing need to understand what is happening at present. These types of personal collections, and now personal digital archives, are the signature elements that distinguish many of the genuinely great research collections housed in libraries and archives. They lend invaluable depth and richness to the broad cultural record.

Both within specific scholarly communities and as a broader society, we need policy discussions about how many digital lives we need to capture, and what organizations should take responsibility for collecting them. This conversation has connections to the evolving missions and strategies not just of national and research libraries, but of local historical societies, public libraries, and similar groups. In some cases, we can see traditional cultural memory organizations seeking personal digital archives of individuals they deem important for one reason or another. But we also see new players—StoryCorps, the Internet Archive, and the BBC in the U.K.—that are soliciting contributions from the general public; as well as commercial organizations such as Ancestry.com that are trying to establish lines of business maintaining digital lives. There are new ideas afoot in areas such as public history, and we need to understand what collections will be necessary to support these activities, where they will be housed, and how they will be curated and funded.

Indeed, we can easily imagine a near future where expectations are established among the general public about a *"right* to archive one's digital life" in some appropriate service. This leads us directly into a final set of questions about the extent to which genealogy, factual biography, national biographical dictionaries (and their successors such as Wikipedia), birth and death records, and similar materials belong to the public or private infrastructure, how they are governed, and whom they represent. Personal digital archives, as they move from private to public, have a rich interconnection with all of these developments.

Mapping these connections and developments leads, ultimately, to a new, but still poorly understood and poorly articulated, research and public policy agenda surrounding the broader nature and evolution of the intellectual and cultural record, which goes far beyond the scope of this chapter. This is much more than personal digital archives made public. But understanding the role that personal digital archives can play in contributing to this record, and the mechanisms by which they might contribute to it, is clearly a very useful source of insight.

Acknowledgments

Don Hawkins has been amazingly patient and supportive yet gracefully persistent in seeing this chapter to conclusion. My thinking on these issues over the past few years has benefited from discussion with people too numerous to list here, but I want to particularly recognize the contributions of the Buckland/Lynch/Larsen "Friday Seminar" at the University of California, Berkeley School of Information on November 30, 2012, in discussing a draft of this chapter. Cecilia Preston, Joan Lippincott, and particularly Diane Goldenberg-Hart provided helpful suggestions on this manuscript. Michael Buckland, who has been an invaluable collaborator as I've developed my thinking in this area, was kind enough to offer not only extensive and insightful comments but also an extraordinary thoughtful set of broader reflections in response to a late draft of this essay. Thank you all.

About the Contributors

Mike Ashenfelder works for the digital preservation division of the Library of Congress, the National Digital Information and Infrastructure Preservation Program. He writes about personal digital archiving, digital preservation leaders, and new developments in digital preservation, and produces public information videos and podcasts. Before joining the Library of Congress, he worked in the San Francisco Bay Area as a technical writer. He has also created music-education content for Time Warner Interactive and has written for the *Whole Earth Review* and the *Millennium Whole Earth Catalog*, published by HarperCollins. He writes reviews for the *Quarterly Journal of the Music Library Association*. As a sideline, Mike co-developed an oral-history program in Donegal, Ireland, training high school students to interview community elders and post the videos online. He also works with the Historic Fredericksburg (VA) Foundation to post its oral history interviews online. He holds a BA in music education from the Berklee College of Music and an MA in music history from San Francisco State University.

Richard Banks is principal interaction designer in the Socio-Digital Systems group (research.microsoft.com/sds), part of Computer Mediated Living (research.microsoft.com/cml) in Microsoft Research's Cambridge facility (research.microsoft.com/aboutmsr/labs/cambridge) in the U.K. Richard's primary interests are the role of digital artifacts in our lives and the potential contribution of design research to social science study. He is the author of *The Future of Looking Back* (Microsoft, 2011), a book focusing on new digital legacies and the impact they may have on how we reminisce about our lives. Richard is honorary professor of design at the University of Dundee and a fellow of the Royal Society of Arts. He is a graduate in computer-related design from the Royal College of Art in London and holds more than 30 patents for Microsoft in user interface design.

Ellysa Stern Cahoy is an education and behavioral sciences librarian at The Pennsylvania State University Libraries, University Park. A former children's librarian and school library media specialist, Ellysa has published research and presented on information literacy, evidence-based librarianship, library instruction, and personal archiving. She was recently awarded a $143,000 grant from the Andrew W. Mellon Foundation to fund the exploration of faculty's personal scholarly archiving practices and needs. She is past chair of the Association of College & Research Libraries (ACRL) Information Literacy Competency Standards Committee and recently chaired the ACRL Information Literacy Competency Standards Review Task Force.

Evan Carroll is an author and consumer advocate in the growing field of digital afterlife. His website, TheDigitalBeyond.com, is the leading online resource for death and digital legacy issues. Evan is also co-author of the book, *Your Digital Afterlife: When Facebook, Flickr and Twitter Are Your Estate, What's Your Legacy?* (New Riders, 2011). As an expert in digital afterlife issues, Evan has been featured in numerous media outlets including the *New York Times*, NPR's *Fresh Air*, *Obit* magazine, The Wall Street Journal's *Smart Money*, Fox News, CNN, *The Atlantic*, and the Huffington Post. A frequent speaker, he has presented to audiences at the Library of Congress, the Internet Archive, and SXSW Interactive, among many others. Evan holds BS and MS degrees in information science from the University of North Carolina, Chapel Hill.

Peter Chan received his MLIS from San Jose State University and holds an MBA from the University of Illinois at Urbana-Champaign.

Prior to his career in archives, Peter worked in banking, serving as vice president of the Operations Planning and Support Division at the Bank of America in Hong Kong and as a full-time lecturer in accounting at the Chinese University of Hong Kong. In 2007, Peter began working with Stanford's Digital Libraries Systems & Services on the Edward Feigenbaum project. Over the next 2 years, he worked in various capacities in the Stanford University Libraries, devoting much of his time to ground-breaking work in capturing and describing born-digital material. In January 2010, Peter became digital archivist on the AIMS Project, a Mellon Foundation grant-funded, collaborative project of Stanford, the University of Virginia, Hull University, and Yale University, focused on developing best practices for acquiring, capturing, processing, and describing born-digital materials. Upon completion of the AIMS Project, Peter became the digital archivist for the Stanford University Department of Special Collections and University Archives.

Danielle Conklin is an independent information professional and trained librarian. She owns and operates Cotton Gloves Research (www.cottonglovesresearch.com), an information services company that offers research, writing, and instructional services. Danielle is a graduate of Saint Michael's College in Vermont, where she studied psychology and history, and Simmons College Graduate School of Library and Information Science in Boston. Her interest in preserving the past began in her childhood. Her personal archiving projects have taken the form of print and digital scrapbooks, electronic catalogs, family history databases, journals, and carefully archived physical collections. She currently lives and works in Massachusetts.

Nathan G. Freier is a program manager at Microsoft in the Office Division. He received his PhD in information science from the Information School at the University of Washington in 2007. His writing has appeared in such journals as the *International Journal of Human-Computer Studies, Developmental Psychology, Journal of*

Environmental Psychology, Interaction Studies, and *Networks and Spatial Economics.* His research investigates the human relationship to technology with a particular focus on both adults' and children's social and moral conceptions of technology.

Sarah Kim is a doctoral candidate at the School of Information at the University of Texas at Austin. Her background is in archives and preservation of digital cultural heritage. Her research interests include personal digital archives, everyday recordkeeping and archiving, and digital technology and everyday practices. She holds a BA in history and art history and an MS in information studies specializing in archives and records management.

Clifford Lynch has led the Coalition for Networked Information (CNI) since 1997. CNI, jointly sponsored by the Association of Research Libraries and EDUCAUSE, includes about 200 member organizations concerned with the intelligent uses of information technology and networked information to enhance scholarship and intellectual life. Its wide ranging agenda includes work in digital preservation; data-intensive scholarship; teaching, learning and technology; and infrastructure and standards development. Prior to joining CNI, Cliff spent 18 years at the University of California Office of the President, the last 10 as director of Library Automation. Cliff holds a PhD in computer science from the University of California, Berkeley, and is an adjunct professor at Berkeley's School of Information. Cliff is both a past president of the American Society for Information Science and recipient of the society's Award of Merit, and a fellow of the American Association for the Advancement of Science and the National Information Standards Organization. In 2011, he was appointed co-chair of the National Academies Board on Research Data and Information; he serves on numerous advisory boards and visiting committees. His work has been recognized by the American Library Association's Lippincott Award, the EDUCAUSE Leadership Award in

Public Policy and Practice, and the American Society for Engineering Education's Homer Bernhardt Award.

Catherine C. Marshall is a principal researcher at Microsoft Research, Silicon Valley. Her current research is on personal information management and on the ownership, reuse, and control of social media. Cathy came to Microsoft in 2000 to work on ebooks after many years at Xerox PARC, where she strayed from her roots in computer science after being indelibly transformed by working with anthropologists, humanists, information scientists, and hypertext fiction writers. She is the author of *Reading and Writing the Electronic Book* (Morgan & Claypool, 2010), which takes a close look at reading and annotation, and how they are changing in a digital age. Cathy's personal homepage (www.csdl.tamu.edu/~marshall) includes a comprehensive list of her publications, new media commentary, blog, and Twitter feed; additional information is available on her Microsoft Research page (research.microsoft.com/en-us/people/cathymar).

Christopher J. Prom is assistant university archivist and associate professor of library administration at the University of Illinois at Urbana-Champaign. He holds a PhD in history from the University of Illinois, and he also studied at the University of York, U.K. He is a fellow of the Society of American Archivists and has received several other research fellowships, most recently a 2009–2010 Fulbright Distinguished Scholar Award. He maintains the Practical E-Records Blog and an active publication portfolio. His research describes the ways in which archival users seek information relevant to their needs and assesses methods that archivists can use to efficiently meet those needs. He most recently authored a technical watch report for the Digital Preservation Coalition, "Preserving Email." Chris is co-director of the Archon project, which developed an open source application for managing archival descriptive information and digital objects, and a member of the ArchivesSpace project, which is developing a next-generation archival management system. He has served the Society of American

Archivists in several capacities. He is currently a member of the editorial board of *The American Archivist*, and in March 2013, he began a 3-year term as publications editor for the Society.

Ben Shneiderman is a professor in the department of computer science, founding director (1983–2000) of the Human–Computer Interaction Laboratory, and a member of the Institute for Advanced Computer Studies at the University of Maryland, College Park. He was elected a fellow of the Association for Computing (ACM) in 1997 and a fellow of the American Association for the Advancement of Science in 2001. He received the ACM SIGCHI Lifetime Achievement Award in 2001 and the Miles Conrad Award from the National Federation of Advanced Information Services in 2011. He is a member of the National Academy of Engineering. Ben pioneered the highlighted textual link in 1983, and it became part of Hyperties, a precursor to the web. His move into information visualization spawned Spotfire, known for pharmaceutical drug discovery and genomic data analysis. He is a technical advisor for the treemap visualization producer, The Hive Group. Ben is the author of *Software Psychology: Human Factors in Computer and Information Systems* (1980) and *Designing the User Interface: Strategies for Effective Human-Computer Interaction* (5th ed., 2010, with C. Plaisant). He co-authored *Readings in Information Visualization: Using Vision to Think* (1999) with S. Card and J. Mackinlay. His book, *Leonardo's Laptop: Human Needs and the New Computing Technologies* (MIT Press, 2003), won the IEEE Award for Distinguished Literary Contribution in 2004. His most recent book, *Analyzing Social Media Networks with NodeXL: Insights from a Connected World* (Morgan Kaufman, 2010), was co-authored with D. Hansen and M. A. Smith. He received his PhD in computer science from SUNY, Stony Brook.

Jeff Ubois is a program officer in the MacArthur Foundation's Media, Culture, and Special Initiatives program, where he is responsible for discovery grants. Previously, he was a consultant to archives, museums, broadcasters, and commercial organizations in the U.S. and European Union Most recently, he worked for Fujitsu Labs in Sunnyvale, California, the Bassetti Foundation in Milan, Italy, and the Netherlands Institute of Sound and Vision. Prior to this, he was a staff research associate at the University of California, Berkeley, and part of the Preserving Digital Public Television Project based at Thirteen/WNET and funded by the Library of Congress. Jeff is a frequent public speaker and was primary convener of the Personal Digital Archiving conferences held at the Internet Archive. In the 1990s, he worked in the software industry, co-founding Disappearing Inc., and as a journalist in Washington, Hong Kong, London, and San Francisco covering new technology. He articles have appeared in *First Monday*, *D-Lib Magazine, Computerworld, Release 1.0, ACM Interactions, Bloomberg Business News*, Ferris Research, and other publications, summarized at www.ubois.com.

Aaron Ximm is a senior engineer at the Internet Archive (www.archive.org). As an engineer within the Collections Department, he focuses on expanding and enhancing the range of material coming into the Archive, with particular attention to developing strategies for preserving non-web materials. Aaron's primary projects have included developing an infrastructure for distributed deep web crawling of high-value/high-popularity web domains, creating a functioning proof of concept framework for active personal digital archiving, and, most recently, extending Archive support for and engagement with the BitTorrent protocol and the communities that use it. In another life, Aaron works with archival materials as an artist; as a field recordist and sound artist, he is best known for composition, installation, and performance work under the name Quiet American, much of which can be found at quietamerican.org.

Jason Zalinger is an assistant professor in the communication department at the University of South Florida in Tampa. His research investigates how communication technology shapes our life stories. Some previous projects include Gmail Adventures, which turned a user's Gmail into a "video game"; Ethnochat, a prototype instant messaging program built for researchers to conduct online interviews; and Super Research Idea Generator, a free iPhone brainstorming app. He received his BA in English from the University of Connecticut at Storrs, his MA in media ecology from New York University, and his PhD in communication and rhetoric from Rensselaer Polytechnic Institute.

About the Editor

Donald T. Hawkins is a blogger and writer at Information Today, Inc. (ITI), where he blogs about ITI's conferences and writes conference reports for *Information Today.* He maintains the Conference Calendar on the ITI website (www.infotoday.com/calendar.asp) and has developed databases and participated in other special projects at ITI.

Don had a distinguished career with AT&T for over 24 years, retiring in 1996 to start his own consulting business, InfoResources. At AT&T, he was the content manager for several electronic information projects. He began his career in 1971, the dawn of the online information industry, in the AT&T Bell Laboratories Library Network and spent 15 years there, developing and managing its information retrieval and current awareness services and conducting several pioneering studies in online searching, bibliometrics, and other related areas. Following his career in the Library Network, he served in the business units of AT&T on projects related to the research and development of econtent products.

Don was appointed Distinguished Member of Technical Staff at AT&T Bell Laboratories in 1986 in recognition of his pioneering work in introducing end-user searching into the Library Network. He won the prestigious UMI/Data Courier Award for excellence in writing in the online information industry in 1987 for his two articles on artificial intelligence and online searching, and again in 1992 for his article on intelligent agents for information retrieval.

Don joined ITI in 1998 upon its purchase of *Information Science & Technology Abstracts* (*ISTA*) and became the editor-in-chief of *ISTA* and, upon its purchase, *Fulltext Sources Online*. He led the efforts to develop a new production process for *ISTA* based on the Microsoft Access database platform, to update and revise its thesaurus, and to improve its quality and coverage of the information science literature. When ITI sold *ISTA* and *Internet and Personal Computing Abstracts* to EBSCO Publishing, he worked with EBSCO to help integrate the two databases into EBSCO's production system and developed the information and computer science component of EBSCO's thesaurus and controlled vocabulary, which is used to index the two databases.

Don is a frequent contributor to the literature, with more than 300 publications, and he has spoken frequently at industry conferences. In June 1996, he keynoted an international conference on electronic publishing in Japan, and he has delivered plenary presentations in the U.S., as well as internationally at conferences in Australia, New Zealand, South Africa, and Israel. Recently, he contributed a chapter on the AT&T Bell Laboratories Library Network to *Special Libraries: A Survival Guide* (ABC-Clio, 2013).

Don was the secretariat for the Association for Information and Dissemination Centers (ASIDIC) before it merged with the National Federation of Advanced Information Services (NFAIS), and editor of the *ASIDIC Newsletter*. He received his BS, MS, and PhD degrees from the University of California, Berkeley.

Index

Italicized page numbers indicate illustrations.
Tables and charts are indicated with t and c following the page number.